ANDRÁS BÍRÓ
NICOLAE GHEORGHE
MARTIN KOVATS ET AL

EDITOR WILL GUY

FROM VICTIMHOOD
TO CITIZENSHIP

The Path of Roma Integration

A DEBATE

ANDRÁS BÍRÓ
NICOLAE GHEORGHE
MARTIN KOVATS ET AL
EDITOR WILL GUY

FROM VICTIMHOOD TO CITIZENSHIP

The Path of Roma Integration

A DEBATE

PAKIV EUROPEAN ROMA FUND
KOSSUTH PUBLISHING CORPORATION

Authors: András Bíró, Nicolae Gheorghe, Martin Kovats, Željko Jovanović

Editor: Will Guy

CONTRIBUTORS TO THE DEBATE

Those listed below contributed to the debate, either by participating in the workshop held at Snagov in Romania (22-24 September 2011) or sending written comments on the core texts. The workshop debates on 23 September were transcribed by Ian Graham.

Gwendolyn Albert, Remus Anghel, András Bíró, Elena Dinca, Gelu Duminica, László Fosztó, Nicolae Gheorghe, Will Guy, Željko Jovanović, Deyan Kolev, Martin Kovats, Cristi Mihalache, Florin Nasture, Gergő Pulay, Christian Petry, Livia Plaks †, Gergő Pulay, Béla Rácz, Nadir Redzepi, Salomeea Romanescu, Iulius Rostas, Valentina Spera, Kristóf Szombati, Jennifer Tanaka, Nicolae Valeriu, Ioana Vrabiescu, Elisabetta Vivaldi

This publication was realised with the support of Open Society Foundations and the Freudenberg Stiftung

Publisher in charge: András Sándor Kocsis managing director
of Kossuth Publishing Corporation

Distributed by the Central European University Press
ISBN 978-615-5225-90-1

Library of Congress Cataloging-in-Publication Data

From victimhood to citizenship : the path of Roma integration : a debate / András Bíró, Nicolae Gheorghe, Martin Kovats et al ; editor Will Guy.
pages cm
Includes bibliographical references.
ISBN 978-9630975667 (pbk.)
1. Romanies—Europe—Social conditions—21st century. 2. European Union countries—Ethnic relations.
3. Romanies—Ethnic identity. I. Biró, András. II. Guy, Will, 1940-
DX145.F76 2013
305.8914'9704—dc23
2013027250

CONTENTS

FOREWORD

The three essays we are presenting here for discussion may prove contentious in some readers' eyes. They trigger a fundamental discussion on the self-image of the Roma activists, and the goals they should be pursuing in the future. They sow seeds of doubt as to whether the Roma movement is on the right track, and they are doing this, moreover, at a time when the EU Commission, the EU member states are tasked with developing action plans for Roma inclusion. Nicolae Gheorghe welcomes the development options created by the EU's initiative. He writes: 'For the first time in history, Roma have prospects of reflecting and playing an active part in bringing about social change. The role of Roma opinion-makers is to suggest new approaches, focusing on integration rather than on being victims.' But then, in the course of his argument, he calls for a moratorium: no more payments from the EU before a new strategy has emerged – an ethically grounded action scenario.

András Bíró, whose essay has triggered a process of reflection which we aim to flesh out in this book, warns in what are sometimes harsh words against continuing the approach that many Roma activists have adopted in the past. Like his friend and long-standing discussion partner Nicolae Gheorghe, he demands nothing less than a new culture, one in which there is no longer a place for ethically dubious instant gratification *(shmekeria)* – the search for devious and not always kosher options for satisfying one's own needs.

Martin Kovats focuses on the politicisation of Roma identity arguing that the European discourse of 'Roma' cannot be understood as reflecting 'Roma' reality, but as a construction of the wider political environment. He advocates reflection on how 'Roma' use ethnic identity in their political activities (after all, national citizenship is a more powerful identity in terms of legal entitlement). Furthermore he urges activists to embrace other, non-ethnic, aspects of politics so they can forge effective political relations with non-Roma (without whom Roma politics is segregated and reflects and even contributes to the general marginalisation/segregation of 'Roma' people).

Now, however, the European action programme for promoting Roma inclusion is indubitably justified with the argument that the Roma are discriminated against and ostracised as Roma, and that this ethnic discrimination and persecution has a lengthy tradition behind it. This is why the EU Commission, in the Common Basic Principles for Roma Inclusion, has formulated as the relevant goal that such inclusion be designed as 'explicit but not exclusive'.

So is a book being planned here that aims to oppose the development of a European inclusion program for Roma?

This impression could perhaps be created when people read that the political linkage to the minority is to be abandoned, that its activists and the groups they represent have to undergo a fundamental change, and that it would be better for them not to receive any more money from the EU until this has come to pass.

This is most certainly not the intention of the charitable foundations involved – the Freudenberg Foundation and the Open Society Institute in Budapest – which are fostering the process of reflection that is exemplified in this book. Nor is this the intention of the Pakiv Reflection Group, which is sponsored and also supported by the Freudenberg Foundation and the Pakiv European Roma Fund.

We are, however, firmly convinced that Roma inclusion is not a self-perpetuating process, that much of the funding assigned to the Roma has failed in its intended purpose, and that a very careful rethink and strenuous efforts are required of the Roma themselves if the hopes pinned on the European inclusion program are to be fulfilled. It would be lamentable if the well-meaning European initiative were to fail and the substantial European, national and private funding earmarked for promoting Roma inclusion in Europe during this decade were to trickle away in futile inefficacy, as has frequently happened already.

The Pakiv and Freudenberg Reflection Group attempted at an early stage to put the cornerstones in place for developing a fit-for-purpose inclusion programme, in the shape of the *Weinheim Declaration: EU Policy on Roma* for the first Roma Summit in Brussels in 2008, and then with their involvement in the recommendations of the European Foundation Centre (EFC) Forum on Roma Inclusion drawn up by European charitable foundations for the second Roma Summit in Córdoba in 2010. While these jointly ratified public statements were being discussed, however, we realised that they would not suffice to assure a successful process of promoting inclusion. This can be accomplished only if at least two conditions are met, which have been addressed but not implemented:

One stipulation is that the preconditions on the part of the Roma themselves be improved: firstly in the category of perception, attitudes and competences among the Roma themselves. What is needed, in other words, is local Roma organisations that are really willing and able to take a proactive role in improving the world they live in. This will often necessitate altered ethnic orientations and a sufficient number of Roma competent enough to act as community organisers.

Secondly, competent and benevolent local administrations are required on the local level. A committed mayor can achieve a lot in conjunction with a strong Roma organisation. Success will indubitably require a framework of national and European responsibilities tasked with reducing discrimination, identifying action thrusts, establishing a monitoring process and creating opportunities for counselling and further education.

The principal focuses envisaged for promoting inclusion, namely housing, employment, health and education, are the responsibilities of different ministries. Whether these theoretical projects can be translated into reality and coalesce to form a holistic, comprehensive approach is something that will be decided on the local level. Whether anti-discrimination will become a dimension of all the action envisaged will depend on the local political culture involved. And this may vary quite considerably from place to place. Without a discussion on the options for and costs of integration, without investment in the capacity building of Roma, and without systematised support from local authorities, no inclusion programme, whatever its nature, can possibly be successful. If the top-down process from Europe to the towns and villages does not encounter a bottom-up process propagating in the opposite direction, the funds will have been spent in vain, and in some cases have done more harm than good. On the local level, the question of identity politicisation does not arise to the same extent. There, you are what you are, and you have an identity, irrespective of how it is expressed. The primary consideration here is the question of whether all citizens will act together in order to overcome unacceptable inequality and discrimination.

What gives us hope is that localities can be found where developments of this kind can take place. What gives us cause for concern is the unresolved question of how such desirable developments can be generalised and put into practice at other locations as well. A process of this nature has to begin by clarifying questions of values and the requisite resolve. It is here that we aim to provide some fresh and hopefully fruitful impetus.

Christian Petry
Pakiv European Roma Fund

Tell him the truth, even if it hurts!

Confucius about the powerful

I reject politics that are based solely
on racial identity, gender identity, sexual orientation
or victimhood in general.

Barack Obama

THE PRICE OF ROMA INTEGRATION

ANDRÁS BÍRÓ

This essay is offered as a contribution to a dialogue of engaged and like-minded individuals, Roma and non-Roma alike. In particular it concerns the future of the integration of this transnational community into a globalised world. As I have been entrusted with the far from easy task of kicking off this dialogue, I feel an obligation to state my biases at the outset, with the proviso that the conclusions I may have reached are nothing else but hypotheses based on empirical experience with no claim to be objective or scientific. Therefore they are open to debate, correction, rejection or in the best case, to being taken into account. Moreover I apologise in advance to my Roma readers if, in its arguments or hypotheses, this essay may hurt their sensitivities or feelings, since its motivation is to unveil some of the reasons for pervasive prejudices and not to justify them.

Returning to Hungary after 30 years as an émigré, during which the fate of the populations of the Third World had become my main personal and professional interests, I was struck by the obvious and widespread discrimination against Roma. My involvement in the development of the rapidly growing Roma civil rights movement started with the political transition of 1989-90. Two decades later it seems appropriate to revisit our thoughts, approaches and actions in a bold attempt at introspection, carried out in a frank and demystified spirit. The title of this essay requires an explanation. My contention is that throughout the centuries the uneven process of integration and marginalisation of Roma in the societies where they live has never occurred without losses – without paying the price – in terms of culture.[1] These changes have been

---

[1] The term 'culture' as a way of life is used in this paper as the 'set of distinctive spiritual, material, intellectual and emotional features of society or a social group' encompassing artefacts, arts and literature, ways of living together, value systems, traditions and beliefs.

generally imposed by the requirements of the host societies, often by exclusion and force – even genocide.

Nowadays, for the first time in history, the Roma, through their movements, activists and leaders, have the opportunity to formulate their independent thinking and strategies about the matter. Contributing to such a development seems to me the main objective of this essay.

The Obama quotation is intimately connected to this objective because, in my opinion, as long as victimhood dominates the spirits of the excluded, and a new civic consciousness does not develop on the basis of the principles of the Universal Declaration of Human Rights, it makes little sense to hope for integration based on respect, multiculturalism and equal opportunities.

Therefore this time it is the Roma who are to be put under the magnifying glass in trying to pinpoint what might be the stumbling blocks on their side in the integration process. 'It takes two to tango', as the saying goes. So attacking exclusively the prejudices and stereotypes of majority attitudes – unacceptable as they are – and ignoring the Roma's own weaknesses reproduces, in my view, the victimhood stance which blocks action and 'explains' the impossibility of changing the *status quo*.

However it must also be emphatically stated that the historic responsibility of the majority vis-à-vis the cohabiting minority can neither be dismissed nor denied, all the less so in societies guided by democratic principles and constitutions.

Trying to explain aspects of such a topic from the viewpoint of an outsider is inherently biased and may be perceived as illegitimate by those in the community under discussion. However the fortunate circumstance of this venture is that this contribution is but one of many and other participants will have the advantage of speaking from the position of insiders. Thus the danger of one-sidedness will be limited and the end result will hopefully contribute to a creative debate.

> The components of the national[2] psyche and char-
> acter are important building blocks of any national
> consciousness. ... [I]t contributes to self-characteri-
> sation, a mechanism of self-suggestion and appears
> since ancient times as a constitutive element of all
> social groups aware of their sense of belonging. In
> this way it is the group itself which ... creates collec-
> tive psychological characteristics via unwritten be-
> havioural and moral norms.
>
> *Jenő Szűcs*

Uniqueness and Universality

To my knowledge Roma are the single socio-ethnic group which is spread all over the globe. Having lost their homeland a millennium ago, for centuries they have represented a culture of *the other* in the countries to which they have travelled and where they have lived, identified by multiple names while speaking more than 150 varieties of Romani. All this time until the modern era they have been intermittently either on the road or settling, meanwhile displaying an unmistakable character and distinctiveness which has been both cause and pretext for their exclusion.

Because of their extreme diversity and complexity, the way of looking at this community cannot be other than multifaceted and interdisciplinary. Thus, as a rule, this essay will try to combine three approaches, looking at aspects of Roma experience from three distinct angles:

the *vertical view*, trying to take into account social stratification within groups or clans (extended families) in terms of the power situation of the players;

the *horizontal aspect*, perceiving the role of belonging to a subgroup or clan often taking precedence over a sense of broader ethnic identity;

the *transversal perspective*, considering the degree of integration into majority society. This has become an increasingly significant factor demonstrating the diversification of the community and is sometimes related to increase or decrease in social mobility.

---

[2] In many countries of Central and Eastern Europe the Roma have the official status of a national minority; in others, as in Hungary, they are classified as an ethnic minority.

An attempt will also be made to combine diachronic with synchronic perceptions of the relationship of the Roma with the majority as a certain aloofness and 'mystery', including the frequent romantic idealisation of envied freedom, which has coloured their image for centuries. If ever there was a community bound up with persistent stereotypes, this one is surely the winner of the contest.

It is highly questionable whether this ambitious method of exploration can be applied throughout this essay, since it requires a consistent methodology which has yet to be developed. Nevertheless it seems worth trying it out in order to avoid simplifying, value-loaded generalisations.

The most salient distinctive factors and basic characteristics of the Roma are associated, in my view, with their relationship to **territoriality**. Solid historical data are lacking, which would explain the reasons for leaving their original homeland, or for their prolonged stay in Persia before their arrival in the continent of Europe in the late Middle Ages. Since then, varying periods of settling and wandering have alternated until the present day, when only a small proportion of Roma has remained itinerant in some western European countries. With few exceptions though, one general statement seems pertinent: *nowhere have significant numbers of Roma turned into peasants or farmers, so that their roots and livelihood have become based on the land.* In this distinctive trait I see the fundamental reason for Roma being perceived by local people as *the other*. Clearly this cannot be the only reason for their fate but their preservation of this intrinsic detachment from the very basis of settled societies is an important and long-standing cultural difference.

I am often confronted with the argument that there exist other itinerant groups, with non-agricultural subsistence strategies. For instance, there are nomadic tribes in Africa and Asia, as well as certain Amerindian pre-agricultural, hunter-gatherer communities, not to mention the Jewish Diaspora. However the nomadic, animal-breeding, itinerant groups are dependent on grasslands and waterholes for their subsistence and thus have a permanent relationship to the land, which is both pragmatic and spiritual – even if the settled peasants consider them as predators. The Amerindian tribes, as well as the Jews, have a basic *spiritual relationship to* land, as they worship their sacred territories. For millennia the latter have repeated: 'next year in Jerusalem' until it became reality with the establishment of the state of Israel. In their case the relationship to the land and the home country coincide, whereas in the case of the Roma the aspiration for a home country is practically absent. Moreover, the rich Roma folklore emphasises and values the 'birdlike', free, itinerant existence,[3] seen simultaneously as a blessing and a curse.

---

[3] It is well worth mentioning that the cartwheel became the unifying emblem of many Roma civil and political organisations symbolising the peripatetic past, a shared history and identity of the Roma people.

For others, intimate connection to territoriality is the traditional way of subsistence, but for Roma their **livelihood** is based on services offered to settled, recipient communities, on which they depend. For centuries and to a great extent until the present day, this basic fact has determined a market relationship where non-Roma are viewed essentially as clients. This appears to be the relevant factor in the relationship and this perception is shared by the *gadjo*[4] as well. Cajoling, persuading the buyer to acquire the proffered goods, is an indispensable technique for achieving success. Therefore linguistic proficiency and delivering a shrewd psychological performance[5] became as important to survival as the quality of the product or the possession of the relevant skills.

Among Roma livelihoods, service activities comprise what I would call the *showbiz* sector: music, dance and circus performances, fortune telling, etc., while the *commercial* sector consists of animal trading, specifically horse dealing, and petty trade. In the crafts sector,[6] skills in iron working and weapon making were once the most valued but adobe brick production and working in wood were also important, as well as several trades like rubbish collecting – often despised by the locals. Various other minor occupations complete the list. Before the industrial and post-industrial revolutions made these professions obsolete, these service functions had been part and parcel of local economies for centuries, filling gaps and responding to needs, especially of rural populations. This model of economic activities pursued by the Roma was characteristically unconnected to a specific locus and thus appropriate to the wandering lifestyle. Yet perhaps the saturation of the local markets also led individual groups to look elsewhere for new customers. However the question whether this type of livelihood determined the itinerant way of life, or vice-versa, is as relevant as the chicken-and-egg dilemma. What does seem equally important to emphasise is that this type of economic activity was oriented predominantly to survival rather than growth. Consequently it had a closed and restricted character. This factor may have contributed significantly to the reproduction of the socially marginalised status experienced by Roma for centuries.

Some of the professions were more highly regarded by client communities, locating their practitioners at the top of the pyramid in terms of social stratification, i.e. musicians and certain categories of businessman. In tune with the continuing fashion for romanticism, the demand for what was called 'Gypsy music' and the fame of its performers were at their height during the eighteenth, late nineteenth and twentieth centuries.[7]

---

[4] In the Romani language *gadjo* is the term for a non-Roma person, *gadje* in the plural.

[5] Some researchers coined the concept of 'utilitarianism' as a requisite attitude in this behaviour.

[6] Strictly speaking this activity does not belong in the service sector, since objects for sale have to be produced, but the direct selling to clients, often in their homes, supports this categorisation.

[7] Bizet's *Carmen* and *Gitanes* cigarettes are only the most prominent cases of exploiting the craze for romanticism.

However other less prestigious professions, like begging, remained at the bottom of the pyramid. These Roma livelihoods and their status may correspond more or less to position of the comparable castes in their original homeland of India.

Another characteristic trait of Roma is their relationship to **religion**. In the course of their stay in different countries the original, probably animistic religion of the multiple groups that arrived in Europe has been formally abandoned in favour of the dominant, monotheistic religion of the host country – essentially Catholicism, Greek Orthodoxy and Islam. In modern times Protestant churches have also gained adherents and more recently the Pentecostal church has recruited large numbers of Roma. This demonstrates an exceptional capacity to adapt to the new circumstances, to diminish friction with the locals and enhance conditions of survival in times when religion constituted the dominant element of identity in society.

This cannot be regarded as an utter 'betrayal' of old beliefs but is better understood as a process of spiritual assimilation to dominant creeds, resulting in a syncretism, where original myths and rites have remained as core elements of their worldview. Over the centuries the presumed and avowed knowledge of the mysteries of life and the universe, has not only been shared by all groups but for many, mainly women,[8] has even embodied a profession. In essence, the deep-rooted beliefs of Roma where natural events are perceived as supernatural phenomena determined by powerful spirits which decide one's destiny – fundamentally a superstitious world view – have melted into the monotheistic religions they encountered on their journeys.

Similar kinds of animistic creeds can be found all over the globe where **oral culture** is dominant and therefore this aspect seems to be relevant in exploring the fate of the Roma too. Minorities lacking literacy, where beliefs, values and technologies of survival need to be transmitted orally, are at a disadvantage in comparison with those possessing a written culture. For the latter, bearing in mind the dominant role played by religious and intellectual elites, literacy is decisive in the global development of their societies. Illiteracy of minorities within these literate societies entails handicaps, inferior status and exclusion. In addition illiteracy performs a double role. On the one hand it preserves traditional lifestyles and values thus identity, while on the other it impedes the growth of its autochthonous literate elite and thereby hinders the competitiveness of the whole group, preventing it from attaining equal footing with the majority. In such cases evidence of historical trends shows that it is by paying the price of acculturation that minority elites reach relative equality with their peers in the

---

[8] Research reveals that the female figure occupies a central place in the mythical representations and religious beliefs of the Roma. Perhaps this explains why an image of the Virgin Mary appears an essential icon on the walls of most of their dwellings.

dominant society. However, they often develop strong assimilative tendencies in the process, losing or denying their roots.

The horizontal **diversity** characterising groups and clans in sub-ethnic terms is even more visible when integration, settling down and wandering have taken diverse forms, which are the consequence of historical changes that the host societies themselves have experienced. The relatively liberal minority policies of the Ottoman Empire stand in stark contrast to the violently assimilative ones of the Austro-Hungarian or the chaotic version of the Russian Empires. These very different approaches have all had a substantial effect on whether varied traditions and rites have been maintained or gradually lost amongst Roma groups.

Nevertheless a pivotal tenet can be detected as both persistent and widespread: the fundamental dichotomy of the worldview – found in many other traditional beliefs as well – which radically opposes the purity of the autochthonous to the *pollution* due to mingling with the *gadje*. In certain cases defilement may even stem from another member of a sub-group of the global Roma community but principally it is the *gadjo*, the other, who is impure. This basic principle seems to have been mainly responsible for the longevity of traditional **codes of conduct** in dealing with members of host societies as well. Accepting the judgements of the *Criss Romano*[9] has been another long-standing factor in identity building and conservation of self-image. Meanwhile Roma have continued to practise rites and rituals surrounding marriage, death, garments, etc. to varying extents, depending on the intensity of the acculturation processes they have experienced.

To obey laws and regulations must appear perverse to a socio-ethnic group which has been excluded from the customary economic mechanisms of the host society, estranged from the rules of mainstream procedures as regards private propriety and permanently exposed to the tribulations of the law enforcement apparatus. Having been in that situation for centuries, especially when enduring the hardships of the wandering periods of their history, Roma often considered themselves to be living on the margins of *gadjo* legality. Consequently they sometimes needed to adopt means of survival that were incompatible with these laws. This detachment from the sacrosanct principles of private property, governing settled societies since the proclamation of the Ten Commandments, has branded the community as a whole as thieves. No doubt these relics of a wandering way of life, without fixed abode and helping themselves to the fruits of nature as gifts of the gods, had remained for some an immediate way of

---

[9] Roma communities have generally followed the rulings of this indigenous court, based on consensual decisions by its members – respected figures within the community. In extreme cases those found guilty were condemned to ostracism and expulsion.

satisfying elementary needs. The relationship to the actual as well as to the symbolic *gadjo*, who represented the fundamental source of income but simultaneously the barrier impeding free access to needed goods, led Roma to adopt a submissive demeanour where cajolery and deception became a technique of survival. The Turkish term *shmekeria* – still in use in all countries that experienced prolonged Ottoman occupation – covers a cluster of attributes (cunning, deceiving, cheating). These have been regarded as valued assets not only in order to obtain material advantages but equally important, psychological recompense in order to get even with the *gadjo*, the power figure. It is powerlessness, regardless of ethnic or cultural factors, which naturally generates such techniques of the weak, the dependent.[10] Simultaneously with *shmekeria*, and in opposition to it, the rules of *pakiv* operate as a moral, self-defence mechanism vis-à-vis the defiling, external rules and mores of the *gadjo*. *Pakiv* comprises a complex of values such as belief, trust, confidence, faith, respect, obedience to the elderly – the fundamental elements of the internal cohesion of the Roma group. In a sense *pakiv* represents the positive mirror image of the negative, defensive behavioural patterns characterising their relationship to the *gadjo*, dominated by doubt, mistrust, fear and disbelief.

It should be emphasised that intimately interwoven with these sketchily drafted, behavioural components of Roma is the systematic discrimination and exclusion inflicted on them by host societies. Here, too, the chicken-and-egg dichotomy appears a salient aspect of the topic under discussion. Nevertheless we cannot ignore the fact that centuries of cohabitation have not been able to overcome – but nowadays to the contrary have dangerously exacerbated – the misunderstandings, conflicts and even clashes between Central and Eastern European (CEE) societies and the numerically increasing, 'alien' Roma minority.

In relation to the hypothesis about the components of uniqueness, the characteristics listed above are only models or ideal types and therefore do not take into account the changes which have taken place in the integration/marginalisation, wandering/settling dynamics of the last two centuries. Eastward and westward movements, enforced and voluntary, long-term and spontaneous settling have all contributed to growing interaction with host communities. Consequently acculturation has taken place to differing degrees, which is particularly evident from the incorporation of local terms or concepts missing in Romani, as well as from the inclusion of vocabulary from the vernacular languages. But for large segments of the Roma population this meant losing the use of their native tongue. Finally the industrial and post-industrial revolutions contributed to the erosion of traditional values, as well of their trades, only preserving them in rare instances as ostracised professions at the fringes of host societies.

---

[10] In the memoirs of Bernal de Castillo, a soldier of Cortez during the fifteenth century colonisation of Mexico, there are incessant complaints about the cheating, no-good, double-dealing Indians.

Two models of enforced integration

Over the centuries several processes have led to greater integration of Roma in various parts of the European continent. These are differentiated both by their intensity and outcomes. I intend to concentrate on two cases of forcible *integration*, which took place in Central Europe. A further reason for concentrating on this region concerns demography. The overwhelming majority of the Roma are by now to be found in Central and Eastern European countries where, depending on the country, they now form 6 to 10 percent of the total population. Consequently the authorities in these countries find themselves in a very different situation to that of their counterparts in the West, where Roma numbers have been, and remain, limited. Relatively smaller Roma populations have meant that the traditional way of life and itinerancy have been more easily tolerated. However in Spain, with the largest Roma population of Western Europe, a slow organic type of integration can be seen.

Power structures with overly centralised administrations, as in the Central and Eastern European region, lacked democratic traditions and in the two cases examined here – the enlightened absolutism of the 18th century and the Soviet model of the 20th century – enforced measures were used. These were motivated as much by ideological as economic reasons. They were claimed to be based on both rational social engineering and humanistic principles, whilst foretelling uniform 'happiness' for the subjects of the experiments. The predicted outcomes did not materialise although there are substantial differences between the two experiences.

The Habsburg monarch Maria Theresa decided to rename all Gypsies in her Empire, giving them the mandatory designation of **New Hungarians** or *New Peasants*. Measures were aimed not only at assimilating Roma but at converting them into taxable peasants while simultaneously revitalising territories which were severely under-populated as a consequence of the war against the Ottoman Empire. Even more forceful decrees were subsequently enacted by her successor, Joseph II. Among others these included prohibiting Roma from marrying, the removal of children from their parents and fostering them among Hungarian-speaking families and a total ban on nomadism. Resistance came not only from the 'New Hungarians' but also from negligent local authorities, while reluctance of *gadje* to mingle with them was yet another factor in frustrating this assimilation. What appears the most long-lasting consequence is the loss of the use of Romani for the great majority of Hungarian Roma.

Settlement was an even more significant outcome of this policy. The 1893 census data indicate nearly 90 percent of Roma as sedentary (and a similar proportion as illiterate). In spite of the astonishingly high figure of settled Roma, which is probably due to flaws in the census methodology, the dominant housing pattern in the Central and

Eastern European region was, and still remains, fundamentally segregated.[11] Since nomadism has been practically eliminated a more or less peaceful coexistence has evolved within the framework of a less harsh integration process.

This period also seems to have contributed to a shift inside the Roma community in terms of most valued professions. Blacksmiths, who for centuries represented a sort of aristocracy, were replaced by musicians who became indispensable participants in celebrations and festivities for all strata of society. A closer, sometimes even intimate, relationship with clients, combining entertainment and pleasurable togetherness, contributed to a shift in perception among the majority, at least as regards this particular segment of the Roma. The lifestyle of these musicians, especially in cities and towns, seems to have cut them off from the core of the Roma community as they identified with their privileged status and even embraced prevalent prejudices. In this way they represented a local variant of the Uncle Tom syndrome. On the other hand, many modern Roma political leaders often come from that privileged background, since formal education had been accessible to them at an earlier stage than for others. Consequently it was among such Roma that a new ethnic consciousness emerged, taking priority over the traditional one, based essentially on kinship.

The road from New Hungarians to **New Proletarians** has not been as arduous as the violent assimilation attempt of the Habsburgs. The period of almost two centuries which separates the two forcible integrations can be characterised as 'business as usual' in terms of social exclusion and discrimination.[12] As already mentioned, the most noticeable change in the status of the Roma had been the settlement of the majority of clans and families, although the category of *semi-sedentary* was to be found in the census, where Roma were registered as settled for most of the year but moved during harvest time, when many found seasonal work as farmhands.[13] Generally, however, self-employment remained the preferred way to earn income, mainly by producing and selling household items and by music and trade. In the context of the local economy of this period, living at the outskirts of the villages formed part of the exchange process, with Roma representing a casual labour force when occasionally required. Here they were generally treated magnanimously with paternalistic condescension rather than

---

[11] In the former Ottoman Empire the *mahala* (quarter) – sometimes amounting to tens of thousands of Roma living in the same neighbourhood – is perhaps an additional reason why a stronger cultural identity and knowledge of the language is maintained than in the geographically more scattered settlements of the former Austro-Hungarian Empire.

[12] With the gruesome exception of the deportations and extermination of Roma by the Nazis and their allies in the region – horrific acts which can hardly be categorised as integration policies.

[13] I have noticed that this still occurs in the South of France where grape picking is a common source of income for travelling Roma.

scornfully, especially when it was a question of *our Gypsies*, not those suspect Gypsies, who still travelled and *stole the chickens*.

Till the end of the Second World War there had been no comparable assimilatory policies to that of the Habsburgs. Regarded as a marginal issue, the *Gypsy question* was handled as a matter of police work with ministries of the interior responsible for controlling their movements as well as their enclaves on the outskirts of villages and towns. Age-old prejudices supported the accepted view of Roma as criminals. A 1938 decree of the Hungarian Ministry of Interior stipulated: 'every Gypsy is a suspect' and a 1942 decree stated: 'a Gypsy is only allowed to leave his settlement to go to his workplace... and shall not sit on town benches'. However this state of affairs was paradise compared with what was about to follow. *Porrajmos* – the Roma Holocaust – claimed thousands of victims, who were first deported and then exterminated. It took a full half-century for this to be officially acknowledged and concrete data is still lacking about those who perished.

Although the new post-war constitutions acknowledged Roma as fully-fledged citizens, governments considered them of minor importance and paid only lip service to their social and educational needs. The Communist-led regimes which were established soon afterwards adopted the Soviet model of treating national minorities as possessing only folkloric significance. This downgraded status was further subordinated under the banner of proletarian internationalism. In practice Roma were barely considered as an authentic national or ethnic minority. The post-war years, characterised by imposed heavy industrialisation and severe shortages of consumer goods, allowed Roma handicrafts some leeway for a brief period. Meanwhile land reforms did not apply to Roma since only landless and poorer peasants were entitled to few acres. However, the truth of the matter is that very few Roma were keen to work the land as farmers. Some did[14] but many others preferred to own just a domestic animal or two.

The extensive Soviet growth model of rapid industrialisation, with its never-ending demand for unskilled labour, soon exhausted the manpower reservoir of remaining landless peasants. The gap was partially filled by turning in the late 1950s to the Roma – a shift which radically changed their livelihood and lifestyle. It was virtually impossible to escape the status of an employed worker as identity cards carried by every adult included not only the employer's name, normally a state enterprise, but even the precise occupation. Punitive work camps were established for those termed 'class enemies' or 'parasites' – people regarded as shirking the construction of socialism.

In contrast to previous governments the ruling regimes did formulate policies for Roma, emphasising the unacceptability of their social and economic backwardness and

---

[14] I had the opportunity to meet some in Bulgaria in the early 1990s.

the need for their social inclusion, although their cultural and ethnic differences were ignored. Unlike the Habsburgs, these totalitarian administrations managed to recruit them into mainstream labour markets, overwhelmingly as unskilled workers.[15] In this area the greatest demands were in heavy industry, construction, mining and state farms. Many Roma women were also employed in textile factories.

From the late sixties an important group of like-minded Hungarian sociologists started to tackle the issue of poverty. These efforts culminated in a 1971 research project headed by István Kemény.[16] This research collected indispensable data on the country's Roma population and represents the most detailed and reliable data on Roma in this period in the whole region. Yet, for lack of an alternative, the definition of the Gypsy target group was that used by officialdom.[17]

Apart from a few novels, poems and short stories written by Roma writers and poets in these decades, no substantive evidence is available depicting the changes which occurred in the behavioural and psychological aspects in the lives of the 'New Proletarians'. Therefore the questions and hypothesis that follow are entirely my own. My presuppositions are based on the conviction that imposition of a dominant alien culture provokes a host of syndromes, primarily in terms of identity.[18] The experience of Roma has been similar but *not identical* to the integration processes suffered by native populations under colonialism. Equally important, however, is the impact made by the new occupations and lifestyle which change the material conditions of those being integrated. During the course of history many of these processes have been gradual and undramatic, moulded by multiple interactions between the actors. But brutal policies, if enforced for a sustained period such as those since 1961, can have a profound influence on the process of change.

Along their sinuous path through history the Roma have never been completely 'broken in' to the ways of *gadjo* mores. For centuries they have retained an exceptional capacity to adapt, giving up what is strictly necessary while maintaining the essence of their indigenous values and culture. However, after previous decades had weakened their capacity to resist, Soviet-style social engineering achieved the greatest success in their acculturation, essentially by making Roma trades obsolescent.

---

[15] Official statistics from the late 1970s give figures of over 80% of Roma males and close to 50% of females in regular employment.

[16] A cluster of well known researchers – Ottilia Solt, Gábor Havas, Zsolt Csalog and others – were involved not only in this research but also launched an independent movement of solidarity with the poor. This critical initiative was hardly appreciated by the regime. The same research was repeated 22 years later after Kemény returned from enforced emigration, a unique case in that part of the world.

[17] Even in primary school registers the names of Roma pupils were accompanied by the letter 'c', for *cigán* (Gypsy).

[18] See Franz Fanon, *The Wretched of the Earth*, MacGibbon & Kee, 1965.

The **perception of time** seems to be the most evident change to have affected them. Standardised production, with compulsory hours spent in a *repetitive manner* at the workplace, was in direct conflict with longstanding flexibility at work which determined the traditional way in which time had been experienced. What was new was not so much the physical effort. On the contrary painful, exploitative or even self-exploitative types of work were not unknown. Instead it was the *systemic and systematic* character of the **new time** which had to be endured and slowly accepted. At first it was not obvious to them that the next day's working hours took priority over a family event or festivity and so a reprimand for absenteeism appeared unjust or inhumane. But now, as regular employees, the 'prison of time' started to oppress them in the same way as it did all other workers.

The relationship to **regular monetary income**, its planned utilisation or accumulation seemed equally incongruous and, paradoxical as it may seem, *irrational*. Their customary situation of permanent scarcity – when even the next day's bread was in doubt – led to an alternative rationale where the immediate satisfaction of elementary needs became the absolute priority. Now, for the first time in their history, families could count on a basic and *reliable income* every month, year after year.

The kinds of **security** offered to all the members of so-called state socialist society became part of the everyday life of the Roma as well. This meant not only job security, but health services, accommodation[19] and compulsory schooling for their children. Such benefits were unknown until then and replaced the hazardous existence to which they had been exposed. Their sense of security was further strengthened as racist statements were made illegal and consequently liable to prosecution.[20] This changed environment encouraged new kinds of personal contact between Roma and their non-Roma workmates, which even included having the occasional beer together in the local pub after work. It also made social mobility more attainable for individual Roma, either through access to technical education or by promotion to team leader in the construction or mining industries. Some Roma also joined the ruling Communist party or were recruited to the regular army and police. For the happy few university degrees were an attainable goal.

---

[19] Czechoslovak governments subjected Roma to an extended series of discriminatory measures. After the Second World War 200,000 Roma were forcibly transported from Slovakia to the industrial centres of Moravia and Bohemia and after the collapse of the Communist regime many were declared stateless after the division of the two states in 1993. Subsequently Roma were often relocated to high-rise buildings, inflaming avoidable inter-ethnic tensions. In contrast, employed Roma in Hungary were offered cheap credit for building family houses by the Kádár regime in its latter period.

[20] Legal measures banning discriminatory statements, in themselves, did not lead to the disappearance of prejudice against the Roma but they did make daily life more tolerable for them.

These trends also had a marked effect on social and cultural traditions within Roma groups. For instance, the influence of powerful figures such as the *vajda*[21] diminished, even among Romani speaking groups – the most steadfast defenders of tradition. Such developments clearly demonstrated the intimate connection between integration and acculturation (here some would use the term assimilation).

In conclusion, the *proletarianisation* experienced by the Roma radically changed their role in society. As a rule, they were prevented from making their livelihood in the service sector, as formerly, and instead large numbers had to join the production process of their host societies. From this point onwards the precise meaning of the term *host society* is questionable, since awareness of a double identity – both national and ethnic – gradually gained momentum. The experience of compulsory school attendance, receiving equal pay for equal work and being called up for national service in the army like their *gadjo* peers all strengthened the feeling of belonging to the nation. Of course discrimination did not suddenly vanish from everyday life but for Roma new opportunities appeared on the horizon. Nevertheless centuries-old separation from mainstream social development still remained a major obstacle to their large-scale inclusion. Consequently disadvantaged strata on the margins of the marginalised – although benefiting from employment and social security – were failing to catch up. However, in a period of less than forty years involving barely two generations, it would have been unrealistic to expect more substantial results. Radical change begged for more time.

Expulsion from Paradise

It is customary to state that the biggest losers from the collapse of the Soviet model in 1989-1990 have been the Roma. In fact the adoption of a neo-liberal model and consequent economic restructuring affected much of the general workforce but primarily the unskilled, amongst which the Roma formed the core. But it is equally true that whereas the bulk of the newly unemployed non-Roma gradually managed to re-enter the labour market, the overwhelming majority of Roma workers have remained in the cold for the past two decades.

In addition, the rapid demographic growth of the Roma population – a pattern characteristic of the Third World – became more visible with its expulsion from Paradise, whereas the majority population declined as elsewhere in Europe. Entitled to the benefits of the social security system, although no longer contributing to it because of their

---

[21] Traditional leader with questionable legitimacy. In Hungary this phenomenon has recently re-emerged from the ashes, contributing to a chaotic scene of self-designated saviours of the community.

enforced unemployment, the Roma in the new democracies were increasingly singled out as *scapegoats* in an atmosphere where the previous ethos of solidarity was evaporating.

The early 1990s were full of illusions as people believed that freedom and wellbeing were synonymous in the West but these hopes soon faded as the laws of the market economy began to operate. Roma groups with trading experience soon took advantage of new opportunities for cross-border petty commerce. However these gaps were soon closed by stricter controls. Nevertheless such dealing established a narrow stratum of successful Roma businessmen making a livelihood from antiques, flowers, catering and small construction firms.

In contrast the marginalisation of the overwhelming majority of unemployed Roma dramatically intensified during this period. This had most impact on those in remote villages in economically underdeveloped regions. There, job opportunities were virtually non-existent and the only means of supplementing meagre family incomes was by illegal casual labouring.

These Roma had forgotten the skills of their traditional occupations and had not replaced these with contemporary entrepreneurial experience, having been 'spoiled' for decades by easily available job opportunities. Worst of all, they had lost *the ability to solve acute problems of survival*. With social security benefits their only regular income, the mass of Roma ex-proletarians fell easy prey to moneylenders and were plunged into limbo. They also lost the conventional sense of time – that had been so hard to acquire – as family heads no longer left for work each morning. Meanwhile a generation of children grew up with no experience of the meaning of regular employment. In this way a substantial layer of the Roma population slid into *slum culture* with all its negative side effects like aggression and crime, which only strengthened re-emerging prejudices about the lazy, useless, no-good, parasitic Gypsy.

In spite of their harmful social and economic consequences, the post-Communist democracies presented the opportunity – for the first time in history – for the Roma to be **regarded as citizens**. Till then their only means of self-affirmation had been so-called cultural associations. Without exception these had been initiated and strictly controlled by the party-state and their leaders had been handpicked from the numerically restricted Roma nomenclature. In the early years after regime change many of the new NGO initiatives launched by local Roma elites preserved the same frame of mind and concentrated on securing funding for their traditional music and dance groups. At this time only a few, intelligentsia-led organisations, based in capital cities, proclaimed human rights, advocacy and discrimination as their agenda. But inevitably it took time to develop awareness.

These initiatives should be seen in the context of the sudden and unexpected changes that occurred in the region with the peaceful[22] establishment of pluralistic

---

[22] With the exception of the Romanian events in 1989.

democracies. Yet democratic institutions and traditions had not been the previous historical experience in these societies, where conflict between the numerous national minorities had fuelled nationalistic trends in the period between the two World Wars. In some countries the Roma remained invisible as a distinct population group but generally the new or amended constitutions acknowledged them as an identifiable part of the nation. In Yugoslavia, for instance, the Roma were categorised as a national minority, whereas in Hungary they were labelled as an ethnic minority.

However Hungary was the only country to establish **minority self-governments** – a move which merits further attention. In 1993 the Hungarian Parliament adopted a law providing adequate financial support to ensure the cultural autonomy of minorities – twelve national and one ethnic – living within the state borders. The real purpose was to protect the cultural autonomy of the numerically far larger Hungarian minorities in surrounding countries and the naive expectation was that neighbouring governments would reciprocate. The Roma were the sole group to be classified as an ethnic minority on the grounds that they had never been a nationality, since no Roma nation state had ever existed.[23] This law enabled a minimum of ten citizens in any municipality, who affirmed their membership of a recognised minority, to establish their own local self-government. However, since all citizens in the municipality were eligible to vote, the majority was able to determine the outcome of elections. This outright inconsistency was corrected in 2006, restricting eligibility to vote in self-government elections to minority members. Nowadays, out of the 3,200 municipalities in the country, there are close to 1,000 Roma local self-governments, headed by a National Self-Government.

In spite of these developments the annual reports of the Constitutional Court repeatedly criticise Parliament for not complying with its constitutional duty to ensure the political representation of minorities in the legislative body. This deficiency has persisted for two decades, epitomising the failure of politicians to take this matter at all seriously. The four Roma MPs in Budapest and the one MEP in Strasbourg all gained their seats on party rolls and are thus bound by party discipline. Other prominent Roma include the minority ombudsman and the press spokesperson of the former prime minister, not to mention the officers for Roma affairs in various ministries. But the numerous Hungarian TV stations do not employ a single Roma anchorman – the perfect window dressing to impress Brussels and Washington.

Although the self-governments may be beneficial for the twelve minorities by safeguarding their mother tongue and folk traditions, individual Serbs and Slovaks are not singled out as such by the rest of the population, as they are regarded as an integral

---

[23] The Greek minority, for instance, amounting to 5,000 people, was also entitled to the status of a national minority. This was an over-reaction, as historically there had been no Greek community living in Hungary until the previous regime offered asylum to Greek political émigrés in the late 1940s.

part of society. In contrast, cultural autonomy – for all its merits – is far from sufficient to counter the daily discrimination and widespread problems faced by Roma. Their self-governments have neither the authority nor financial means to offer effective support to Roma families. Municipal offices frequently refer Roma citizens in need to Roma self-governments with the excuse that these bodies are responsible for the provision of assistance. As I see it, the main advantage of such self-governments is that, in cases where Roma representatives are invited to attend local government meetings, they can provide an apprenticeship – a sort of leadership training in dealing with communal problems. By now many Roma are ready to participate in decisions related to local developmental investments, if asked to do so. While a few enlightened mayors adopt such practices which promote social harmony, these are exceptions that prove the rule.

For two decades Hungarian governments, led by whatever party, have drawn up short and long-term plans to improve the situation of the Roma and have even made budgetary resources available. The results have been dismal and according to a recent Treasury report, this is due to local authority mismanagement of these funds. The most positive initiatives have been in the field of education with an extended grant system for Roma mid and higher level students and also attempts to end segregation in primary and pre-school institutions through funding for minority quotas in their operational budgets. However successes are few in number and in 600 primary schools segregated education still continues.

Whatever the eventual fate of the self-governmental model, its introduction provoked mixed feelings in Roma. This system was imposed from above as a by-product of a broader policy without consulting them or anticipating its role or effects on them. On the other hand the creation of minority self-governments established the only elected – and thus legitimate – local and national representation of the community. However as their effectiveness is questionable, their acceptance by the community continues to be weak. In the meantime they remain the only local institutions offering immediate protection against violent racist attacks on Roma – a recent dangerous development. As regards progress towards a functioning Roma civil society which is genuinely democratic, their status as semi-governmental representative institutions diminishes the space in which NGOs can operate, creating conflicts of interest amongst bodies speaking for Roma. Blessing or curse? Even after seventeen years of their existence, this remains an open question.

Roma civil society – or to be more precise the Roma sector of the civil society in a given country – burst into life and is still growing in terms of NGOs set-up. These can be numbered in their hundreds in some countries, although only a few are well established. Even these admit their inability to collect membership fees, explaining this by their members' desperate economic circumstances. But by accepting this they have abandoned one of the main pillars of democratic practice within organisations. With the appearance of the post-modern model of *service delivery NGOs*, funded exclusively by governments or private donors, the essence of an independent civil sector has been substantially weakened in the new democracies. Professionalisation – concentrating on writing funding applications, project proposals and reports – has taken priority over mobilising, raising awareness and developing a culture of participation. This shift in focus is by no means exclusive to Roma organisations but with their ethnic movement at a formative stage, these practices appear more as obstacles than aids to progress. Consequently it is often hard to defend Roma against hostile accusations of conducting ethno-business.

The present state of affairs came about when a significant group of educated young Roma slid – whether willingly or not – into the donor-recipient paradigm, as there seemed no viable alternative. In the early years of democratisation Roma leaders mostly came from the generation educated under the previous regime, where democratic practices were unknown. As in majority societies – though even more evident due to traditional power relations within Roma communities – the spirit of cooperation based on partnership was virtually absent. Since Roma were unprepared to make the most of new opportunities, the cult of the leader was reinforced. This probably explains the emergence of so many extremely short-lived NGOs and political parties. Eventually more and more women became involved in organisations and public life, unsurprisingly generating positive results. This significant new trend had a radical influence in challenging this traditionally male-dominated culture.

The mere existence of a Roma civil sector and its presence in public life both encouraged and strengthened the voice of those who had been silent before. Likeminded *gadjo* organisations also appeared,[24] mainly concerned with human rights, legal defence and advocacy but also with education, training and housing issues. Other NGOs, mainly from the US, limited themselves to funding Roma-related projects. With time Roma established and staffed similar organisations but this often led to unhealthy competition between Roma and *gadjo* organisations for funding.

---

[24] The *Open Society Institute* (OSI) has played a unique and ground-breaking role, both regionally and nationally, in supporting the Roma cause. This organisation has been the main donor and initiator not only of the Decade of Roma Inclusion, in cooperation with the World Bank and now 12 governments in the region, but also by launching and funding the European Roma Rights Centre and the Roma Education Fund. Likewise national foundations of the OSI operate in many countries of the CEE region, funding a host of programmes and projects. Lately the Roma pavilion during the Venice Biennale, also an OSI-funded initiative, has attracted international attention. Nevertheless some questions are asked regarding the funding policies of the biggest private donor for Roma projects in the region, suggesting that these do not always correspond with what some Roma organisations identify as the most pressing needs and priorities. Others would prefer more horizontal methods of empowerment, oriented towards small-scale, local partnerships and initiatives as well.

However such financial support diminished as EU membership for these countries drew closer. The new type of dependency is now centred on securing EU funds.[25] This involves meeting onerous bureaucratic requirements, leading to the growth of new administrative hierarchies within local organisations instead of strengthening their role as community organisers. It is time that donors, too, recognised that without appropriate communication and empowerment techniques, funding in itself often fosters dependence in recipients rather than promoting their genuine, autonomous development.

An attempt at empowerment

When the Autonómia Foundation (AA)[26] was established in the summer of 1990 there was hardly any experience of this kind of activity in Hungary. Nor did any other foundation set out to become a donor and development agency in partnership with the Roma. The Foundation set itself the objective of developing Roma civil society through income generating projects and the donors[27] supported this approach.

> ### The **Pakiv** *project*
>
> The AA initiated the *Pakiv* project because it recognised the need in the region for a well-trained young Roma cadre capable of giving new impetus to the developing Roma movement. Funded by the World Bank the project began with nine months of training in leadership and management for young Roma from Bulgaria, Hungary, Romania and Slovakia. Two rounds of the instruction resulted in around 45 Roma, aged between 19 and 32, being trained in English language, leadership, needs assessment, community organisation, participatory development methods, fundraising and project management skills as well as knowledge of existing practices related to income-generation and job creation among Roma in the CEE region. Since completing the programme, over 90% of former trainees have been working in governmental and non-governmental agencies at local, national and international levels.

---

[25] Despite the substantial funding available to the governments of Member States, the impact and effectiveness of national policies for improving the situation of the Roma remain extremely disappointing.

[26] The Hungarian title of this foundation, of which the English version is the *Hungarian Foundation for Self-reliance*.

[27] Initially the Rockefeller Brothers Fund, followed by the Ford Foundation, the Mott Foundation, the Mellon Foundation and several anonymous US donors became our regular sponsors. Afterwards the European Union, the Soros Foundation and some state funding also increased the scope of our actions.

At that time there were over 80 Roma registered organisations in the country, most of them local. The obvious first step was to support these NGOs in the hope of encouraging democratic practices in their procedures. One possibility was to 'teach' democracy by means of courses, seminars and publications. On the other hand a private foundation could not even think of creating jobs, therefore AA invited local Roma organisations to submit grant applications for income generating programmes and projects. This enabled the NGOs to tackle practical concerns by launching their own initiatives while easing the economic problems of their members and developing solidarity amongst them. Such an approach was a way of making autonomy and income generation compatible. Based on previous experience, the technique of good old Socratic maieutics was adopted as the most efficient tool. Using this pedagogic method trainers – acting almost as midwives – put focused questions to participants, allowing them to discover and draw on their own latent knowledge.

Nevertheless this approach was not suitable for all kinds of Roma. Local NGO members were drawn from the most integrated among the former skilled and semi-skilled workers of cooperative and state farms, construction firms and industrial plants who started mostly small-scale agricultural and stock rearing projects. In certain cases, where the community was more cohesive and know-how and organisational abilities were above average, some production-based projects managed to target the local market. However the most marginalised families believed that 'Roma money' was coming into the village and so thought it should be distributed amongst them all by virtue of their ethnicity, whether or not they were organisation members.

Some ethical and technical aspects of the method used seem worth mentioning:

It is their life, not ours characterised the overall approach. The customary top-down aid techniques were rejected as failures; instead *'provoke' not persuade* was the guiding principle. Consequently funds were provided on condition that projects were initiated by local organisations and not by the staff of the foundation.

Dialogue not monologue governed communication among the partners. They were required to listen and be open to dialogue, to ask questions rather than give answers and to provide orientation rather than advice. In general the intention was to create space for the self-realisation of Roma partners in formulating and executing their initiatives. The parallel objective was to develop self-confidence – an attitude so rarely found among the socially excluded. AA's approach required close contact and permanent dialogue with partner organisations. Therefore a group of coordinators or facilitators were hired who had to be trained in methods of horizontal communication, patient dialogue and refraining from imposing their own views, i.e. to seek consensus with Roma partners. The individual coordinators had to question their own *do-gooder* tendencies – not an easy task – and encourage autonomous decision making at each stage of the project.

Loans not grants. Interest free loans fulfilled several functions at the same time: they presupposed an agreement on the rate and instalments of the loan repayment, thus improving planning ability – an essential element for changing the here-and-now culture; they developed know-how in money management, including dealing with bank accounts, expense documentation, submitting financial and other reports – all those management activities totally alien to partners till then; they contributed to growing self-respect as well as to mutual trust in Roma-*gadjo* relationships and by the formal signing of contract documents established horizontal links between partners by defining their mutual rights and obligations.

The empowerment process. Dialogue began between applicant organisations and AA as soon as their requests reached the foundation. Indeed AA has never funded a project that was not proposed by local people. Several meetings took place before final applications were formulated and contracts signed. For example, if a project was for pig rearing then there were further questions to be answered, such as: Do the members prefer to act jointly or individually? Are the pigsties in an operational state? Can any land be leased for growing maize since no fodder is currently available? The contract was then based on the answers to these questions and mutual responsibilities were laid down. The basic premise was that a well-managed process would encourage Roma to feel they owned the projects and having agreed the conditions, would take assume responsibility for them.

AA's unusual approach was viewed with suspicion by certain local Roma, since they had never experienced anything similar – particularly from *gadje*. The initiative often stimulated exaggerated expectations or fantasies of easy money. Later it became evident to most that AA grants were given on the basis of the merits of the project, irrespective of the political or institutional affiliation of the applicant organisation.[28] In the beginning loan repayments were negligible but by the third year, when the partnership between the coordinating team and Roma NGOs was well established, the repayment ratio increased to 76%. This was a striking success if compared, for instance, with Canadian government funding over decades for projects aimed at American Indians, where the corresponding repayment rate was 8%.

Going too far. Certainly reality did not always match the ideal picture that this account has suggested so far. Sometimes it was not only lack of experience but also going too far that prevented successful outcomes. For example, coordinators might fail

---

[28] Out of the 301 Roma organisations supported by AA, 37 projects were allocate to the local branches of the national organisation like *Phalarope*, 33 to *Lungo Drom*, 4 to *MCKSZ* (Cultural Association of Hungarian Roma), 3 each to *MCISZ* (Justice Organisation of Hungarian Roma) and *FICA Noi*, and 2 each to *Zsutinász*, *RISZ* (Association for Roma Integration) and *Igaz Szó* (True Word). The remaining 215 organisations, the substantial majority, were local independent associations, suggesting that those not relying on their parent organisation seemed to be more active and enterprising.

to contact local mayors or priests at the beginning of projects as they were so protective of the autonomy of their partner organisations. They were afraid of these functionaries taking over the projects, or even sabotaging them – fears not entirely without foundation. Besides this, some Roma politicians accused AA of harming their organisations or favouring competitors. In particular they objected to funding being given directly to their local chapters rather than being channelled through central bodies. The evident public relations failure by AA to explain its mission and methods hardly helped diminish mistrust and misunderstanding in the Roma political establishment, let alone the *gadjo* equivalent. To sum up it can be said that *AA's methods proved that ethnic and cultural specificities are no impediment to integration, provided that the integration process is based on cooperation, participation and trust, instead of 'business as usual'.*

Some remaining questions. Evidently AA's experiment is neither the only approach, nor *the* way to proceed under all circumstances. It is not as much the *what?* but the *how?* What matters is the practice of horizontal communication. With hindsight one might even say that perhaps this initiative could have had a much bigger impact nowadays, when the movement has reached a more developed stage and the income of Roma in rural areas has drastically plummeted. In the early 1990's the accustomed sense of job security provided by the previous regime was still too close for more radical initiatives to emerge from below.

If we look at the quantitative indicator of success, i.e. the repayment rate of loans, the results are more than satisfactory. But if we want to measure the qualitative aspects – the sustainability of these projects, the extent to which partner organisations adopted democratic practices in their procedures, the projects' impact as a role model for local Roma communities, or whether these projects contributed to the social, economic and political participation of Roma in everyday life where they lived – then we have to admit that the achievements were far more modest.

Qualitative benefits are hard to assess because gathering such data is expensive and there was insufficient funding to carry out this kind of evaluation. However a more important reason is the *relationship between funding and the time factor*. Donors, whether private or public, support projects lasting only one or on rare occasions two years, which inevitably raises questions about their sustainability. Likewise the funding of loans in AA projects only lasted a year, although exceptionally this was extended for a further year. In the case of marginal groups such a short time span for projects – even with competent support – conflicted with the aim of bringing about culture change and at the same time achieving economic benefits for participants.

As regards the adoption of democratic practices the main obstacle was that all too often membership of local organisations was recruited from within the same extended family. In such circumstances 'election' of the leadership was a hollow formality and 'control from below' was entirely absent.

The original objective of the training was to stimulate local income and employment initiatives among local Roma but this goal was never realised to the desired extent. Perhaps the project's over-generous funding had the opposite effect to that anticipated, since the sense of serving the local community ceased to exist in most cases. The value of leadership training, conceived and financed from 'above', remains very dubious when trainees are not selected on the basis of their past performance but in the optimistic hope of elite building. This would suggest that deprived and marginal communities in need of trained leaders capable of promoting their development cannot rely on the few amongst them with relevant professional experience. Yet another puzzle in the Roma riddle.

Nevertheless, in spite of these structural disadvantages and problems of prejudice, as well as the inevitable weaknesses of a path-breaking initiative, the AA programme offered Hungarian Roma their first opportunity to develop their own collective initiatives and to become autonomous agents in the wider context of civil society. This was demonstrated in subsequent years, when successful leaders of AA projects were prominent among regional and national cadres of the Roma movement.

Anti-Gypsyism is haunting Europe

Various reasons explain the perceptible growth of discrimination and intolerance directed against Roma in the CEE region. Predominant factors are the effects of globalisation and social reactions reflected in increased anxiety about security, which has now become the main concern throughout Europe. These coincided with social and economic problems and the recent financial crisis, as well as growing and visible abnormal manifestations of the *wretched of the earth* all over Europe, feeding the demand for more effective security policies. These anxieties have been accompanied by widespread Euro-scepticism in new Member States – a consequence of wishful thinking about the magical powers of the Union, which failed to meet expectations as a provider of unlimited resources. So in these circumstances it is worth reviewing the situation of the Roma in recent decades.

The now accepted official status of Roma as an ethnic or national minority, as opposed to their previous categorisation as a sub-ethnic group, has grown in significance since the birth of the Roma civil movement. Generally speaking, in this new phase two main lines of thinking emerged within the Roma movement – *culturalist* and *modernist*. Modernists are mainly drawn from a younger urban elite who see themselves as representatives of an ethnic minority group facing multiple social, economic, educational but primarily discrimination problems. Consequently their concerns focus on equal opportunities, human rights and integration. Culturalists are located primarily in rural areas and while less visible, are a significant presence in Roma communities. Headed by an older leadership, these prefer retaining tradition to integration. Many people have remained undecided between the two tendencies, which were not easily identifiable as such since they were often expressed as personal confrontations. Disagreements remained at this low level rather than developing into a debate about alternative strategies, which is characteristic of movements with a limited number of educated members.

The present state of ethnic identity building among Roma shows some, even if remote, similarities to the African nation building processes of the 1960s, where the task was to establish a new national awareness in place of localised tribal loyalties. Those who championed this idea took as their model the colonial powers and saw raising awareness as the royal path to establishing a nation state. The price to pay was to accept the norms of modernity requiring a radical transformation from archaic, pre-modern societal patterns. The bloody tribal wars that followed demonstrate the manifest failure of the dreams cherished by the great generation of post-independence African leaders. This example is given only to indicate stumbling blocks in the way of imposed integration. In any case this template cannot be applied directly to the situation of the Roma, as their niche in society has never been that of the colonised. But their historical experience of marginality, while maintaining their social institutions of 'clans', *familias*, and *kumpanias* and only recently having been officially identified as an ethnic minority, suggests that some of the potential pitfalls mentioned above may be relevant.

Launched in the early 1970s, the international Roma movement provided little guidance at first because it was dominated by Western European Roma. Their historical background and preoccupations were quite different and consequently cultural traditions and protection against discrimination were prioritised above the socio-economic conditions of CEE Roma communities. However, with the widespread increase of anti-Gypsyism in recent times, the idea of a separate European status for Roma has been proposed, although unsuccessfully as yet. Some Roma even began to dream about a possible nation state to be established on some unspecified territory. EU statements, although expressing concern about the situation of Roma, have failed to adopt a clear position on such matters. While Brussels did exert pressure earlier on the governments of applicant states to give higher priority to the situation of the Roma in their countries, it was sadly not able to exert the same extent of leverage after accession as before.

However, from the standpoint of the developing Roma movement, this institutional sphere remained remote from the daily life of rank-and-file Roma and had minimal impact on their status of unemployed post-proletarians. With Roma unable to exert effective pressure from below, CEE politicians preferred to keep a low profile for fear of losing 'white' votes if advocating expenditure on Roma. Likewise, without real bargaining power, Roma representatives were unable to ensure that an appropriate share of the budget, corresponding to their population numbers, was devoted to Roma affairs.

Nowadays the most striking, conflict-provoking phenomenon has been the aggressive anti-Gypsyism that has arisen in recent years. In Hungary Roma have been savagely hunted down in the manner of the Ku Klux Klan. In one chilling incident in 2009 a house was set on fire to drive out the occupants and the fleeing Roma father and his child were then shot dead. Such attacks mark a new stage in the deteriorating situation, which has been inflamed by the growing spread of hate speech in the media. Drastic reductions in social benefits (Slovakia 2004), cutting off electric power to an entire settlement because of unpaid bills (Bulgaria 2002) and naked racist aggression (Bulgaria 2007) have all provoked riots by Roma in retaliation – an unprecedented reaction in the past – indicating a transformed consciousness among present-day Roma. The mounting danger of a self-perpetuating cycle of violence demands radical rethinking of the future role of the Roma movement.

Paradoxical as this may seem, the growing threat to Roma individuals and communities may even have a positive outcome by instinctively forging stronger ties of solidarity amongst them. Although there is no firm evidence to support this supposition it can be expected that, in time, a positive response to such aggression might be the emergence of a strong, well-organised Roma movement at international, national and local level to combat the imminent risk of genocide. The exemplar seems to be the US Afro-American *civil rights movement*, the only successful case in modern history in democratic societies. Building a Roma movement, based not only on democratic rhetoric but also on empowerment, transparency, participation and trust, calls for a strong and effective grassroots approach. Unless this happens in a disciplined way, impulsive reactions by Roma become increasingly harder to avoid. Such inflammatory incidents increase in proportion to the mounting attacks against Roma.[29]

---

[29] In Hungary (Olaszliszka), after a high-school teacher's car had struck a local Roma girl, a group of Roma from her community retaliated by lynching the driver – killing him in front of his small daughters. This incident provoked an unprecedented campaign of anti-Roma hate speech. Without excusing this barbaric act, the press failed to report that the year before a local Roma child had been killed by a hit-and-run car in the same village. This at least could explain, if not excuse, the reaction of the girl's parents.

What now?

Unlike the 1960s and 70s, when economic growth and social well-being reached unprecedented levels in the US and the West and the prevailing climate was multi-culturalism and tolerance, the present globalised crisis kindles nationalistic, inward looking protectionism where fears and xenophobia gain ground. The negligible attention paid by CEE governments to the sorry situation of the Roma until now has little chance of improving in the future. Who should then think about a vision and strategy for the future? Is there a possible global path for Roma – at least for the countries in this region?

With rare exceptions the Roma elite that has emerged since regime change has not shown a noticeable willingness to engage with this challenge. At least publicly there is no sign of an open debate on such topics among its representatives. Much more vocal, and duly publicised by the media, are the personal attacks and mutual accusations, which are often based on political allegiance of the individual leaders.[30] In this respect the new *gadjo* post-Communist political class has offered the worst of examples, only to be imitated by civil leaders. Consequently it appears essential to acquire the spirit and skills of cooperative methods, allowing caucuses, coalitions and platforms to be built. This alliance-building should take place amongst Roma organisations as well as with the like-minded *gadjo* allies, leading to common policies and actions. These can produce the necessary snowball effect for the rank-and-file – a formidable force when mobilised – to gain the necessary conviction to participate in significant collective action and demonstrations in order to make the voice of the community heard. At this point we should recall Obama's blunt statement about victimhood at the beginning of this article.

Lenin declared: *misery does not revolutionise*; I would add, neither does it democratise. Those who have lived and worked in the midst of marginalised communities, as many Catholic priests did in Latin America, can bear witness to this. The tragic new exclusion of Roma, triggered by regime change in CEE countries, affected large segments of their population. As this process intensified the demoralising effect was to deepen still further their sense of being passive victims, leading to a noticeable growth in slum culture. Core aspects of their outlook include lack of self-esteem, searching for scapegoats, feelings of helplessness – as individuals as well as collectively – and loathing and hatred of others. This cluster of key elements, characterising the psychological state of powerless social individuals and groups, now appears to be the main obstacle to their mobilisation.[31]

---

[30] A relic of the communist regime is 'colonisation' by political parties, particularly when in government.

[31] Incidentally this is also a characteristic of ethnic Hungarians which has been much criticised down the centuries, particularly by leading national poets.

The ambivalent attitude of Roma officials to the increase in petty crime among unemployed Roma in villages and cities illustrates this barrier. They explain, and even excuse, this highly publicised behaviour simply as a consequence of endemic poverty. Their acceptance of such delinquency as a normal response to harsh economic situations, strengthens the community's self-image as victims. Worse still, accepting delinquency as an ethnic characteristic (Roma are poor, so they steal!) offers a justification for racism, which is ever more widespread among the general public.[32]

Another delicate issue should also be mentioned, i.e. the evident contradiction between deep-rooted, traditional social practices and the requirements and values of the Declaration of Human Rights. In other words there is a gap between the presumption of equal rights for all as regards wider society and the failure to confront remnants of pre-modern societal patterns found amongst less integrated strata of the Roma population. The relationship to children is a case in point. Although the great importance of children for Roma is acknowledged even by the majority population, the lack of interest of parents in school attendance or their exploitation of child labour are taboo subjects for Roma leaders, who shy away from dealing with them. This provides ammunition for right wing arguments that it is futile to provide support for this community.

Roma women's emancipation is steadily growing in strength, although still in its embryonic stages. Nevertheless the submissive demeanour that many women consider traditional and therefore proper behaviour seems to remain the predominant pattern.[33] Despite this, or even because of it, woman community organisers are now becoming instigators of change and are more open and energetic than many male leaders. In addition they are usually more sensitive to democratic, horizontal activism than most males and, as such, represent an asset which is insufficiently taken seriously by many national leaders.

Roma leaders' competitiveness and unwillingness to cooperate is also a major obstacle. Such attitudes may explain their inability to establish alliances on an equal footing, not only with other Roma organisations – a fundamental flaw – but markedly with like-minded, non-Roma associations as well. At this point a question of mutual responsibility arises. Well-meaning *gadjo* partners frequently take the role of donors and offer generous help, which can be motivated by a desire to expunge white guilt

---

[32] A recent poll in Hungary asked the question: 'Do you think that criminality is in the blood of the Roma?' (sic). In the 2010 parliamentary elections Jobbik, the acknowledged champion of anti-Gypsyism, won 17% of the seats, campaigning with the slogan 'Let's fight Gypsy criminality!'

[33] The 2007 documentary '*Barishey*' by Krisztina Bódis, an activist film maker working with Vlah women, included the following declaration by one of her participants: 'A woman is different from a man. A man can allow himself more things that a woman shouldn't!'

feelings. In this way they seek to offer recompense for the succession of historical wrongs inflicted on the excluded. However such reasons for involvement can often lead to patronising, *do-gooder* hierarchical relationships, instead of reciprocal democratic partnerships as equals. This paternalistic tendency, casting Roma in the role of passive recipients, only reinforces their sense of dependency.

Another aspect worth mentioning is the arrogance frequently displayed by leaders in their dealings with their fellow-Roma, which helps explain their lack of legitimacy. The role of representing the community often conflicts with that of serving it. Such patterns persist because of poor undemocratic election practices within organisations and reliance on the remnants of traditional family ties. In these circumstances control from below is non-existent.

It is hardly worth adding that appropriate role models in majority society are equally absent.

Numbers of well-qualified young Roma with university degrees and English language proficiency have recently started to emerge from higher education and are frequently offered career opportunities in national and international governmental offices or private institutions. Removed from the control of their communities and with prospects of attractive salaries, these graduates understandably prioritise career considerations over the goal of serving their communities. Their dilemma of split loyalties is sharpened by the facts that their appointment is largely a token gesture by their employers and their peripheral posts allow them little chance of influencing policies. Hopefully the sheer presence in growing numbers of these graduates may eventually create a critical mass.

The fundamental issue remains the lack of political clout of the Roma movement. In CEE countries the potential number of Roma votes, if they could be combined, are sufficient to sway the composition of elected national governments. Demographic trends will increasingly strengthen this possibility. In democratic systems the only way the voice of the excluded can be heard is through the ballot box. Therefore, by focusing mobilisation strategies on elections, two goals can be attained: achieving the necessary level of representation in parliament and, equally important in my opinion, making ordinary Roma aware of their rights and duties as citizens.

Apart from the fragmentary state of the Roma movement within countries, the main concerns remain the overall lack of vision as well as the need to list and prioritise strategic objectives relating to the future of the community as a whole.

In reviewing the prospects several general and specific questions need to be considered, analysed and debated. Some require immediate answers, such as: How can we counter increasingly frequent violent attacks against Roma individuals and neighbourhoods? Is this not the time to forge closer links between communities and organisations? Should self-defence groups be organised and if yes, should these consist of

Roma alone or together with local authorities? What should be done if there is an upsurge in violent retaliations by young Roma?

But other longer-term but no less important issues also require serious attention. Is there any answer to endemic unemployment? What local income-generating projects, even if small-scale, should be initiated to alleviate poverty? What kind of alliances between key actors (local authorities, non-Roma NGOs, regional development funds) can be made? Should not Roma parents attend school board meetings? Is this not the time to establish within municipalities effective care procedures for the infirm and elderly, working together with the local communities and likeminded individuals?

Then there are the broad strategic questions: Is integration the royal path to achieve equal status, and if yes, what does it entail? Is there something called *essential Roma culture and identity*, independent of time and space, to be modified and adapted to worldwide trends in globalisation, or is this a fantasy – just wishful thinking? Will future changes always be those that suit external interests and will they be imposed by the scenarios of others or is there a possibility that Roma might design an alternative future of their own?

In conclusion, even if it is not for an outsider to tell the democratic Roma movement what strategic decisions it should make, it is at least permissible to express his opinion to the reader of this essay. I find it useful to reiterate the ancient Athenians' credo: *Power lies in front of you, so reach out and grasp it*. This proto-democratic rule is as relevant for the Roma today, as it is for any other citizen in whatever country. During elections there is no reason for not attempting to gain positions of power, such as the post of mayor, especially in places where there are many potential Roma voters. Even though this has seldom happened in northern Balkan countries, this dictum remains valid. But to me the establishment of a Roma *ethnic* party or parties, movements and coalitions, seems an indispensable prerequisite for stepping onto the stage of political competition. However, this is provided that these bodies apply bottom-up techniques, their policies are transparent and consensual and their leaders are accountable to their constituencies, and trust – *pakiv* – becomes the route to success.

It may seem ludicrous to suggest such an idea as ground-breaking as there is nothing revolutionary about it but in Hungary such a position appears heretical, even among liberal Roma. No one questions the important political role played by Hungarian ethnic parties in neighbouring Romania and Slovakia but when it comes to a possible Roma party at home, all sorts of fears are voiced. Foremost amongst these is fear of arousing the deeply entrenched anti-Gypsyism of the majority. Yet governments put forward Roma programmes, strategies and policies as a matter of course and a European Roma Strategy is now on the agenda. Nevertheless, for reasons hard to understand, the idea of Roma political parties based on ethnicity is rejected as illegitimate.

The course of history teaches us that minorities have only succeeded in obtaining their rights if they stood up for them. Why should the Roma be different? There are no magic shortcuts. Only a sustained effort by dedicated leaders and activists – often lasting generations – can step by step cement the solidarity of their brothers and sisters. Why should the Roma be any different?

While history has never evolved on the basis of blueprints, this has not prevented humanity from trying to define the required parameters of *the good society*. For the first time in their history the Roma, who have already paid a heavy price for their survival, are in a position to reflect on the trade-offs resulting from the different options they could choose. It is up to them, to their movements and leaders, to determine what price they are ready to pay for fully-fledged integration.

CHOICES TO BE MADE AND PRICES TO BE PAID: POTENTIAL ROLES AND CONSEQUENCES IN ROMA ACTIVISM AND POLICY-MAKING

NICOLAE GHEORGHE
IN COLLABORATION WITH GERGŐ PULAY[1]

In search of language

The time has come to suggest some serious changes in Roma civil society. This paper is written as a response to the compelling need for a language that goes beyond political correctness and challenges the assumptions of liberal human rights discourse. Recent polemics over Roma integration are mingled with a reluctance to address 'touchy' or 'risky' issues – sometimes even 'taboos' – by those who strive to defend the rights of Roma or by Roma themselves.[2] We need to forge a new language, based on a frank and critical revision of previous approaches, to understand the origins of this crisis and move forward.

This is why we really need to talk about such controversial topics as the links between Roma international mobility, chain-migration, human trafficking and criminality; the inequality of women and men amongst the Roma; the 'begging-business', in particular the forced involvement of children and teen-agers in activities such as begging; the practice of early marriages in some traditional communities; and the exploitation of child labour by certain families who sometimes take advantage of the elderly or disabled as well.

What makes certain Roma economically redundant and others economically productive in their home countries or on their journeys abroad? What kind of cultural patterns lie behind these differences? Do notions like 'Gypsy work' (*romani butji*) or 'cunning' (*shmekeria*) only refer to a form of fraud? Is it possible to accept such

---

[1] This text is primarily based on the interviews and discussions I had with Nicolae Gheorghe in Bucharest and Salerno during 2009 and 2010. It also includes certain fragments from his previous writings, notes and speeches that he delivered to various audiences. Throughout the process of transcription and editing I was following his personal suggestions regarding the structure of the argument. (Gergő Pulay)

[2] See amongst other examples the media coverage of Roma-related debates and diplomatic arguments between France, Romania and the European Union during the Summer and Autumn of 2010.

mentalities and practices as *opportunities* – or even as legitimate and profitable sources of income in competitive market environments? What has made informal or 'traditional' Roma leaders like the *vajda* or *bulibaşă* so powerful recently? What has helped them re-emerge as potential partners for policy-makers and national, regional and local authorities? Why have they gained legitimacy, especially when European agencies and public opinion demand 'good practices' and 'concrete measures' with the expectation of quick results, which in reality may be no more than window-dressing? Why are these patriarchal Roma leaders secretly envied by their *gadje* partners when they occupy posts in unstable public bodies and face confused Roma and non-Roma voters – some of whom may even have been bribed? How do Roma experts, activists and policy-makers use the concepts of culture, identity and tradition when discussing those they claim to support and represent? On the other hand how do Roma themselves use their social networks and cultural capital in changing contexts at home or abroad? What are the enduring markers of Roma ethnicity, and what should be changed in this regard if we wish to achieve wider political mobilisation as active partners of further civic initiatives? How do Roma activists function as facilitators and mediators between their different social worlds? Do they expect to be hired to implement projects or to become community organisers to inspire grass-roots movements? What should be the further aims of Roma mobilisation – particularly in relation to nation-building and citizenship roles? Politically correct speech proved too abstract and simplistic when trying to resolve dilemmas about rights, welfare, poverty and exclusion, as well as extended disputes about 'civic' versus 'ethnic' Roma elites. Public debates and policies have continued to ignore a wide range of important issues, yet these have been haunting me since I claim to be part of that Roma elite.

This text is based on discussions with colleagues – in particular with András Bíró – on recent events that have complicated the relationship between particular Roma groups and majority populations and also their home states or where they migrated. The argument is primarily dedicated to fellow activists, policy-makers and engaged Roma experts in order to stimulate further discussion. In the social sciences at least two alternative and verifiable theories are required, precisely because they can disprove each other. Instead of ultimate answers or an all-encompassing theory, what I offer here is more of a subjective, partial account or mosaic, based on previous dialogues as well as the story of my life and work as a Roma activist.[3]

---

[3] For further sources on the life story of Nicolae Gheorghe, see: Beck, Sam (1993). Racism and the Formation of a Romani Ethnic Leader. In George Marcus ed. *Perilous States: Conversations on Culture, Politics, and Nation.* Chicago and London: The University of Chicago Press, 165–186. Heinschink, Mozes F. – Karoly, Mirjam (2001): Interview with Nicolae Gheorghe, source: http://ling.kfunigraz.ac.at/~rombase/cd/data/pers/data/gheorghe.en.pdf.

If anything connects the different sections of this paper, it is the complementary approach I have adopted. Each section starts with controversial issues which have been topics of extensive public debates, either between Roma and non-Roma or amongst members of Roma NGOs, other civic organisations and governments. My main intention is to understand what makes these issues controversial, to spell out alternative approaches and to articulate choices that might be made in finding solutions. Each and every choice implies different prices to be paid when decisions have to be made. How can we achieve reasonable levels of success, dignity and personal fulfilment while dealing with these issues? How can we make better and decent lives, not just for ourselves, our families and for the 'Roma people' as a whole but also for others with whom we live together – our non-Roma fellow citizens?

Throughout our discussion the common aim of the Roma movement should be clear: the organisation, mobilisation and eventual re-mobilisation of Roma, based on pursuing the struggle against racism and discrimination. Part of this process is to unite the various often competing groups in the Roma movement in flexible but effective ways. This will enable Roma groups to collaborate and work together with local authorities, civic associations, churches and political parties. Agreement on common interests is a prerequisite for Roma at local and higher levels to define a coherent policy agenda. In other words, Roma themselves should take increased responsibility for initiatives to improve the situation of their people. It would be hard to overestimate the importance of activists, economic entrepreneurs and intellectual and moral Roma elites in this process. Poverty and exclusion are usually presented as insurmountable barriers to social mobility or political mobilisation. Activists tend to think decision makers can only be made aware of the situation and stirred by dramatic images of Roma as victims of their societies. I also played a part in backing these ideas, especially during the 1990s. But we seem to forget that some of our people have already achieved economic and educational success. Like us, they are part of an emerging middle-class, both amongst the Roma and in mainstream society. Our common projects, self-funded initiatives and voluntary associations have a crucial role in identifying future prospects for Roma civil society.

Most of us working in this field are Roma through our discourse; because we *talk* about being Roma and not because we *live* as many Roma do. We often have to describe the Roma way of life and culture to others. So, for many of us, discourse and language are basic assets for legitimising our positions and building our careers. At the same time we feel a sense of urgency, created by the need to provide evidence of action in promoting 'good causes'. We should be aware that the language we use touches other people's sensitivities and has actual consequences for their lives. However appreciating possible consequences should not prevent us from speaking frankly and admitting our failures while explaining the context. Tackling controversial issues in order to renew the vocabulary of human rights is part of *the price* we have to pay.

Recent political developments – particularly the re-emergence of nationalism and populism after EU-accession – suggest that the liberal, human rights-oriented approach to Roma integration failed to achieve many of its expected goals. The rise of anti-Gypsyism and violent attacks on Roma in the Czech Republic, Hungary and Romania are evident signs of crisis. Re-examination of the origins of these tensions is needed to prevent further exploitation of the 'Gypsy question' by right wing extremism and populist leaders in their quest for electoral majorities.[4] This would benefit not only Roma but our democracies too. One source of contemporary anti-Gypsyism and hostility towards Roma has been our own unwillingness to mention certain issues. This has allowed them to become the exclusive domain of extremist politicians, the police, populist justice and mob-violence. Putting them on our agenda is a step towards resolving them. The language we are searching for should not arouse hostility to Roma but instead should provide alternative frames. This allows thoughtful treatment of controversial issues, which would otherwise be labelled 'Gypsy crime' or attributed to the 'genetic force of Gypsy nomadism'.[5] Certain statements in this paper might be criticised as reinforcing stereotypes although my intention is quite the opposite. I want to start developing appropriate language for tackling previous taboos or *open secrets*.

It is hard to take this step because going beyond the limits of political correctness requires a considerable effort. It might be argued that this endeavour is doomed to failure from the start, since no alternatives yet exist to already established discursive frames. Renouncing certain basic elements of the human rights approach to Roma appears dangerous, since it could lead to unpredictable consequences both for how we speak and in practice. The natural assumption is that this discursive change opens Pandora's Box, leaving Roma defenceless against racism where the victim is blamed or subsequent pogroms legitimised. This is why many Roma activists and engaged experts fail to acknowledge or even mention these issues. Instead of seeking viable solutions, we restrict our role to *policing thinking*. In cases where certain Roma deserve blame, we intervene and demand that racist statements should be condemned. This strategy can be seen as reducing freedom of speech, since it conveys the message that Roma cannot be criticised. Many core concepts of our anti-racist vocabulary are eroded in the process – including the very notions of 'racist' or 'racism' – since these are often used without any proper definition of their meaning or scope. Such confusion results from a lack of reflection and critical analysis of previous or continuing anti-racist initiatives. This is one reason why no public agreement could be reached on identifying principal forces behind contemporary forms of racism. As is often seen,

---

[4] See András Bíró's paper, *The Price of Roma Integration*, in this volume.

[5] As could be seen, criminality amongst some groups of Roma was often a topic of extended political discussions in countries such as Hungary, particularly during local or national electoral campaigns.

public figures – including representatives of the extreme right – can easily reject the racist label by pointing at someone else as 'the racist'. Now we are witnessing an apparent resurgence of tensions and hatred directed at Roma and other European minorities without knowing what exactly should be categorised as 'racist'.

Roma activists, policy-makers and other engaged experts are often haunted by visions of holocaust, ethnic cleansing or genocide. Discussions are constrained by fear that certain ways of speaking can make the recurrence of such tragedies more likely. Liberating ourselves from these fears does not mean denying the Holocaust or treating it differently. The idea of holocaust is familiar to all, regardless of ethnic identity or particular historical and political contexts. Holocaust as an operator allows an immediate switch from local experiences to the disturbing spectre of concentration camps and allows us to portray the plight of Roma communities as part of a greater historical narrative. Nevertheless, actions to raise public awareness about the social and historical implications of the Holocaust are not equivalent to reducing the whole Roma issue to the tragic experience of World War Two. Racist discrimination has been decisive throughout Roma history but it does not exhaust its entirety. Such a reduction runs the risk of losing sight of the internal dynamics and particularities of different Roma communities in their own social contexts.[6]

On denominations

I have to clarify my choices about how I refer to the people I discuss or address in these pages. I might be seen as inconsistent in using different denominations in parallel – employing both correct and pejorative terms simultaneously. However, being identified as Gypsy – or the various equivalents of *Tsigan* – is perceived as neutral by many. These terms can be the glue that binds people together provided they use it for themselves in contrast to the derogatory usage of others. But once external, powerful actors – whether the parliament, state or administration – begin to utilise such denominations, hierarchical authority takes precedence. Instead, in the first place, individuals should be offered freedom of choice about their own preferred denomination – that is whether they wish to be formally identified as Rom, Gypsy or *Tsigan* – instead of being labelled with an imposed classification. This choice should not be limited by any restrictive conditions such as those advocated in recent statements by the Romanian parliament and Romanian Academy.

Those who argue in favour of the term 'Roma' being used in public and official contexts usually claim that formal usage of this denomination they regard as correct

---

[6] For further discussion, see the section on local and universal knowledge in this text.

would partly compensate for previous discrimination. So, even if people are using 'Gypsy' or other equivalents of *'Tsigan'* in private, the term for public discussion would be 'Roma'. For this reason, the latter term can be also considered as a concept belonging to the world of NGOs and politicians – and their supposedly universal concerns. We might say that 'Gypsy' or *'Tsigan'* and its equivalents belong to the world of close kinship ties, extended families and neighborhoods where many things – such as property relations and marriage arrangements – are negotiated informally beyond the scope of legal systems. In this sense *'Tsigan'* can be seen as a 'subhuman' category but it also invokes the familiarity and intimacy associated with close interactions between kin and friends. However the term 'Roma' implies another type of association altogether. In contrast to direct relationships, such as those based on blood, to use it implies a claim to membership of an ethnic group and recognition of its top-down categorisation and supra-local political bodies in mainstream society.[7] Together with notions such as 'democracy', 'good governance' and 'the rule of law', the term 'Roma' is part of an official rhetoric which is detached from everyday life. Indeed it might even be considered as part of the language of domination and power that should not be trusted – just like a lie. Consequently I am not going to restrict myself to a single type of denomination in this text but prefer to use several, depending on the social and political context of the discussion.

Shared responsibilities

The way out of the vicious circle of blaming an undifferentiated racist 'other' and making claims merely on the grounds of eternal Roma victimhood is to take into account our *shared responsibilities*. These are not limited to the general and frequently oversimplified categories – 'Roma' and 'non-Roma'; local communities and the authorities; the media and NGOs and activists – but they have implications for each and every one of them. Even if these responsibilities are always unequal, asymmetrical and often even hierarchical, taking them all into consideration is one step towards confidence-building and the renewal of the social contract amongst all actors. One part of this process is to acknowledge controversies *within* Roma communities which are part of their dynamism but also threaten to undermine relations with their external environment. What I mean by responsibility is related to the way we think about common concerns. For instance, I am personally not a police officer nor a member of an agency opposing the trafficking of children. Nevertheless, I consider it my task to examine the

---

[7] For further discussion of ethnic nationalism and civic rights and the question of the Roma *ethnos* and *demos*, see the section on the reinvention of culture.

processes leading children to beg at Italian churches or railway stations and – with supporters – to raise this as an important issue for public debate by creating a language based on solidarity and desire for change.

Racist ideologies suggest that crime is not a matter of exclusion, deprivation and poverty but of ethnicity or genes, implying that Roma are hereditary criminals. People forget that the primary victims of such crimes are members of the very same communities: relatively wealthy Roma robbed by other Roma; wives beaten by alcoholic husbands; the weak exploited by stronger people – such as those in debt to local moneylenders demanding exorbitant interest rates. On the other hand middle-men in human trafficking networks are not all Roma, which means that these issues cannot be dealt with simply as ethnic problems specific to 'Roma'. In general the framework of shared responsibilities is not diametrically opposed to the liberal human rights discourse. Rather it is meant to overcome the pitfalls apparent in many of the anti-racist projects since 1989, including those initiated and coordinated by myself.

Associating Roma with criminality has a long social history in Europe. In the Third Reich it underpinned a racial ideology that Roma were biologically inferior, parasitic and asocial by nature.[8] These deviant characteristics were often attributed to *nomadism* as a cause of their detachment from wider society and petty criminality. The Communist regimes of Central and Eastern Europe tried to eradicate this supposed heritage – sometimes by force – by turning Roma into regular workers and sending their children to school. But after 1989 the dominant discourse regarded the Communist approach as completely mistaken. Nevertheless, this view conflicts with the nostalgia for those times of many former industrial and agricultural workers and public service employees – with their memories of full employment and accessible social housing. During post-socialist transition Roma started to make claims for their emancipation. They were soon granted various rights – firstly as citizens; secondly as acknowledged national, ethnic or cultural minorities of their respective states; and thirdly as victims of previous persecution for which they were compensated.

Criminality was attributed to social causes and any supposed link with ethnicity was rejected. If Roma, by definition, are victims of society and its institutions, they are not to blame for being poor, or for the fact that some of them make their children beg. However, excusing them can prevent us appreciating that criminality, exploitation or human trafficking is inevitable in conditions of long-term unemployment and structural exclusion. Social excluded communities are largely perceived by outsiders as Gypsy and so it is natural that popular 'folk-theories' will assume a link between

---

[8] Uses of this ideology were not limited to Fascist Germany since it also provided conceptual grounds for action by the Vichy-government in France and wartime deportations in Romania.

exclusion and Gypsiness. But what actually is the nature of this relationship and what is the legitimate – and not only the *correct* – way of speaking about it?

Roma activists and experts sometimes appear to be hesitant about the prospect of this discursive shift. Some think that our language and epistemology is not yet capable of dealing with an intermediate level between individualisation and generalisation. Although we might sense these distinctions and frequently discuss them in private, we are not yet sufficiently confident to express them openly. My view is that, even if we still lack a sufficient vocabulary for public debate, we have to start searching for its elements. One condition for discursive change is to avoid victimising the entire Roma population but this is what we are seemingly afraid to risk. Among themselves human rights activists and other experts might agree that it is unacceptable to defend human traffickers or those exploiting other Roma. But then they retreat to safer ground, maintaining that criminality is primarily a police domain and any discussion should remain 'colour-blind', leaving ethnicity aside. My suggestion is that, as civic activists or social workers, development of our language and practice are equally important aspects of crime prevention. Do I betray my people if I say so?

The rigid stance of many activists, clinging to their politically correct discourse, has historical origins. After 1989 the principal task of human rights organisations had been to dismantle the institutional frameworks of Communist regimes and control the emerging practices of new post-socialist governments.[9] However, in my opinion, their activities contributed to the persistence of a cold war-like mentality within civil society. Being in action is always a powerful motivating force but simply to oppose governments and public authorities is to ignore the fact that although we have competing concerns, we may also have shared interests.

Entering into debate with racists is not the same as justifying or supporting them. Paying attention to what they say is legitimate in order to develop an alternative account. It is not the same as a public official taking discriminatory action against someone or using discriminatory language. Bear in mind that *discrimination* by the human mind is necessary in the sense of differentiating or distinguishing, for example between colours, smells and sounds. Discrimination turns into something to be opposed once it disadvantages a group of people because of their age, ethnicity, race, gender or social origin. Sometimes those who aim to represent and defend the Roma give the impression that each and every act of discrimination – including all differentiations and distinctions – is necessarily negative.

I might try to express this in other words but I cannot avoid discrimination once I realise that my own self-presentation as Rom requires others to differentiate and

---

[9] Organisations such as Helsinki Watch and other US NGOs, among others, were some of the main players in this field.

acknowledge me in this identity. A first step in effective self-affirmation by Roma is for them to be recognised by others as someone different. As a second step we have to be careful that this act of self-identification and its acknowledgement by others is not going to bring disadvantages. This explains the need for affirmative action – another aspect of discrimination – in particular initiatives to compensate for a legacy of group disadvantages by ensuring that individuals have equal opportunities. Affirmative action is part of a negotiation process that needs to be monitored in order to protect the interests of those who were initially targeted by such a policy. Today human rights work concerning Roma has to target the vulnerable and to be reoriented towards the rights of children, women, the disabled, the elderly and victims of drug abuse. The problem is that these rights are not yet codified and monitored as strongly as civil and political rights such as the freedom of association or the freedom of speech.

Imagined cosmopolitanisms – some biographical remarks

As mentioned, instead of a systematic theory this paper consists of a collection of personal reflections. Throughout my life I have been trying to explain myself, my own subjectivity and the experience of being different from others – even if I did not exactly know the roots of this difference. Maybe I am not a 'true' Rom because I have been assimilated through my education and occupational trajectory, because I do not live in keeping with Roma values and I also had a non-Roma wife. I grew up as part of a group in which Romani was not spoken as a first language, my relatives did not live in extended families and my parents did not follow traditional occupations. Previous generations in my family were already integrated into the social life and economy of their villages as blacksmiths and musicians (*lăutari*). My first cousins, sisters and their in-laws took their first upward steps on the ladder of social mobility as industrial and construction-site labourers, cleaners and handicraft workers. Our identity and memories of being *ţigan* were based more on the experience of discrimination and external stereotypes, less on commonly shared meanings of being Roma in a vernacular, ethnic sense. Why am I different then as a Rom or *Ţsigan* if I feel in many other ways similar and equal to others? This is an enduring dilemma for me and for many of my kin and fellow Roma, even if we live with this difference day by day. Sometimes it is an obligation imposed from the outside and not necessarily a personal choice. It might be perceived as a cultural deficit that is damaging for the individual or the group. Some might try to find an escape by hiding it or striving to assimilate to mainstream society. Others try to explore it, speak openly about it and eventually legitimise it. To solve this dilemma I decided at a certain moment of my life that I am a Rom, although I was not necessarily obliged to be. Activism meant an opportunity to come into terms with the meaning and heritage of being *țigan*. To relieve the tensions that went along with using this category, I affirmed my social and cultural background and projected it onto Roma social history and culture.

I was educated in an era when Romania was following the Soviet model – before the emergence of Ceausescu's national Communism. I believed the Communists had the means to create equality, to improve the lot of the poor and to support people with disadvantaged backgrounds, including the Roma. I internalised the dogmatism of the official ideology with the international proletariat as its core. Alongside this, I also embraced the internationalism – or cosmopolitanism – and anti-nationalism of those times. This ideology was obviously aimed at legitimising the imperial structures of the Soviet Union but as a teenager I saw it rather as an entry point towards a kind of universalism which embraces the ideas of revolution and humanism, the renaissance and the French era of encyclopedism. In the late 1970s and then during the 1980s I established contact with experts on Roma culture, including sociologists and activists in the International Romani Union. I learnt to consider the Roma as people who form a genuinely world-wide diaspora. After the fall of Communism, I started to argue for a cosmopolitan – or at least European – perspective in Roma activism on these grounds. Following the international proletariat, my self-portrayal as part of this widespread Roma diaspora was another form of imagined cosmopolitanism. My mobility between international organisations and the various places I have been has been part of this. I thought: I have my own adaptive techniques as I know several languages; I have people to meet in many places in the world and I know how to manage my life while living out of a suitcase. However, I never intended to represent the Roma as nomadic people. After two decades of mobility, working with international organisations, I am back in Romania. Yet throughout my life I have maintained my genuine allegiance to my Romanian citizenship, to my home and family in this country.

My life story is hardly unique. In countries such as Romania, Hungary, Slovakia and Serbia – but also in Spain and France – many Roma are familiar with the historical experience of co-habitation and co-existence with others – even if it was full of ambiguities most of the time. The same peasant might drink together with you in the local bar today but tomorrow he might say that you are just a bloody *țigan*. Racial differentiations cannot be fully eliminated by law or state policies; to a certain extent we have to live with them. As long as someone accepts the fact of being Rom, *Țsigan* or Gypsy, it also involves an expectation of being treated as different by others – with all of its advantages and disadvantages. As long as you want to be a Rom, *Țsigan* or Gypsy, you must know that it entails a cost. This cost was paid by common people such as the Roma victims of murders in Hungary or the riots in the Czech Republic, in Slovakia and Romania. Our goal should be to diminish these costs as much as possible, to keep them to acceptable limits and eventually eradicate them. Nevertheless, being Rom or *Ţsigan* or Gypsy is not solely a destructive or damaging experience. It also brings advantages and resources, such as being more flexible than others or knowing how to use one's brain instead of pure force alone. At the same time these features do not provide any grounds for claiming some unlimited forms of freedom: the rule of law applies to everybody and being someone who travels around or claiming to be an 'eternal nomad' is no excuse for neglecting this fact.

On Roma experts

Since I gave up my posts, the organisers of international meetings have adopted different strategies to include me in their programmes although I have no institution, organisation or association to legitimise me. At the 2008 European Roma Summit in Brussels I appeared in the programme identified simply by my name, without any further title or status. It might sound narcissistic but I considered it a challenge to appear without anything placed after my name. At the 2010 European Roma Summit in Córdoba the organisers felt uncomfortable with this, so they listed me in the programme as a 'Roma expert'. I think it was a rather worse solution than the previous one: 'Roma expert' is one of the titles to use if there is nothing else to say about a person.

The concept of 'Roma expert' can easily take on pejorative overtones. Sometimes this notion refers to a kind of *'gadjo'* figure who only pretends to be Roma in order to take advantage of this label while building a personal career. These 'experts' could always be criticised for not being familiar with the life and culture of Roma in a more genuine sense – no matter how smart and effective they are or how many relatives they mobilise in their projects. On the other hand they tend to feel more comfortable in the middle-class environment of NGOs and policy-related meetings. In these contexts their belonging is taken for granted as they can rightfully claim to be Roma since they came from Roma organisations. Meanwhile their identity and position are often contested by those Roma – including some leaders – who base their legitimacy on their origins from ethnically 'unambiguous' and more traditional family backgrounds. These are the forces at play which explain the split between Roma activists – or the elite – and the very communities they are supposed to represent. We are not yet in the position of possessing a *functional elite*, as our ability to mobilise effectively is limited. Our parents moved upwards from the lowest strata of society as service providers or members of the working class. As a continuation of the same trajectory we moved one step further by becoming part of the non-Roma middle class as bureaucrats, intermediaries or middle-men. Advancing further on this social ladder is part of a historical trend and, as such, is not a negative development in itself.

However, these trajectories are highly divergent from the lives of many people we aim to represent.

In spite of their identification and their efforts to create links that bridge differences, the lives of Roma intermediaries belong more to mainstream society – even if they claim that they do their work in a more considerate, friendlier or more effective way than others. In spite of this in most cases they are as remote from other Roma as any other social worker. At the same time in their dealings with non-Roma they have to conform to the role designated by their ethnicity and are often questioned by others as to whether they share the cultural characteristics or behaviour regarded as 'traditional' for this ethnicity. If they are honest, they acknowledge that they don't share most of these features. Another way of dealing with the dilemmas of this schizoid situation is to start dressing or behaving in a way that is assumed to be 'traditional'. The apparent risk of this attempt at 'authenticity' is that in the end it turns into play-acting where 'Roma identity' is constructed by means of imitating stereotypical aspects of an ethnic culture. Representations of Roma culture are often simply responses to other people's expectations of the performance of otherness. Conjuring up such exotic or folkloric images – including making a joke of oneself – can be detrimental for the Roma, precisely because it is done in order to satisfy the expectations of others and serve them as customers. Many of these cultural representations have no connection with the people at grass-roots level, since usually they are neither the main audience nor the primary market for them. My own answer to these dilemmas is that Roma intermediaries can perform occupational roles and achieve personal fulfilment, primarily at an individual level, if they are able to articulate a coherent set of values and principles. These values do not imply any strict adherence to mutually exclusive concepts of being Roma, Romanian or Hungarian, since they can be defined in more universalistic terms such as respect and the creation of bridges between different cultures.[10] However, even in such a dialogue, it is necessary to clarify the potential contribution, specific markers and 'uniqueness' of Roma. Various attempts have been made throughout history to specify these ethnic markers. The concepts that have been used most frequently to resolve this dilemma are *nomadism* and the *relationship of Roma to land and territory*.

---

[10] See: Acton, Thomas – Gheorghe, Nicolae (1999): Dealing with Multiculturality: Minority, Ethnic, National and Human Rights, In *The Patrin Web Journal*, source: http://reocities.com/Paris/5121/multiculturality.htm

Slavery, nomadism and territory – reflections on the Romanian case

In his essay, Bíró suggests that the uniqueness of Roma is related to their status as 'eternal nomads' and to their lack of a relationship with land, both in a spiritual and economic sense.[11] As he understands it, the relationship to land has to be a productive one, which rules out selling one's labour and remaining a service provider instead of becoming an owner, farmer or manager. Roma are considered to be attached to land, a country or a state only in superficial ways and this disconnectedness gives them the potential for various kinds of mobility – as is happening nowadays when they migrate to Western European countries or Canada. Since Roma are constantly liable to move around, in this sense they correspond to the stereotype of the nomad.

I must admit that when I first read this argument of Bíró, I reacted emotionally and rejected it. I still feel this opposition while seeking plausible alternatives, although I acknowledge the consistency of his approach. At the same time I also recognise the limits of my own argument, especially in terms of its emotional or identity-related aspects. To summarise the main point of this section in advance: Roma in the Romanian principalities had been slaves, which means that they had been collectively bound to land – even if this link appeared rather indirect, making it easier for them to leave a specific place and move elsewhere. Roma *are* connected to territory – and not only in the Romanian case – so the concept of nomadism is not the key to their specificity.[12] Instead of denying this link, I argue that different kinds of relationship to land and territory should be taken into consideration. Consequently large segments of the Roma population can be regarded as settled, without them having been farmers or landowners. In this context I take into account several historical regimes – the two Romanian principalities of Wallachia and Moldavia, the Habsburg and the Ottoman Empires and the Western world. Here the connection to land is articulated mainly in juridical terms rather than the organic terms used by Bíró.

Roma slavery in the Romanian principalities

I grew up as a descendent of *țigani vatrași* (settled Gypsies) in Romania. The history of these people cannot be understood without taking into account *robia* (slavery), both as an institution and as experienced in these Romanian principalities. I discuss *robia* not

---

[11] András, Bíró: *The Price of Roma Integration*, in this volume.

[12] I regard this as valid for both the direct and metaphorical senses of the concept 'nomad'.

to complain about it, or denounce it or even to claim to be a victim, but simply as a matter of fact. *Robia* was an economic and social institution which produced the group of people to which I belong. These *țigani* had long-term connections with local territories and the associated social history, precisely because of their position as settled *robi* (slaves).[13] From the end of fourteenth century until the mid-nineteenth century they were tied to land owned by *boiars* (lords) and monasteries, while working as servants in the courts of the lords, blacksmiths and field hands, etc. Enslavement produced *țigani* as *robi* by historical and social categorisation, and not as a category containing 'ethnic stuff'. The process reached its apogee in the period between the end of the eighteenth century and the mid-nineteenth century.[14] In those times the terms *țigan* and *robi* became equivalent, referring to the Roma and their socially subordinate status. It was a period when these principalities entered the European capitalist wheat and cattle markets and larger landowners were looking for a labour force to exploit in an overwhelmingly agricultural market economy.

The institution of *robia țiganilor* (Gypsy slavery) was an important element of the feudal class structure in Wallachia and Moldavia. These principalities had a unique position since they had not been occupied by the Ottoman Empire like Bulgarian territories or what is present-day Dobrudja. Their relative autonomy generated massive additional labour requirements, which could only be met by the intensive exploitation of the local population by the Vlach and Moldavian princes. Similarly, in the Habsburg Empire during the era of Maria Teresa, agriculture and local industries also needed far more workers and supposedly unproductive Roma were forcibly settled to provide additional labour. To mark this change in status, they were renamed in German as *neu bauer* and in Romanian as *neo-rustic* (new peasant) or in Hungarian *új magyar* (new Hungarian). As in the Romanian principalities Roma were tied to land owners. Meanwhile the more technologically advanced and less labour-intensive economies of Western Europe allowed more opportunities for small groups to continue following a travelling way of life. However these mobile bands were far less numerous than the Roma populations of Central and Eastern Europe[15] and the basis of their nomadic life style was that they were peripheral, if not redundant, to the wider economy. In Western Europe they were tolerated as people who were often on the move and they are the ancestors of today's *Gens du voyage*, *nomadi* and

---

[13] The historical account presented here is based on the following paper: Gheorghe, Nicolae (1983): The origin of Roma's slavery in the Romanian principalities, In *Roma*, 7 (l):12-27.

[14] The institution of slavery did not exist anywhere else in nineteenth century Europe; slavery was practiced only in times of war and on an individual basis, even in the Ottoman Empire.

[15] Although in Romania a significant part of the Roma population maintained a travelling life style up till the 1950s and 60s.

Travellers. However the travelling populations in these countries also have non-Roma groups.

In the Romanian principalities the status of *ţigani* accompanied that of *romîn* (peasant serfs). These two groups formed the lowest level of the feudal social hierarchy. In contrast to the way in which Romanian peasant serfs were bound to the land, *ţigani robi* (as slaves) were tied to owners as their property or chattels. It was impossible to sell or exchange individual serfs, as they were always part of the village and the village formed part of the land. If land ownership changed hands, as a gift or dowry, the inhabitants had to be included in the transaction. In contrast *ţigani robi* could be donated or received as dowry without any accompanying transfer of land. These practices made slavery a collective and hereditary juridical and economic institution concerning the person. From a juridical point of view, the status of *ţigani* was defined in terms of personal dependence on the owner who had legal rights of total authority over the *robi*, their families and their possessions (with the exception of the right to kill them, which was punishable). Land ownership was not only the basic condition for social and juridical freedom, it was also the requirement for full citizenship. To be a native-born subject of the Romanian Principalities with political rights meant being a landowner. In the Romanian language, the original term for this was *pământean* – a 'man of the land'. Being connected to the land was to be a full member of the political community and Roma were denied the legal possibility of land ownership. As 'aliens' or 'new arrivals' they became dependent on the local prince, acquired legal status and were subjected to particular taxes which were similar to the collective taxes paid by other villagers. The ruling prince owned the whole territory of the principalities and he was considered to be the nominal owner of these 'foreigners' who had settled in his country – hence they were treated as part of his property. Even if some of the *robi* could move around pursuing certain occupations and trades, their way of life was far from today's stereotype of Gypsy nomads.

Roma slaves were affected by the process of enslavement in different ways depending on their occupational categories. The *ţigani domnesti* ('prince's Gypsies') had more freedom than those who belonged to monasteries and landowning *boiars*. *Ţigani* owned by monasteries were treated worse and exploited more than the *ţigani* of boiars, because monasteries had fewer local peasants to work in their fields. Amongst the *ţigani boieresti* (landowners' Gypsies) one group worked in agriculture (known as *ţigani de camp* – Gypsies of the field). Their living conditions were worse than those of the *ţigani vatrasi* (settled Gypsies), many of whom made their living as traders. Amongst them a large number of *ţigani curteni* (Gypsies of the court) lived in cities and had access to the urban resources unavailable to those in rural areas. Large numbers of Roma settled during this period while others maintained a nomadic way of life, although all had varying forms of *robie* status which influenced their identity.

Meanwhile these people managed to preserve and reproduce their cultural heritage and distinctive identities.[16]

The deportation to Transnistria

In 1930s a debate arose about the 'nomadic' Roma with some arguing that they contaminated society. This view rapidly gained popularity. Meanwhile within the Great Romania of that period an even more heated debate focused on the disputed status of the Jews and Roma. To demonstrate legitimacy it was even possible to apply to a special Commission for Romanianisation for a document certifying the bearer's full membership in Romanian society. At this time a new legal category was introduced, that of the *țigan romanizați* – the Romanianised or assimilated Gypsy. This phrase is used to this day by some groups as a means of self-categorisation.

During the Second World War Romania fought on the side of Germany, an alliance based on shared fascist ideals and Romania's pride in the fact that after 1918 it had finally gained world power recognition. Following the German army's southern thrust into the Soviet Union in 1941 Romania strengthened its position as a regional power by occupying Transnistria. This Governorate became the destination for deportations of Roma[17] and Jews from Romania but these expulsions were different from those in other Axis-controlled countries: the Romanian Roma and Jews were not sent to concentration camps. Instead the process was described as the *colonisation* of Transnistria.

These newly acquired territories needed Romanians to populate and work the land. The logic behind the deportations was to transport Roma 'nomads' in the hope that they would become tied to the land, abandon their status as nomads and become useful peasants. Accordingly the so-called 'nomadic' Roma were deported collectively, whereas settled Roma were only deported on an individual basis. During the war approximately 25,000 – 35,000 Roma were expelled to Transnistria in this way. However lack of organisation and supplies resulted in a third of them (about 11,000) dying of cold and starvation.[18] After the war had ended the survivors straggled back to Romania.

In the 1950s the newly installed Communist regime felt it still had a serious problem of 'nomadism'. To counter this anachronistic way of life, an assimilation pol-

---

[16] Distinct cultural customs or symbols of identity varied from one group to another – for example the tent for the *cortorari*.

[17] Some Roma were able to make use of their classification as *țigan romanizați* to avoid deportation.

[18] The situation of the Jews in Transnistria is a separate issue and is much better documented as it is considered part of the *Shoah* (Holocaust).

icy was adopted aimed at 'humanising' these Roma and transforming them into examples of the 'new socialist man'. This approach regarded Roma from a social rather than ethnic perspective and was imposed on the whole population, imitating what the Soviet Union had done in the 1930s.[19]

Connection to land as compulsory integration

Many examples from the times of *robia* and the deportation form part of a history of victimisation. A neglected aspect of such a history is that Roma actually managed to survive such experiences and this gave them a distinctive sense of identity. Therefore, if we characterise Roma solely by the image of a nomadic life, the experience of *robia* – which lasted for centuries – was quite the opposite. For generations these people worked as agricultural labourers, just like ordinary peasants. Their social and economic integration was derived from their social status *as* slaves. Through this institution, Roma became part and parcel of their local societies and economies, even if only in a marginal and inferior position. After the abolition of slavery they continued living in their local communities but as inhabitants, which was a step towards becoming citizens of modern Romania – even without owning land. Not all Roma groups were involved in agricultural work and some were traders. However, they retained cultural, economic and religious links to their local societies. Roma fought in both world wars – as did my grandfather in the first and my father in the second – and some were even given land in the post-war land reforms. In this way Roma were gradually integrated as part of Romanian society and in many cases eventually assimilated into today's Romanian nation.

The trajectory of the social status of these Roma could be understood as a process that developed from a necessary connection to land, as *compulsory integration*. They did not lack a relationship to land, as such – as suggested in the concept of nomads – but rather a relationship to land as *patrimony* that can be owned and inherited over generations. In this sense there are long-settled Roma communities all over the Balkans, in Central and Eastern Europe and in Spain. However, this relationship is hardly unique to Roma since it is the common condition of the agricultural proletariat throughout Europe and beyond. These people were selling their labour wherever it was needed, while still experiencing emotional attachment to their land and territory. I share this sense of belonging with many other Roma in Europe. My argument is that one

---

[19] In the 1930s the Soviet Union banned Roma craftsmen and their extended families from travelling around the country in search of work. The Soviet authorities used the term 'nomad' in referring to these itinerant Roma to justify their actions.

consequence of Roma subordination is that we have a level of integration and assimilation which has made us part of our societies, justifying our claim for full rights as citizens in the contemporary sense of the word.

The experience of those generations of Roma who worked during and after slavery and later throughout the twentieth century – including the decades of Communism – is proof that they, like other people, can be factory or agricultural workers and not just service providers. Their history demonstrates that Roma can be productive in economic terms. However their fate depends largely on the state of economy and contemporary social structures, as well as their ability to integrate as citizens. Instead of labelling Roma as 'eternal nomads', it is more accurate to say that they have the capacity to be flexible workers. Whether their way of life is nomadic or settled largely depends on economic, social and historical circumstances. The same people who were regular workers during the Communist era often became migrants after 1989, simply because altered economic conditions in Eastern Europe had made them redundant. Indeed such people were just as likely to travel abroad as their non-Roma fellow citizens, who also migrated to Western Europe for employment.[20] The concept of nomadism as an explanatory factor has been used mainly to refer to some tens of thousands of Roma in France and Italy, often living in squalor. However, such insanitary conditions have nothing to do with 'nomadism' but, as with many non-Roma migrants, are the inevitable outcome of being forced to live in severely overcrowded accommodation or densely packed camp sites.[21]

On shmekeria and 'Gypsy work'

The argument in the previous section might be read as ignoring the fact that different relationships to land can affect work-ethics. Roma worked as service providers in European societies where historically land was seen as a main way of legitimately accumulating wealth. Service providers adopt a quite different approach since, first and foremost, they need clients to exploit. To be successful in this ambiguous relationship they might also need to cheat. The concept of 'cunning' *(shmekeria)* refers to this behaviour: deceiving clients for a short time, before moving on and using the same tricks elsewhere. Subordinated groups such as women, nomads or people without an

---

[20] In recent years an estimated 3-4 million Romanians sought work in Western European countries. However distinctive characteristics make Roma migrants more visible than others, such as whole families with children travelling together.

[21] For the further discussion of the current forms of Roma mobility, see the following section: Nomads of European Union?

inheritance often turn to similar strategies and survival techniques in response to feeling excluded and oppressed. Being in this situation somehow seems to justify cheating the exploiters and the more powerful, being unreliable or untrustworthy – '*La donna è mobile*', as the famous Verdi song goes. In this sense *shmekeria* or what is known as *romani butji* ('Gypsy work') is hardly unique to the Roma. The concept of *shmekeria* is known and in some contexts considered admirable in Balkan peasant societies.

In other words, *shmekeria* is an ambiguous term as it can be used in very different ways. Its actual meaning only becomes apparent from the context. It functions as an operator that can create cultural understanding between very different peoples. An insecure Romanian businessman might find it appropriate for describing how he has outwitted someone he generally despises as a *țigan shmeker*. Being cunning is not only a character trait but is also displayed as a technique. If a strategy of fooling around is adopted, then informal social connections and kinship-ties come into play as a form of social capital. In this sense some people play the 'Gypsy' role very skilfully.

Work ethics and the role of Roma leaders

Controversially, Roma leaders, activists and representatives often utilise, justify and eventually legitimise the formal and informal strategies for economical success by explaining this as the 'culture' of the Roma. To say that Roma are 'cunning' is to say that they prosper using *romani butji* ('Gypsy work'). If people make money in this way to have a good life and secure the well-being of their families, it means they are good Roma. In our circles we rarely question these self-protective strategies for success, although this means we cannot claim citizens' rights or equal treatment. By behaving in this way we place ourselves beyond mainstream society. Exploiting the resources of the periphery also entraps us at the periphery. Does this mean I want to say that Roma are at the periphery from choice? Perhaps sometimes this is the case. People are not always forced to remain in the ghetto or at the periphery, sometimes they choose to stay there. There are certain opportunities at the margins, various ways of moving around in the shadows which are no longer available once you move to centre stage or into the spotlight.

Some Roma lead their horses to the fields of the *gadje*, steal their potatoes while the children make off with the peasants' hens – this is part of our internal knowledge. How should we talk openly about those Roma who make their living by such 'Gypsy work'? The attitudes of Roma activists towards these issues resembles the situation where all family members are aware of what the 'bad guys' are doing but avoid talking about it to preserve family unity. These defensive techniques are reproduced and can even be a source of pride amongst Roma activists, who are supposed to follow a different ethical code in their life and work. To be a *shmeker* in this context means to be unpredictable, to manipulate money, influence and symbols and gain power by cheating rivals if necessary. This is not so far removed from the kind of liberal, individualistic attitude that puts winning before behaving ethically and results in switching political alliances or abandoning values to further one's own or family interests. Roma activists sometimes play games of *shmekeria* amongst themselves. They speak about policies to be implemented to unify the Roma nation, while in practice they mistreat and abuse each other in ways that Roma are meant to use in 'Gypsy work' to exploit *gadje* resources. Some Roma leaders still indulge in populist rhetoric, suggesting that *gadje* should not be trusted and that any offers they make – including European Union programmes – are deceitful or plain lies. Such attitudes can lead us to believe it is acceptable to squander external funding, since this money is not our responsibility. This is one of the reasons why I think that in future Roma NGOs should increasingly turn into self-help organisations, funding activities with donations from their members.

Sometimes particular activists are not accepted by others as genuine Roma to be trusted. In comparison with some of the so-called 'traditional' Roma I might appear to be a *gadjo* or a kind of a hybrid, rather than a 'true' Roma. Some might think this justifies treating me as an idiot to be exploited. To others I might be seen more as a *gadjo* who exploits Roma by obtaining funding and implementing projects opposed to the interests of authentic, traditional community members. As I argue throughout this paper, the Roma civic movement is still in its formative stage and still lacks a code of conduct for alliances and partnerships between different actors. Developing an organisational culture means defining common interests, morals and ethics, establishing coalitions and partnerships, and acting reliably within these networks. Yet as long as our status remains subordinate, employing survival techniques such as mistrusting others is understandable.

However nowadays we find ourselves in a different situation. Over the last twenty years various opportunities have been created for Roma which might continue in future decades through the European Union. This is our chance to find other ways of successfully adapting in place of the familiar survival techniques. For the first time in history Roma have prospects of reflecting and playing an active part in bringing about social change. The role of Roma opinion-makers is to suggest new approaches, focusing on integration rather than on being victims. These opportunities include education, possibilities of free movement in Europe, employment in state administration or various other programmes based on principles of affirmative action. To benefit from these opportunities, we need to have confidence in standard legal procedures, to trust others with whom we share fundamental goals and come to an agreed understanding on values, duties and rights. If our aim is integration there is a definite price to be paid, such as making the effort to mix with others to gain a sense of security and solidarity. This is not easy. But if, in this new situation, we cling to traditional survival techniques, this can undermine and harm our relationships with others. If we do this, the cost is remaining socially excluded even though there are now opportunities for us to be accepted. Either we cheat others, while remaining loyal only to our own people, or we take the opportunity to trust others and their institutions. We should take this risk.

Traditional survival techniques continue in reinvented forms in migration and welfare-dependency.[22] Adopting new economic strategies and seeking integration might be difficult for Roma, especially during the current economic crisis when mainstream populations also suffer unemployment. At present the standard approach is for Roma to attend school, followed by vocational training or further education, as preparation for entering the mainstream labour market. In the meantime we fight discrimination and racism, seeing these as the main obstacles to their employment. In the short term traditional strategies might appear more attractive to them, at least until economic growth makes it possible for a younger cohort of Roma to find work.

A further paradox is that economic success and social integration – or even assimilation – are not necessarily linked. Some Roma who continued making a living in traditional ways proved more successful than others. They managed to adapt their family-based way of working to current economic conditions and discovered new occupational niches. During the last two decades the losers during transition and those most dependent on welfare support have turned out to be those Roma who had been drawn into mainstream economies by the process of Communist proletarisation, mainly as unskilled workers in agriculture or the construction industry. However, it is unhelpful to think in terms of 'winners' and 'losers' in considering the range of economic strategies pursued by Roma. During the Communist period the *kalderash* or *gabor* dealers of Transylvania became prosperous due to their occupational skills and culture. This process was quite separate from the parallel proletarianisation of other Roma. During the period of transition these dealers became small-scale businessmen – trading in metal or becoming other kinds of entrepreneur. This gave them advantages over other Roma groups and, to a certain extent, even over some of the majority population.

Using cultural capital to generate economic capital demonstrates the capacity of Roma to adapt. These strengths should be recognised, encouraged and developed, especially since they stem from self-reliant, entrepreneurial strategies. Roma musicians in Romania, too, were only marginally integrated into the Communist economy. They used false documents to prove they had jobs in factories or other workplaces to avoid

---

[22] Patterns of welfare dependency are reminiscent of ways in which Roma slaves were formerly reliant on their lords.

police checks but actually made their living as entertainers. Many of the Roma migrants in Italy, Spain and France had been industrial workers before they lost their jobs in the 1990s, while the Roma middle-men helping them to reach their destinations are from different groups which had escaped proletarianisation and so were able to gain more experience of travel. Migrants regard these people as role models for commercial success. Likewise, although Roma from the Romanian city of Craiova had regular jobs under Communism, they were also engaged in trading at fairs or informal markets which were not legal in the strictly regulated command economy. The *spoitori* around the Romania town of Calarasi were formally employed on co-operative farms or as street-cleaners but retained their culture of dealing involving an extended kinship network. People who lost their jobs during transition were not entirely dependent on state welfare benefits since their families continued to support them. Family and kinship ties are social and cultural capital in times of crisis or when seeking new ways of making a living. Romanian Roma rubbish collectors in Italy did the same work back in Romania but perhaps gathering different types of rubbish in their new country.

As these examples suggest, the capital derived from kinship ties can be used in different ways in the mainstream economy, either in the informal labour market – which is especially wide-spread in countries like Italy – or in criminal activities. Members of different families might have achieved similar levels of economic integration under Communism before they joined the mainstream, informal or criminal labour markets during transition. These different paths were often chosen by chance. Also, perhaps the only kinds of economic activity visible to police, social workers and policy-makers are criminal acts, while the 'grey zones' – especially the less clearly defined, intermediate areas – remain unnoticed. In the local and regional labour markets of Western Europe, sectors like agriculture, the construction industry, recycling and seasonal work are characterised by informal economic practices that would not survive unless they were controlled by members of the host population.

Understanding how Roma utilise social and cultural capital is crucial if we intend to reorient their use for integration into mainstream society. Otherwise Roma might remain trapped in the informal economy, which in some cases would mean criminal activities. These are the choices to be made, primarily by policy-makers and Roma representatives. As is evident from sociological research, combating discrimination and concentrating on the structural forces that generate poverty and social exclusion are not enough to provide viable solutions. In striving for integration there are gains to be made but also losses and the former often seem less evident. Making choices is a shared responsibility – of the state, of mainstream society and of authorities guilty of racism – but it is also a responsibility of individuals.

Nomads of the European Union?

Recent debates about migration, particularly from Romania and Bulgaria to France and Italy, show that continuing beliefs about Roma nomadism and their parasitic ways of making a living are stimulated more by recent events than by historical experience. Based on the treatment of migrants to Italy, this section argues that as soon as they enter the country Roma are automatically labelled *nomadi*, as a legal classification – even if they live settled lives in their home countries. Furthermore intermediaries, foundations and organisations themselves require the existence of *nomadi*. While leading representatives of Roma civil society denounced governments' treatment of migrants as racist persecution, closer examination of actual cases suggests alternative interpretations. Many Roma migrants are part of larger economic networks and some might even choose to remain in nomad camps.

Historical backgrounds and the 'Europeanisation' of Roma issues

From the start of the 1990s I was often quoted as lobbying for a European and transnational approach to Roma. Today I have to acknowledge both continuities and discontinuities with my previous statements. Europeanisation of Roma issues allows individual states too much scope for shedding their responsibility for these problems by passing this to other states or higher levels of European institutions. For example, Romania can be seen as giving Roma an implicit message encouraging them to leave for France or Italy and seek social inclusion there as European citizens.

It could be said that there is nothing new about this covert government strategy. After the First World War the aim of government policy in Romania was to establish an ethnically Romanian nation state. This policy was intensified, more violently during the 1930s and 40s and in milder forms in the 1950s and 60s, only to reappear more aggressively during Ceausescu's national Communism of the 1970s and 80s. Jews emigrated to Israel and elsewhere in the 1950s and 60s, while Saxons from Transylvania and Swabians from Banat left for former West Germany. During the Ceausescu era Romanian authorities dealt with minority-related problems by sending them 'home'. Meanwhile cold war propaganda represented the Western world as the realm of freedom, motivating Romanians to emigrate for human rights reasons. As well as ethnic minorities, many others migrated for political or economic reasons including dissidents and Protestants. Going to the West was associated with economic success, personal fulfilment and active support from Western states. The Romanian authorities, the government and police all quietly assisted this process.

In going abroad Roma are behaving like Jews, Swabians, Saxons and some Hungarians and Romanians in the past. Now is their time for leaving to enjoy the benefits of the West, while millions of Romanians are doing the same. However Germans, Jews, Hungarians and Turks all had a nation state of kinfolk to defend their rights but Roma are assumed to be protected as a 'European minority'. In line with earlier Romanian ethnic nationalism Romanian authorities and politicians tolerated and even tacitly encouraged their departure. Following a visit to a nomad camps in Italy Romanian President Basescu declared that the status of their inhabitants had been legalised and that the children were attending school. This message could be interpreted as approval – claiming that Roma migrants had successfully achieved social inclusion as *nomadi*. It was as if he was urging others to take same opportunity to emigrate voluntarily. The argument of the extreme right was that Roma should travel where their rights are most respected – a viewpoint also expressed by several officials. The concepts of European citizenship and freedom of movement can be misused in an attempt to legitimise this kind of discourse by emphasising the 'Europe-wide' nature of the problem while completely ignoring local responsibilities. Indeed some Roma activists contribute to this controversial 'Europeanisation' of Roma issues by urging that freedom of travel should be extended to the maximum number of Roma and by urging host countries to improve social inclusion amenities for migrants.

Travellers, Nomads, Voyagers and the Roma of Europe

Policy-oriented debates about Roma began during the 1960s and 70s, initially in Western Europe. At that time discussion focused on people known as Gypsies and Travellers (in English) and *Tsiganes* and *Voyagers* (in French). These debates were mainly concerned with the situation of travelling people in Western Europe or Roma migrants from Eastern Europe. Policy-makers in all European states shared the common assumption that the terms *Roma, Travellers* and *nomads* were equivalent. Widespread popular notions about nomadism were stimulated not just by policy resolutions but by the media and experts' publications.[23] During the 1990s we witnessed an unprecedented flood of Roma-related documents from international organisations, human rights activists and EU policy-makers. As well as raising the profile of Roma claims on the international stage, this upsurge of interest also encouraged oversimplification of Roma experience and haphazard labelling of diverse groups to make Roma issues more intelligible to an English-speaking, globalised world.

---

[23] In the early 1990s some of the work I did with Jean-Pierre Liégeois was also about *Gypsies* and *Travellers* or *Tsiganes* and *Voyagers*.

Today a main challenge for activists, policy-makers and members of the Roma elite is to correct the many misconceptions that still flourish. For example, settled Roma live in various European regions and are as widespread in the Balkans as in Central and Eastern Europe or Spain. In the USSR and other former socialist states the last remaining nomadic groups were settled during the Communist era. Their experience is quite different from that of many Gypsies in Western Europe still following a nomadic way of life. These include *Travellers* in the United Kingdom, *nomades* or *Gens du voyage* in France, *nomadi* in Italy, and other travelling groups in countries such as Germany and the Netherlands. In Western European countries these groups are officially classified by administrative, occupational and legal categories. In contrast, Roma in Central and Eastern Europe are regarded as ethnic or national minorities and this is reflected in their legal and political status.

In spite of this diversity, most discussion about Roma usually uses terms drawn from political and policy-related discourse. Activists and political leaders portray Roma above all as a *non-territorial minority*, or a *nation without territory* or a *stateless people* in need of special international protection. This lay behind a call for the establishment of a European Charter of Roma Rights, and other similar initiatives that seek to establish a transnational and culturally inclusive, political constituency representing the entire diaspora.[24]

With the collapse of Communist regimes, first the Council of Europe and then the EU began to discuss the issue of Central and Eastern European Roma. Since the dominant Western European conception of these people was in terms of Travellers or *voyagers*, this perspective was initially applied to these Roma as well. It was only when Roma from Central and Eastern Europe attracted the attention of the general public and policy-makers that the framing of discourse and initiatives was gradually corrected by referring to Roma and Sinti rather than Travellers. From the late 1990s onwards EU enlargement became a dominant concern and as a result the situation of Roma in candidate countries rose higher on the agenda.

Over time less attention was paid to Western European Roma issues, which was partly due to Roma activism but also the political context. The problems of Roma in candidate countries, particularly their poverty, exclusion and discrimination, increasingly seemed more pressing than those of Western Europe's Travellers and nomads. I, too, played my part in drawing attention to Roma issues in Central and Eastern Europe, while neglecting those in Western Europe. I later realised my mistake for older Member States need to acknowledge their responsibilities towards their own Roma populations.

---

[24] For example, the European Roma and Travellers' Forum involved Roma representatives from European states working with the Council of Europe between 2000 and 2005 to develop such a frame.

The new cohort of Roma activists from Central and Eastern European were better educated, more articulate and had more professional experience than their less skilled counterparts from Western Europe. Consequently they were more effective at making international organisations aware of their problems. They had benefited from the greater resources available for training and establishing NGOs in post-Communist Eastern Europe. Meanwhile the main advocates and policy-makers on behalf of *Travellers*, *nomadi* and *Gens du voyage* had been non-Roma intermediaries, such as human rights activists, social workers, philanthropists and academics. Subsequently their clients came to resent these *gadje* experts, who dominated their organisations as the main interlocutors in dealings with national authorities. However now we have to support Western European *Travellers*' and *voyagers*' representatives in becoming self-reliant to narrow the gap between them and Central and Eastern European Roma activists.

Nowadays the European Union is the main source of Roma policy-making and the most crucial policy issues concern the new Member States' substantial Roma populations and their westward migration.[25] The most acute recent case is Romanian Roma taking advantage of the EU right to freedom of movement. The Italian 2008 declaration of a state of emergency, aimed at *nomadi*, was a political use of legislation to deal with the consequences of EU enlargement.[26] But all such migratory waves between states contribute to the current construction of Roma as *nomads* in the reluctant host countries.

In an earlier paper we argued that the fundamental source of Roma identity-construction and political action in the 21st century should be citizenship that also guarantees the status of minorities as an integral part of their respective nations and nation-states.[27] An alternative approach suggests that political action should be based on the claimed status of Roma as a nation of stateless people – similar to refugees, asylum-seekers, or diasporic populations. The argument runs that Roma are *sui generis* Europeans and only citizens of certain states at a subsidiary level. In Western-European semantics to be a full member of a state means to possess citizenship. If the politically distinct status of Roma is based entirely on the idea of statelessness, it means renouncing the claim to citizenship – as with migrants and refugees seeking asylum in countries such as France or Germany. For instance, in France and Italy many Roma from former Yugoslavia still hold Yugoslav passports. Some have no intention of

---

[25] E.g. when Roma from the Czech Republic – although their origins were in Slovakia – sought asylum in Canada, prompting the reintroduction of visa restrictions there for all Czech citizens.

[26] Prior to Romania's accession to the EU in 2007, some Member States abolished visa requirements for Romanian citizens as early as 2002.

[27] Nicolae Gheorghe and Andrzej Mirga (1997): *The Roma in the twenty-first century: a policy paper*, Princeton: Project on Ethnic Relations (PER).

applying for French passports since they still feel a sense of belonging to their home-land, even if it no longer exists as a state. Nevertheless they are proud of the way in which Roma nationality was recognised during the Tito era. They might ask for resi-dential and legal rights and social security in France, but not necessarily French citizenship. In such cases freedom of movement and European minority status become questions to be negotiated and defined at ground level. If Roma are stateless people but free to migrate as European citizens, then the institutions of the European Union bear sole responsibility for them. Therefore could these refugees represent a vanguard for the entire Roma population?

The construction of Roma as nomads in Italy

In Italy the official term for Roma is *nomadi* (nomads). Originally this applied to *Sinti* – Italian citizens who travelled within Italy and lived on campsites. In this respect the status of *nomadi* or *itineranti* in Italy was similar to that of *Travellers* in the United Kingdom or *Gens du voyage* in France as autochthonous, itinerant populations. Instead of referring to ethnicity, special regulations often categorise them by their occupations with the aim protecting their itinerant way of life and associated trades.

However, following an influx of Roma migrants from Yugoslavia in the late 1970s and 80s, the arrangements for nomads were extended to the newcomers. A second wave arrived in the 1990s after the Balkan wars and a third from Romania and other Eastern European countries was more recent. All of these migrants were formally categorised as *nomadi* as soon as they entered Italy. In this way the migrant population of Italy grew continuously, increasing pressure on the legal sites designated by the authorities for the accommodation of all migrants. The construction of these camp-sites was initially well-intentioned, aimed at suiting the migrants' supposed 'nomadic character'. Local and regional councils have taken steps to finance legal nomad camp-sites, constructed and maintained by NGOs with regional authority funding.[28] To establish these sites, not only must land be acquired but also the caravans, infrastruc-ture, services, health and schooling facilities. In this way these associations, sometimes linked to the Catholic Church, gradually expanded in response to the growing numbers living in camps. Many NGOs have now become an established institution acting as intermediaries between local, regional and national authorities and commu-nities of people categorised as nomads. These associations are also enlarging their own organisations; this is a market for them where they need mounting demands to justify more recruitment.

---

[28] A major foundation is *Opera Nomadi*.

Pressure steadily grew on the legal sites permitted by local authorities as they could not offer enough places for the needy. Illegal camps sites started to mushroom as Central and Eastern European borders opened, visa requirements were lifted and EU enlargement gathered pace. Many newcomers only found shelter in abandoned industrial buildings, under the bridges or next to highways. The more visible their destitution, the better it was for organisations that catered for them, since this increased the pressure on authorities to fund even more legal camp sites. But increased public visibility was accompanied by growing public awareness of activities such as washing car windows, petty crimes, begging and aggressive behaviour, creating tensions in everyday life. Negative perceptions were reinforced by media manipulation of stereotypes and prejudices. The press also focused on the role of parents, emphasising the hazardous circumstances of children and their exploitation in begging networks. Finally the issue became an intergovernmental problem in 2008 when Giuliano Amato, Minister of the Interior in Romano Prodi's government, arrived in Romania to discuss Roma migration with the prime-minister, including criminality of Romanian citizens in Italy.[29]

In Italy the Prodi government passed a package of special laws in response to these unwelcome developments. Roma migration and its visibility has been used to pass a more restrictive regulation on immigration in general, first for non-EU citizens and from 2007 for EU citizens as well. A major promise in Berlusconi's 2008 campaign was to deal with migrants in general and with Roma in particular. In May 2008 security measures treated Roma as an emergency. Three commissioners were appointed as regional prefects of Rome, Lombardy and Campagnia, with special powers to take exceptional legal steps. The measures were to benefit as well as punish migrants as they treated children's school-enrolment and education as an emergency issue by speeding up customary procedures – but they also gave prefects the right to expel those without legal status.

As part of the emergency measures, the ministry of the interior proposed a survey to count the people in legal and illegal settlements, since some migrants were illegal residents of legal camps. As some had no identification documents, it was impossible to verify their age, especially in the case of children and young teenagers. Eventually fingerprinting was chosen for a 2008 census to ascertain the age of young people, legalise their status and provide them with identification. Fingerprinting of legal and illegal nomads was also suggested but became a hotly contested issue and provoked

---

[29] Similar debates have taken place between France and Romania. In 2002 Nicolas Sarkozy, as Minister of the Interior, came to Romania to discuss Roma migration, criminality and begging. After he became president these issues had an even higher profile. The latest episode in this intergovernmental debate accompanied the expulsion of Romanian Roma migrants from France in 2010.

NGO campaigns and many debates, also in the European Union. The project was even denounced as a fascist act directed against the entire Roma people.

Some Italian municipalities adopted an alternative approach and demolished camp sites as ghettos where criminality proliferates. In their place they built social housing projects with public funds to promote the social inclusion of migrants. This does not necessarily diminish tensions since there are always local citizens in sub-standard living conditions who might compete for the same resources. Nevertheless, in general, authorities in host countries have mostly refused migrants' claims and sent them back to their home countries.

Throughout these debates the nomad designation has been confused with the ethnic connotations of the Roma category. Roma activists have contributed to this confusion, either by their terminology, for example the European Roma and Travellers Forum, or in the case of the Roma National Congress, by portraying the Roma as a stateless European minority with a cultural tradition of mobility, which entitles them to unlimited freedom of movement as a right. One possible reading of the Roma Rights Charter suggests that because Roma have been discriminated against throughout their history – including the experience of slavery and the Holocaust – they are the victims of European societies which are now obliged to repay them for inflicting such suffering. According to this logic, demolishing a shantytown is nothing less than a violation of human rights, unless alternative local housing is provided. However in discussions where Roma migration is framed entirely in terms of freedom of movement, the issues of economic migrants, refugees and asylum-seekers tend to be totally confused and ethnicised.

Do Roma have special entitlement to travel around, apart from the right to freedom of movement as EU citizens? Are they entitled to receive social facilities, housing, education, health-care and other services from the authorities of host countries, simply because of their history as victims of discrimination? Migration can be an individual choice in accordance with state regulations. Any attempt to legitimise it as a collective solution for a whole ethnic group can lead to dangerous and unintended consequences.

The way to resolve these confusions is to make clear distinctions in terms of who are migrants or nomads and who are not. Confusions begin once the status of the autochthonous travelling populations of Western European states is not distinguished from that of the Roma migrants. In Italy the category of *nomadi* is imposed on these arrivals, even if they had lived perfectly settled lives in their home countries, as this is the only administrative category available to Italian authorities. Yet, migrants might not object to this categorisation since *nomadi* status entitles them to claim accommodation on legal campsites. Since these sites are indeed like ghettos or concentration camps, as a next step they might claim social housing, which can be also done on the basis of their status as nomads. These confusions make various manipulations possible using the double status of being settled in Romania and nomadic in Italy. People might play the role of nomad while looking for resources just like any seasonal migrant – including the prospects of work, social welfare or the informal economy – and then go home, remain on the level of day-to-day survival, improve the family house or maybe even have some economic success.[30]

In my view attempts to institutionalise the status of Roma on the basis of state-lessness are not real alternatives to citizenship. A strong citizenship means to have an identity card, to be registered with a family doctor, to have one's children enrolled and well-treated in school, to have access to employment and to pay taxes. There is no way to become a full citizen in any state by being mainly a consumer of social services and not a contributor them; to make claims for being part of a society with free access to medical services and to the education system without paying taxes or working regularly. At the same time, from an economically rational perspective, it is obvious that by begging abroad one can gain much more than by doing many of the steady jobs in a country like Romania, even with an employment contract accompanied by medical insurance and other benefits.

My suggestion is to provide full rights for Travellers, *voyagers* and itinerants as autochthonous, occupational and cultural groups of the United Kingdom, France or Italy, based on their citizenship in the respective states. In this case a status like the *nomadi* in Italy can be preserved for those Roma and Sinti who are citizens there and have maintained a tradition of itinerant occupations for generations. Italian Sinti or Roma, with a proven record of their occupation over time, might have the right to stay at a certain camp site. Others might not have this legal and administrative status since they lack such a license or depend on social welfare but are also part of the grey or black economy. Romanian Roma migrants in Europe should be treated according to Romanian law and citizenship, since the main responsibility for their integration is borne by the Romanian state, even if they happen to be in other countries. Obviously, the living conditions of Roma need to be improved first of all in the countries where they are citizens. The responsibility of these states is to fulfil their obligations in accordance with the laws of the United Nations and the European Union. The role of these European institutions is to reinforce these mechanisms by making the individual states aware of their duties and responsibilities towards the Roma at local level.

The problems associated with Roma from Romania in Western European states are largely due to their own vulnerability to informal economic practices, including human trafficking and petty criminality. In my view, those who stay on completely ille-

---

[30] This is the case with the *spoitori* Roma – a former itinerant group, traditionally galvanizers of metal pots – from the city of Călăraşi in Romania. At one point almost the entire Romanian Roma community in Naples was made up of *spoitori*.

gal sites, and have nothing to do with traditional itinerant occupations, are abusing the right to freedom of movement. However, Roma are not the only people abusing certain rights and opportunities, for they themselves are also abused by others.

I think many Roma have been used and misused in this process, which on the one hand is about drawing on public funds to enlarge a particular market of services and on the other being exploited by traffickers. These migrants arrive in large Italian cities through a cycle of reproduction, which is partly spontaneous but partly organised. Migrants have to pay in order to travel to their final destination and to have a place to stay, even if it is an abandoned warehouse or a factory. Their journey would not be possible without those who make a living by trafficking people in conditions of extreme poverty. Others might also have to pay off debts with high interest rates to money-lenders back home. These people are in a highly vulnerable situation and need protection not only against the authorities but also against the social forces of the illegal economy. As a result of such migration, stereotypes of Roma are not only maintained, but exaggerated and exploited by populist politicians and the media.

NGOs are involved in combating racism and populism at both national and European level and several have played a significant part in bringing about two resolutions about fingerprinting in Italy that were adopted by the European Parliament. However, more needs to be done about the trafficking of organs, women and people in general as well as the exploitation of children – all constituting contemporary forms of slavery. The main goal is to get Roma children into schools and kindergartens instead of passively witnessing their mistreatment in various kinds of street work and the illegal economy. Governments are often ill-equipped to deal with these problems, so established NGOs need to explore areas where Roma are most at risk, starting by establishing how many Roma are victims of trafficking or vulnerable to exploitation by abusive gangs.

A Romanian problem, not a European one

The issue of migration is now at the top of the political agenda. Migration is the subject of debates in national parliaments, bilateral talks on inter-state affairs and declarations by EU institutions.[31] In 2010 controversy on this issue intensified following the expulsion of Roma migrants from France. While France does have the legal right to close the camps where they were living, since these are illegal under French law, it is questionable whether such actions are morally legitimate. An associated concern is

---

[31] Such as the resolutions of the European Parliament following the fingerprinting of Roma in Italy, decisions of the European Council and communications of the European Commission.

French repatriation of whole groups of Roma to Romania. From a strictly legal point of view this practice cannot be classed as expulsion or deportation, since France offers each adult 300 Euro to return home voluntarily in an attempt to counter large-scale migration.

My point is that underlying these events is a Romanian 'problem', not a European one. As argued above, in Romania the idea of 'getting rid of the gypsies' existed ever since the deportations to Transnistria during the Second World War. From the point of view of the Romanian government mass Roma emigration following EU accession in 2007 serves a similar purpose. The expectation is that the Roma will leave, the Westerners will have to shoulder the burden and then they will 'understand our bitterness'.

The argument for considering the Roma as European citizens is complex but first of all a solution has to be found in Romania. Western Europe wants to see more controls and a reduction of east-west migration. But as a consequence will Romania retain freedom of movement for its citizens? Will it be accepted into the Schengen area? It is quite possible that the Roma issue might be used as a pretext for restricting this freedom – an argument that would be acceptable to both politicians and public in the West, as well as to some political groups in the European Parliament. This tendency may strengthen in the coming years, which makes me apprehensive.

I believe that the leading politicians in Romania are ready to re-invent and manipulate the 'nomad' label as a bargaining chip. They might argue that the country has a social segment of nomads who don't like to work but who do like to travel – and we call them Roma. A problem with generalisation is that distortions can arise when an ideological view already formed is then put into practice. So, for example, when journalists cover the 'Roma story', they head for the most visible sites. Although there are virtually no 'nomads' in Romania anymore, we can always find groups who are mobile and living in poverty. Therefore journalists try to meet with mobile Roma since this makes it much easier for them to do their job – that is to reproduce the stereotypes about nomads and show the contrast between poverty and wealth.

In my opinion the Romanian government should not develop a new Roma strategy, even though this has been promised since February 2010 in successive high-level negotiations between France and Romania. There is no need for the type of political strategy that was adopted in 2001. Instead what is needed is an effective system of public administration that works for everyone. If the Romanian social services would only function as they should by following their own regulations, this would be far more beneficial – for everyone – than any specific Roma strategy could be. If the government does unveil a new strategy this will probably be with the aim of attracting a few helpful headlines and will be used as a bargaining chip in the Schengen negotiations. It is highly unlikely that a new Roma strategy would ever be implemented, if only because the institutional capacity to realise this does not exist. Such empty rhetoric does not help but has precisely the opposite effect by reinforcing negative perceptions that vast sums of money are being allocated to 'hopeless Roma problems'. So yet again the majority of the public will claim that Roma are undeservedly benefiting from positive discrimination. So, to repeat my main point, what is needed is simply an effective public administration guaranteeing access to public services for all. This should be run by properly trained civil servants in senior positions, some of whom could be Roma.

In fact, the social inclusion of the Roma in Romania is essential. To 'Europeanise' the problem of the supposedly itinerant Roma is particularly misleading. For example a local policeman might encourage a Roma citizen to leave home and travel west, as this makes his task easier. But this is hardly a solution. To make Romania more effective, its standards must be improved to European levels. That is a meaningful way to Europeanise the situation. In this way the so-called 'Roma problem', including the debate around European Commission funds for Roma, could become an entry point for raising the general level of public service standards in Romania.

The idea of 'nomadic' Roma is a myth but, as in all myths, it also contains some truth. As explained above, mobile Roma groups do exist and there are some who use this myth to legitimise their strategies. While it is their right to express such opinions, it is not acceptable to extend this mythology to cover the whole population and promote images of the Roma as 'eternal nomads', 'children of the wind', 'people without a state', or 'stateless, uprooted, true Europeans'. The simple fact is that the vast majority of Roma in Central and Eastern Europe are settled, they are citizens of their respective countries and they have nothing whatsoever to do with these nomadic stereotypes.

Churches and sects

The analytic concepts of 'churches' and 'sects' are utilised here to explain the recent dynamics of the Roma movement.[32] An established church is a mass organisation in contrast to a sect, which is a small group splitting from an established church in a return to fundamental religious principles.[33] As in any other smaller social grouping, sect members are rigidly controlled. Established churches are characterised by codified rules and courts to enforce them, enduring beliefs and rituals such as gatherings and pilgrimages. The institutional structure of churches is maintained by boards,

---

[32] These are used metaphorically without reference to actual forms of Roma religious mobilisation.

[33] Christianity was originally a sect among various Jewish ideas and beliefs.

administrators and a hierarchical leadership[34] but to survive as institutions churches need to attract, include and keep together a large and varied membership of believers. This wide constituency is precisely what provokes the breakaway of charismatic leaders in pursuit of the true credo of the founding beliefs. Initially sects have few adherents following a charismatic leader but, if successful, eventually grow in numbers and become a rival church. Alternatively, the mainstream church can absorb such challenges by implementing the dissidents' agenda.

For Bíró clusters represent some of the traditional survival strategies. Historically, Roma clusters are based on mutual separation and lack of communication, because in the past Roma were oriented towards their own clients rather than each other. These clusters occupied different economical niches with distinct professions according the kinds of services they provided or the kinds of materials they worked with – such as gold, metal, wood or the bones of animals. These distinct resources are implied in different occupational identities. Such belongings are embodied in closed caste-like forms of social organisation backed up by different genealogies, so it might be only the external stereotypes that hold them together under the umbrella of the same ethnic category. Here, the cluster-like distinctions are associated primarily with Roma organisations and activists but they also characterise Roma society and culture in a broader sense. Nevertheless one of my main goals is to emphasise that we, as members of the Roma civil movement, also reproduce the cluster-mentality in the sense Bíró uses the concept. However I also employ the concept of *sect* to identify these tendencies for the analytic purposes of this section.

Clusters and Roma nation building in international organisations

Attempts to construct the Roma as a cultural nation can be traced back at least until the early 1970s when the emerging international Roma movement took this concept as a valid ideological basis for mobilisation. The commonly shared belief in the emancipation of Roma and their recognition as a cultural nation with its own language, traditions and Indian origin was the obvious motivating force among activists in the 1970s and 80s. Events like the cultural festivals in Tito's Yugoslavia could be described almost in spiritual terms as affirmation of the Roma nation and glorification of its customs, which made us emotionally involved and committed. The idea of Roma emancipation followed the model of romantic nationalisms, based on the assumption that a specific group of people with a distinct culture already exists but their status is

---

[34] For example priests, bishops and the Pope.

that of an oppressed group. Therefore the task is to gain recognition and turn them into a nation. This belief provided the main ideological background for our activities until the start of the 1990s. Later this position was taken for granted as more and more associations had been organised with different agenda issues such as housing, education or infrastructure. A new generation of Roma activists grew up in the NGOs with rationally designed projects and more focused aims than the general emancipation of Roma. The social integration of the Roma depends on the bureaucratic processes of policy making so it cannot arouse the kind of enthusiasm experienced in previous times. In other words, it cannot be the base for a social movement in terms of spontaneity, dedication or a fight for commonly shared goals.

In the mid-1980s Rudko Kawczinsky and his followers broke away from the International Romani Union's (IRU) establishment. In May 1990 Kawczinsky openly confronted the IRU leadership during the fourth International Roma Congress in Serock, Warsaw and founded the Roma National Congress (RNC) in the same year. In terms of the analytical framework given above, this was a 'sectarian' split by the RNC from the IRU, which in many ways was then in decline. The radical discourse and actions of the RNC included street protests and sit-ins similar to those organised for Roma asylum-seekers in Germany. During the 1990s such actions served as reminders of the Roma movement's initial militant, rights-oriented agenda, embodied in the manifesto and spirit of the first World Romani Congress (WRC) held in London in April 1971. The strength of the RNC was that it remained a relatively small-scale but well-articulated body of committed activists, devoted to their leader. Their criticisms were catalysts for the movement's internal political struggles while also encouraging the partisan realignment of various national organisations and certain compromises between factions. The RNC initiated new forms of activism which included attempts to reform and revitalise the IRU and re-organise its leadership during their fifth IRU congress held in Prague in June 2000. The *Declaration of a Nation* was launched at this congress, strengthened by the stirring political symbolism of the Roma flag, anthem, International Roma Day and the Romani language[35] with the aim of inspiring millions of Roma people world-wide.[36] The fact that these symbols have been adopted by very different segments of the Roma movement over time, and particularly from the 1990s onwards, demonstrates that the ideology of striving to build a nation is not solely the fantasy of a few zealots.

In 2000, we established the International Roma Contact Group, which included the leadership of the IRU, the board of the RNC, and a couple of independent Roma

---

[35] These were all adopted at the first World Romani Congress in 1971.

[36] The Declaration was later reiterated at the sixth congress in Lanciano (Italy) in October 2004 and also at the seventh congress in Zagreb (Croatia) in October 2008.

activists and experts. This structure worked quite well for about one year and a half. This group facilitated the first discussions between Finnish diplomats and Roma representatives in August 2001 about the creation of a pan-European Roma body which, with the support of the Council of Europe, led to establishment of the European Roma and Traveller Forum (ERTF) in 2003-2005. With this significant achievement the Roma movement reached a different level.

The ERTF is a broad umbrella organisation which includes the IRU, the RNC and other international organisations, such as the International Roma Women's Network, the Forum of European Roma Young People, the Gypsies and Travellers' International Evangelical Fellowship, as well as national Roma political parties and NGOs. However it remains to be seen whether the ERTF will be able to expand and develop within existing institutional frameworks or whether the need for political creativity and effectiveness will require newer forms of political 'dissent'.

My earlier conception was that both the IRU and the ERTF should have a parliamentary structure under the supervision of the Council of Europe's parliamentary assembly, to prepare the way for an elected European Roma Parliament. At present the ERTF is at an early stage, resembling an international NGO where delegates are appointed not elected. But as soon as we manage to establish in each country representative organisations, based on inclusive networks of Roma NGOs, political parties or churches, then we can join the Council of Europe as a genuinely parliamentary body with locally elected delegates from these national organisations.

The ERTF is often seen as not being involved with certain major Roma-related issues. For example it does not tackle questions such as poverty and exclusion which feature prominently in media coverage and political debates. Many Roma dismiss ERTF activities as insignificant in comparison with electoral contests over positions of real power in national politics, which are seen as more important than attempts to unify Roma. My suggestion is that the Romani diaspora can be considered as a nation, which although not homogenous resembles a *bricolage* or mosaic of varied colours.

The IRU and RNC still have the vision of gaining recognition for the Roma as an autonomous nation, an aim incorporated into the ERTF's Roma Rights Charter. Nevertheless, the Charter deviates from the fervent romantic language of Roma emancipation of the 1970s and 80s in seeking a compromise with governments of EU Member States and proposing a weaker version of the RNC's initial proposal for recognition of a Roma nation. Nevertheless, the continuity is evident with retention of the demand for the right of self-determination, following the example of former African colonies of the colonial powers.

In my opinion it is still too early to evaluate the merits of the ERTF and therefore we should continue to maintain friendly relations in supporting this organisation while retaining our critical faculties. However, just as with the Roma movement in general, the ERTF also needs to move beyond its own cluster mentality. In practical terms this means setting standards and creating precedents for national Roma organisations by initiatives that strengthen the position of the ERTF as a role model. This also requires finding answers to crucial dilemmas confronting Roma – such as questions of assimilation, integration and cultural separation. In particular, it means taking a consistent position on whether to argue for the non-discriminatory application of general human and citizenship rights for Roma, or develop transnational networks[37] or strengthen the minority status of Roma in their own countries.

As a former club member I now appear a heretic for challenging prevailing orthodoxy by suggesting a more genuine, credible and legitimate type of Roma representation. This is the form my activism takes nowadays – by reinventing myself and working at national level in Romania but drawing on my familiarity with European structures and developments over the past years in the belief that the ERTF can be a key factor in the development of Roma political culture at a European level. In this way I remain consistent to my original agenda of the 1990s to establish institutions at European level concerned with Roma.

In the 1990s one of our main goals was to re-launch Roma politics in terms of greater participation both in politics and in public policy-making affecting Roma by the recruitment of more professional Roma administrators, officers and experts in ministries and governmental offices. Since the beginning of the 2000s there has been a gradual but steady increase in Roma representation in local and national parliaments[38] and Roma employees in government and administrative offices. Slow progress in electoral representation is partly due to Roma politicians not making greater efforts. However international organisations such as the Council of Europe, the European Parliament and the Organisation for Security and Cooperation in Europe (OSCE) regularly invite Roma participants to their meetings – usually to draft texts or to make comments – but usually don't take the opportunity to involve them in political debates and controversial issues. The naïve assumption seems to be that rights are guaranteed simply by the adoption of laws and policy documents.

Reviving Roma civic activism cannot be achieved simply by confronting governments – as we did from the 1990s – but also means criticising newly established Roma groupings in parliament or government, even if these are largely our own creations. Citizenship status also creates space for political disputes between Roma officials in positions of power and those in opposition.

Amongst many others, I took part in establishing the ERTF but in mid-2003 I withdrew when I started to feel it was changing its character. In promoting the idea of the

---

[37] As advocated in the RNC's European Roma Rights Charter from the mid-1990s.
[38] This is true of Bulgaria, Hungary, Macedonia, Slovakia and Romania.

Roma nation, activists had become increasingly obsessed with European institutions such as the Council of Europe in Strasbourg, the EU in Brussels, the Open Society Institute (OSI) in Budapest and the OSCE in Warsaw. In the 1990s I had travelled to these cities for meetings and perhaps some of the younger activists were keen to follow my example. Later I was appointed to a senior position as Head of the Contact Point for Roma and Sinti Issues in the Office for Democratic Institutions and Human Rights (ODIHR) in Warsaw. Lívia Járóka and Viktoria Mohácsi also served as role models as MPs in the European Parliament. Many talented Roma were attracted by opportunities to appear on an international stage and we supported them since their involvement with intergovernmental agencies was the most visible sign of our success. This was a milestone in the development of the Roma movement and in my life story as well.

When the borders opened I was already in my fifties. Nowadays invitations to meetings, seminars and other events are widely offered to young Roma activists, many of whom acquit themselves very creditably. I contributed to the creation of these European structures by putting Roma issues on the agenda of mainstream international organisations. Today I am more sceptical about encouraging talented Roma to seek international posts instead of working at national and particularly at local level. This is because I believe the next stage, in the development of the Roma movement and for those involved, is to reconnect with the people we represent. Working hard in an international office – as I did for seven years in Warsaw – remains invisible to communities at grass-roots level. Instead of acting as a Roma ambassador in Strasbourg or elsewhere and duplicating previous successes, the ERTF must become an umbrella organisation supporting local groups.

Bureaucratisation and the prospects of re-mobilisation

Most Roma organisations still operate as 'sects' and rather than 'churches', since they are not yet part of a broader mass movement. As argued throughout this paper, for the time being there is a dramatically widening gulf between the 'clubs' of Roma political elites – both at national and transnational levels – and the communities they are supposed to represent. Their initiatives, projects and discussions still have too few participants as most activities take place amongst small, restricted groups of fervent activists. Instead of operating with the tired dichotomies of 'modernist' and 'traditionalist', 'good' and 'bad' or 'pure' and 'dirty' Roma, our associations should work towards a collective transformation including all kinds of Roma people – money-lenders as much as human rights activists. A church is able to embrace all types of members in its congregation, always in the hope of change for the better. Like any other corporation, a church needs to treat everyone as equals whether they are idealists or opportunists, true believers or hypocrites. Leaders are expected to find ways of involving all these different actors.

The concepts of churches and sects also imply centrifugal and centripetal forces, fissions and fusions that determine relations in organisations. Centripetal forces consolidate by attaining mutual acceptance of rules and procedures. However, where factions compete, becoming director of one's own 'heretical' association is a more attractive prospect than submitting to the discipline of an established organisation. This is especially true of movements in their early stages, such as Roma activism. While disagreements and schisms are inevitable, the overriding goal should remain keeping in touch with reality to be able to mobilise large numbers of potential recruits. Today 'sects' and 'heresies' are more evident and successful than 'bishops' defending orthodoxy and the hierarchy of an established church. A main challenge facing Roma activists today is moving beyond their cluster-like mentalities and practices, which can hinder further development of the movement as a whole. In order to become more effective and influential, the Roma movement needs to become more like a church – or churches – instead of a group of dogmatic sects, which although intolerant of their rivals are nevertheless very similar to them.

There were also practical reasons for the growth of factionalism in Roma civil society. Over the past two decades many Roma organisations have become more specialised, concentrating on education, legal procedures, health, infrastructures or electoral participation. Although the aim was to increase effectiveness, this narrowing focus gave the impression that they were working in separate worlds. However cooperation – starting at local community level – might help to link their different agendas and lead to a more holistic approach. We have to prevent our organisations becoming as autocratic as the politicians we criticise by reinventing democratic processes amongst ourselves – which is different from being politically correct.

In the 1990s I was in favour of having large numbers of NGOs but their proliferation was flawed since most are still not self-sufficient. Instead of being funded by membership fees they became dependent on external donors, governments and subsequently European funds and subsidies. Some NGO workers are better paid than governmental officials. This illustrates the paradox of a higher level of welfare-dependency amongst Roma NGO workers. In my role as lobbyist and consultant, I saw how Roma civic associations gradually lost their moral autonomy and organisational capacity and became dependent clients – or protected customers – of their 'paymasters'. NGOs in Romania were said to be actually helping de-mobilise Roma while[39] many

[39] Rostás, Iulius (2009): The Romani Movement in Romania: Institutionalization and (De)Mobilization. In Nidhi Trehan and Nando Sigona. *Romani Politics in Contemporary Europe: Poverty, Ethnic Mobilization, and the Neoliberal Order*. Palgrave Macmillan, 159-185.

NGOs serving the Roma movement are not part of it. Instead of organising Roma communities they provide contracting services for the EU, national governments or other funders to support Roma associations on the ground. Consequently Roma associations became fearful of confronting and criticising governments and other authorities and refrained from 'naming and shaming' those proven human rights violations against Roma and other victims of social exclusion, oppression and racial discrimination. Therefore it is doubtful whether this technocratic elite of Roma fund-raisers would be capable of inspiring youngsters to work for the Roma movement.

In order to re-mobilise ourselves we need to agree common aims and procedures for building collective realities. Sometimes it is necessary to take a 'heretical' stance and return to fundamentals to renew institutions that cling to an established orthodoxy but have lost their connections with the grass-roots. In the case of Romani CRISS, an NGO I helped found but which became increasingly bureaucratised, I opposed those in power in heretical ways (although within the rules). Bureaucratised NGOs resemble dinosaurs with heavy armour-plating, so even if trying to act radically they can only move slowly, unlike smaller, more agile actors. The leadership of such organisations have to discard opportunism, focus on their constituencies and become accountable. As already stated one way to achieve this is to introduce and rely on membership fees.

The reinvention of culture

In the 1970s and 80s my main links with the Roma movement were through writing, travelling with friends from Yugoslavia and making personal contact with leaders in the struggle for Roma emancipation such as Romani Rose, Rudko Kawczinsky and Jean-Pierre Liégeois. Until the first half of the 1990s I was deeply involved with issues of cultural rights and emancipation, with history and traditions and less with human rights. That explains the name of our organisation, the *Romani Centre for Social Intervention and Studies*. The outbreak of anti-Roma violence in Romania during the 1990s changed our direction. Then our priority had to become the protection of basic human rights. Such interventions made the Roma Federation and later the Romani CRISS pioneers of projects for education, health and income-generation as alternatives to migration or the informal economy. Our growing activities were influenced by various international organisations, particularly the United Nations and Open Society Institute – both of which played a major role in guiding the initiatives of Roma NGOs.

The place and the meaning of *culture* has remained controversial in debates on Roma policy making. Integration into mainstream society can take different forms.

Assimilation is not a necessity, although it is one of the options. Another is to reaffirm Roma culture and claim respect and recognition for minority rights. This assumes that integration is not only an individual process or achievement but also a collective one. In the case of the Roma it usually implies the status of a national minority, teaching of the Romani language in schools and organising cultural festivals and other events. A further stage might be to use these various forms of expression and representations as a basis for Roma claims to be recognised as a cultural nation. Personally I believe in this affirmation of Roma as a nation in the cultural sense, as an *etnie* unrelated to territorial units or nation states but sharing a common set of cultural values. Indeed activists are deeply concerned with such issues since they need justification that their goal is not the full assimilation of Roma.

Ethnic nationalism, civic rights and the fiction of unity

Two main opposing paradigms of Roma mobilisation or nation building have been proposed over the past two decades. One uses the language of ethnic nationalism, aiming at the recognition of Roma as a distinct, Europe-wide entity, supported by EU-funds. The other is a civic paradigm where national governments bear the main responsibility for Roma based on their rights as citizens. In this case the role of activism is to support civic associations that monitor both governmental and Roma bodies – primarily at local rather than at the European level. The clash between the two positions stems from the contrasting approaches to Roma rights. In the civic model the concept of rights refers above all to rights of citizens. In the ethnic nationalist model rights also include national minority rights and legal protection of the codified cultural patterns known as *Romanipen*. Proponents of this view tend to give equal priority to human rights activism and cultural preservation – or revivalism – concentrating on the Romani language, the heritage of traditional occupations or family-structures. In other words, they combine both political paradigms. Nevertheless, conflict between the two approaches frequently surfaces in debate, where the ultimate argument against proponents of the civic paradigm is that they underestimate the importance of ethnicity and culture – after all their problem is that they are not really 'genuine' Roma.

From the very first World Romani Congress in 1971 Roma activists have shared a dream of creating an ethnic nationalist agenda, following the example of earlier nationalist movements in Central and Eastern Europe.[40] These were seen as models for

---

[40] Such as those in Hungary, Serbia or Romania. They were also influenced by the recent success of Kosovo Albanians in gaining their independence from Serbia.

achieving nationhood, with or without a territory. Many Romanian Roma leaders had viewed the post-Communist political strategy of the Hungarian minority in a similar way. There ethnic Hungarians had successfully achieved many of their aims due to their disciplined behaviour at elections. The Romanian Roma Party *(Partida Romilor Pro Europa)* imitated this in prioritising ethno-political mobilisation of Roma. Roma identity takes many local forms, but differing from other people doesn't automatically mean being a Rom. The category 'Roma' is constructed by the very act of classification which gathers a wide range of different groups and individuals. Institutionalising this categorisation results in reifying fluid identities and varied characteristics. However public policy making needs to be based on a clearly defined target group to be supported by funding, programmes and rights. To create a concept of Roma, covering vernacular identities and all those suffering racist discrimination for being regarded as *Gypsy* by others, is an ongoing process. But once completed, everyone labelled as such can be automatically assigned to the category of Roma.

The flexible concept of Roma is actually an ideological construct and does not signify any cultural homogeneity. It is mainly an administrative term serving policy-making requirements. For example officials and project leaders seek partners – perhaps a Roma MP or traditional Roma leader such as a *vajda* or *bulibaşă* – in order to validate their efforts for the 'Roma community' in general. Such misleading impressions of fictive unity bear little relation to the actual diversity of the people in question but give those in power the feeling that their target population is easy to demarcate and control. Yet at the same time Roma activists from Central and Eastern Europe try to persuade others to think of themselves as Roma – with the sub-text that this implies acknowledging the linguistic and cultural dominance of Romani speakers from their region.[41] In spite of competing factions they conceive of Roma as an all-embracing, homogeneous community, which is a fantasy. The attempt of a hegemonic group to homogenise populations resembles 19th and 20th century forms of nation building in France, Germany, Italy and Romania when nationalists spoke as if for the whole nation, while concealing and repressing internal diversity to strengthen their claims.[42]

Following the 2005 riots in Parisian suburbs the situation of Roma in Europe – particularly in Central and South-Eastern European countries – was compared to that of young Muslims in EU countries. Undoubtedly both groups suffer racism and social exclusion but Roma have been part of the settled populations of Europe for centuries, while Muslim migrants mostly arrived after colonial regimes had ended. As a recent

---

[41] Certain groups, like French *Manouche*, object to being called Roma since for them this term signifies Central and Eastern Europeans.

[42] Similar aims can be detected in the work of the ERTF or the text of the Roma Rights Charter.

problem Muslims prompted new anti-discrimination policies in France in contrast to Roma whose political status remains unclear.[43]

In Western Europe the multiculturalism of the 1970s and 80s provoked a backlash from nationalist and right wing extremist organisations in the Netherlands, Denmark and Belgium, which saw multiculturalism as a threat to their supposedly homogeneous national identity. We should not wait twenty years before having similar arguments about Roma, who are in many ways more vulnerable than migrant communities. As already noted, how minority languages are treated by the state is a crucial factor in gaining official minority status. This allows Hungarians in Romania, Slovenians in Austria and Germans in Italy to be protected in law as communal groups.

Teaching the Romani language in school, as is done for Hungarians and Germans in Romania in separate schools, might seem a basic right. However to set up separate classes for Roma – or even separate schools – appears segregatory and in contradiction to the general campaign for desegregation. Nevertheless we might push for schools with Romani as a first language, at least in larger, more concentrated Roma communities. This could be a first step towards establishing autonomous, self-governing municipalities, where Romani is used as an official language.

In the past Roma were denied the status of a linguistic minority on the grounds that they were a social group defined by a nomadic way of life rather than cultural characteristics. An Italian parliamentary commission has now been convened to decide whether to grant Roma this status, already enjoyed by Albanians, Slovenians and Germans. This initiative might be seen as compensation for their harsh treatment in recent years but also as an attempt to counter the racist reputation of the Italian state. But who will be entitled to this new status? Will it be all Roma and Sinti Italian citizens, even though not everyone is a Romani speaker? Some only speak the majority language[44] although it could be argued that they had been deprived of their language over the course of time and could relearn it. And what of Roma from former Yugoslavia who migrated three decades ago and whose children were born in Italy? These Roma are mostly tolerated since they are expected to leave for Serbia, Croatia and Bosnia, when democracy is restored. Yet apparently very few intend to return to their homelands, in spite of their diverse legal statuses in Italy. Furthermore the European Roma Rights Charter supports a claim that they are more 'genuine' Roma than some of the autochthonous Roma and Sinti populations of Italy since, though not always Romani speakers, they have nevertheless preserved many ethnic cultural traits entitling

---

[43] The French state introduced positive discrimination measures for French Muslims and a government official is responsible for them.

[44] Like the *Manouche* in France and *Gitanos* in Spain and France.

them to protection as members of a European minority. Romanian Roma might also claim protection as European citizens with the right to freedom of movement. Their case would be that they are 'more European' than Roma from former Yugoslavia. These dilemmas need to be resolved for Roma to be granted a legal status entitling them to rights and funding. However such a process inevitably provokes rivalry amongst potential beneficiaries, who have considerable scope for manoeuvre by presenting themselves in the guise of various identities.

Roma have no mother country and they don't even want one. If anything they are a non-national minority without boundaries since they are spread out in diasporas, without even forming large-scale concentrations in regions or towns. They are quite different from the Hungarians in Romania and Turks in Bulgaria, whose national minority status was a side product of nation-building and state-formation when boundaries were redrawn. For Roma the best prospect is to become a political entity or *demos* linked to intergovernmental organisations – such as the Council of Europe or now the European Union. These organisations take the role of a mother country, standing up for the rights of ethnic kinfolk in other states. However practices that may function well for others may not necessarily work with Roma. Simply adopting such patterns is hazardous as it ignores the internal divisions within Roma populations that make them more fragile and vulnerable than other European minorities. These risks are partly related to legitimising 'traditional' forms of power amongst the Roma – the domineering 'king' or 'big boss', the *bulibașă* or *vajda*. Such institutions are often inherently corrupt and lack democratic transparency.

The reinvention of culture and grass-roots mobilisation

Religious mobilisation is one important form of Roma activism where charismatic leaders become preachers, pastors or church moderators. These find project-based activities unsatisfying and so turn to what might be seen as another kind of entrepreneurship. Sometimes I almost envy these leaders and also feel challenged, since they are amongst the few whose followers are real rather than fictive. The reinvention of tradition is another major mobilising force based on a revival of *Romanipen* as a codified set of genuine Roma cultural patterns. However Roma at grass-roots level have also drawn on tradition, reinforcing the clan structure and kinship-ties, because they provided resources supporting adaptive strategies. And speaking of international migration, traditional Roma might have greater opportunities to travel abroad than most ethnic Hungarians or Romanians.

At the same time reinforcement of the clan-structure and other traditional institutions has negative consequences, like the lower age of marriage in many Roma families.[45] Twenty or thirty years ago this rarely fell below fourteen years amongst girls but nowadays it can be around ten years of age. Such arranged marriages can be a way of bringing women and other family members to Western Europe and gaining residence permits for them. The clan-structure can help in finding accommodation but these forms of social capital can be also exploited in the informal labour market through human trafficking, begging and other semi or illegal activities. These developments, even if unintended, pervert Roma traditions to support organised crime. As a result media debates reinforce stereotypes about the high crime rates of Romanian Roma in France and elsewhere, providing political ammunition to racists.

Trafficking and other criminal networks, which handle the whole delivery operation, would not function so effectively without the middlemen and other organisers to whom migration is just a business. Once in Italy or Spain Roma from Romania meet Roma from Serbia or Albania, who had migrated twenty or thirty years earlier. Back then they had done the 'dirty work', as beggars and petty criminals, but they have since become middlemen, recruiting the newcomers. A considerable amount of knowledge is being traded in these ethnically mixed groups – how to bring people into the country; where to find scrap metal; how to share begging pitches; or how to find accommodation.

When it comes to the issues of criminality, we usually warn the public to avoid generalisations: not all Roma are criminals and not all criminals are Roma; not all beggars are Roma and not all Roma are beggars. But this goes to the other extreme and individualises everything, avoiding the question of criminal responsibility. We also need to understand individuals as parts of a social fabric with cultural patterns, kinship and ethnic ties. A Roma woman, with children in her arms, does not appear in front of an Italian church by chance. While she might be acting on her own initiative she could be part of wider group, organised around human trafficking. Beggars have to pay fees, so what they end up with is never the whole amount they collected. Nevertheless she will earn far more in a successful day than a woman cleaner in Romania.[46]

Instead of concentrating on the individual, it is crucial to explore how these networks operate to understand the ways in which informal economic practices – and certain forms of criminality – become socially embedded. Certain organisers need to be put on trial but their responsibility to others should also be recognised for these

---

[45] See: Bitu, Nicoleta – Morteanu, Crina (2010): *Are the Rights of the Child Negotiable? The Case of Early Marriages within Roma Communities in Romania*. Report realized with UNICEF Romania support within the Project 'Early Marriages within Roma Communities: Rule of Law, Cultural Autonomy and Individual Rights (of Children and Women)', source: http://www.unicef.org/romania/Early_marriages_Romani_CRISSCRISS.pdf

[46] Apparently 30 to 50 Euros are considered to be average daily takings but a skilled beggar might collect even more on a successful day in an advantageous location.

people cause much of the damage suffered by the whole community. The approach of some NGOs is distorted by concentrating overwhelmingly on complaints against the police and legal procedures. Actually we need more successful prosecutions but communal debates with local churches, associations, NGOs and political parties can use such cases to raise social questions and add another dimension of prevention.

Another negative instance of the reinvention of culture is the recent public appearance of self-proclaimed traditional Roma leaders, indicating deterioration of democratic institutions at local level. This is a sign of substantial public mistrust of local Roma self-government bodies and NGOs, due to divisions between Roma elites and local communities. The rising Roma-related organisations are based in centres such as Budapest or Bucharest and even if their projects are successful, their links with the grass-roots tend to be weak. The reappearance of traditional Roma leaders fills this gap and police, local councils and politicians often legitimise their declared role by cooperating with them. Once more this is a reinvention since, historically, the *vajda* and *bulibaşă* were authorised by non-Roma officials to control their communities, collect taxes and obtain information. Nowadays these traditional and separate leaders are sometimes legitimised in multiculturalist discourse as part of 'their culture' which has to be respected. This same argument is also used to justify the practice of early marriage. My view is that early marriage and school attendance are human rights issues not cultural questions.

Arguments based on culture can easily become a reactionary, socially counter-productive force as demonstrated by the growing popularity of nationalist mythologies in many European countries as a consequence of disillusion with pluralist democracies or the outcomes of post-Communist transition. The legitimising of 'traditional Roma leaders' resembles the retrograde tendencies of majority nationalisms – such as nostalgia for Greater Hungary or regarding orthodox legionnaires as the 'truest Romanians'. This should be borne in mind by those who base their plans on a supposedly genuine Roma culture.

Not all Roma communities participate in the reinvention of traditions to the same extent. Least involved are groups which over the centuries have been most integrated into wider society, albeit as inferiors, like the *Romungre* in Hungary or the *Vatrasi* in Romania. These people are not seen as Roma, if this label means following traditional customs. They only speak the language of the majority and attend Catholic or Orthodox churches as the others do. Yet they are not fully accepted as Hungarians or Romanians: socially they seen as inferior and treated differently as *cigány* or *ţigan*. Nowadays these kinds of people are most at risk.

While traditional Roma still have the safety net of their traditions and kinship systems, these Roma are caught in between for although not traditional, they are also racialised since their deprivation is explained by racial traits. This racialisation is partially fed by Roma activists when we tell them that the solution to overwhelming social tensions is to affirm their Roma identity and persuade their children to do likewise This brings advantages like access to special quotas in the educational system. We give this advice even if people were integrating or assimilating with some success. And they might adopt the Roma category as the politically correct way of avoiding the labels *cigány* or *ţigan* but may well not know what this word actually means. In relation to the actual social and personal histories of these people the prospects of their re-ethnicisation and claims to be Roma are based on lies and misunderstandings.

Addressing social problems – in the way we discuss migration and exploitation – as 'Roma issues' contributes to the ethnicisation of these phenomena, which are really common to many ethnic groups in different countries. One advantage of claiming the genuine and powerful status of citizen is that we are able to build alliances with other citizens who have different ethnic and social backgrounds and then tackle these issues together with them. In this way we can escape the ghettoisation of Roma activism. Instead its narrowly focused agenda can extend to embrace a broader, generalised human rights approach tackling problems like the exploitation of children irrespective of their ethnicity. Nevertheless, our efforts are mainly targeted at the Roma people as such, in other words we are still caught in the ethnic trap.

Roma ethnos and demos

The ethnic nationalist paradigm assumes a collective entity as the bearer of rights: the nation or national minority is in itself the subject of law and history, so it is the community that needs to be protected and not the individuals who belong to it. To accept this, we need a legal definition of who is Roma and who is not. Who is entitled to provide this definition? As already noted, this soon turns into arguments about the criteria for being – or not being – 'genuine' Roma. The real point of these disputes is to monopolise the role of making political decisions on behalf of those possessing acknowledged rights. In any case it is a contradiction on the one hand to demand collective Roma rights – such as freedom of movement and settling in any EU country – but on the other to denounce treating Roma collectively as racist, while arguing for individual treatment when it comes to fingerprinting, evacuation or group repatriation.

The civil rights paradigm does not exclude the strengthening of Roma national identity nor using cultural elements by mobilising people on the basis of their ethnicity. Individuals are entitled to join associations as citizens but in this model cultural elements are parts of a broader civic and democratic structure, where the citizens' rights take priority over minority or cultural rights since individual states bear the major responsibility for Roma. We favour this approach since citizens' rights are codified and can be upheld and monitored by the various institutions supporting them, while potential rights of ethnic minorities are still to be clarified using the Council of Europe's convention on national minorities.[47] However, the civil rights-oriented movement amongst the Roma has not yet become a social movement with wide grassroots support. NGOs like the European Roma Rights Centre and Open Society Institute support this approach by training courses, seminars and by helping various other civil society organisations. Yet such bodies fail to make a significant impact since, as part of the human rights-oriented liberal establishment, they not only promote this agenda but sometimes also impose it on Roma recipients.

The civic approach to Roma nation building offers a way of reducing the costs of traditional or ethnic nationalisms – such as competing claims for 'authenticity' and intra-ethnic struggles for hegemony exemplified in postcolonial history. We have to choose whether to pursue ethnic nationalism and define our claims accordingly or utilise existing institutions based on citizenship and then try to modify and strengthen them. Part of this process is building civic and voluntary associations where people with common interests can maintain specific cultural values consistent with the rule of law. In my view we cannot follow 19th and 20th century ethno-nationalisms in nation building based on a Roma *ethnos*. This agenda is based on separatism and can lead to territorial claims for the ultimate goal of a nation-state – an outcome somehow inherent in such discourse.

Instead I propose continuing our cultural work for the creation of a Roma *demos* in a political sense. Nowadays we can use cultural arguments in conceptually less rigid, non-territorial ways. We may have municipalities with local autonomy which, although lacking full sovereignty of nation-states, nevertheless provide lessons in self-government.[48] For effective mobilisation such local knowledge is a crucial resource.

The uses of local knowledge

In the early 1990s my work was linked more closely to the grass-roots than afterwards. We intervened where there had been conflicts and wanted to comply with legal requirements. Our aims were to rebuild Roma houses, create schools, promote income-generating activities and pioneer the role of health mediators and community organisers. My time was split between local communities and meetings in EU capitals. I travelled in order to lobby and back again to see whether this had results at local level.

---

[47] See: Gheorghe, Nicolae – Mirga, Andrzej (1997): *The Roma in the twenty-first century: a policy paper.* Princeton: Project on Ethnic Relations.

[48] Such as Luník IX in Slovakia or Stulipinovo in Bulgaria.

The connection between universal principles of human rights and understanding of small-scale communities or *local knowledge* is not always obvious. Such experience is sometimes ignored or rejected by human rights activists as parochial and conservative, reactionary and racist. Nevertheless, local knowledge can also be used to explore differences in Roma communities as they are far from homogenous. Distinctions can be drawn between dissimilar social and economic behaviour and between individuals, families and lineage clusters, bearing in mind local norms and values. One obvious risk is that identifying people as different means drawing boundaries and creating divisions between 'us' and 'them'. Therefore local knowledge has to be documented, acknowledged and validated – after all it is usually at local level that most solutions have to be found and applied. Roma inclusion needs to happen in local communities and not just in courts of law or other official contexts. The phrase 'building Europe' means supporting people in their local neighbourhoods before giving them freedom to move anywhere in Europe.

Many NGOs often provoke controversy by thoughtlessly applying broad universal principles to local people – Roma and non-Roma alike – to whom they can seem like an occupying force sent by the EU. In many ways this is comparable to earlier invasions by Communist cadres, charged with imposing the ideology of the international proletariat. What these situations have in common is the asymmetric roles of authorised supervisors, requiring compliance with approved courses of action, and those expected to submit to them. Local knowledge must be taken into account in detailed negotiations about aims and implementation, leading to a better fit between actual situations and general principles. This means making alliances with local actors for any NGO claims that they can handle everything by themselves are implausible.

The role of local knowledge – reflections on a Transylvanian case

These reflections on examples of local knowledge draw on local conflicts and attempts to resolve them in two Transylvanian villages.[49] On 31 May 2009 there was a violent clash between groups of Roma and the local Hungarian *(Szekler)* majority population

---

[49] The following summary is based on the following two reports: *Inter-ethnic Conflict in Sânmartin, Harghita County*, Working Document by the Romani CRISS Roma Center for Social Intervention and Studies, published in 2009; László, Fosztó – Mária, Koreck – László, Magyari Nándor – Stefánia, Toma: *Kettős kisebbségben és konfliktuális helyzetben, a székelyföldi romák* ('Double-minority in conflict situation – the Roma of Szeklerland'), Research Report supported by the Open Society Institute (OSI-ZUG), treaty number: B0092, published in 2010. An earlier report on the conflicts: Nicolae Gheorghe – Gergő, Pulay: *Racist Peasants and Discriminated Nomads? Draft Report on Analysing anti-Roma violence in Harghita County, Romania.* (manuscript, 2009)

in the village of Sânmartin (Harghita County). Several hundred Hungarian villagers raided streets where local Roma are concentrated, damaging their houses and cars. The attack was provoked by the discovery of six Roma pasturing their horses in Hungarian-owned fields. No-one was injured since the Roma had already fled to a nearby forest or neighbouring settlements. Some returned home soon afterwards and agreed to the Hungarian demand to give up their horses and carts but others camped in the forest for several weeks waiting for tensions to subside. The police restored order and there were no further clashes. Relations between Hungarians and Roma remained strained until inter-communal discussions established a basis for peaceful co-habitation, which included an agreement that Roma should no longer keep horses unless they owned at least half a hectare of land for fodder.

About a month later there was a similar conflict between Hungarians and Roma in the nearby village of Sâncrăieni (Harghita County). In this case the Hungarians' anger was directed at only some of the Roma inhabitants. It all began when a Roma man injured a Hungarian in a scuffle in a local pub. The incident led to further tension and a group of Hungarians burned down this Roma man's barn, where kept his horses and fodder. Although the conflict was initially intense, further escalation was prevented by firm police action and tensions calmed down sooner than in Sânmartin.[50]

In both villages members of the local majority and the Roma communities signed contracts to agree rules of future co-habitation, based on their mutual awareness that in the past there were good relations between *Szeklers* and Gypsies. However human rights activists disagreed with these local initiatives, so it is instructive to compare contrasting approaches to these events, focusing on the encounter of local knowledge with universal principles of human rights.

The Romani CRISS and other organisations' initiatives in these villages had two aims: on the one hand, to win court cases against those guilty of violence against Roma citizens and on the other, to develop local programmes involving human rights, confidence-building and the reconstruction of inter-communal relations. Local knowledge was to be a key ingredient in the development plan for rebuilding trust but in such a context this is not the same as re-establishing the often romanticised yet essentially unequal 'good relations' between peasants and Gypsy labourers, where the former had the power of patrons. The aim was rather to redefine the prin-

---

[50] Two major events were initiated by civil actors following the conflicts: one was a demonstration against anti-Roma violence in Miercurea-Ciuc on the 30th of July 2009, organized by several Roma NGOs from Romania; the other one was the international workshop with the title '*Shared social responsibilities: Economic crisis and anti-Roma violent attitudes. Insights from Romania and Hungary*' held in Târgu-Mures on the 18th and 19th of August 2009.

ciples of co-habitation, where both Roma and non-Roma could co-exist in function-ing local communities.

Instead of using the stereotype by contrasting 'enraged', 'racist' Hungarians with Roma suffering 'discrimination', distinctions were drawn within both communities. Among Roma there were differences between locals and outsiders, 'more' or 'less inte-grated' inhabitants, those with property and ordered household-economies and those who relied predominantly on gathering and harvesting. As is common, Hungarian villagers distinguished between 'our Gypsies' and 'strangers', who were known new-comers – or even outcasts – from elsewhere in the region.

Not only Hungarians but also local Roma representatives made similar distinctions between these two categories, when aiming to identify the troublemakers. Therefore in both villages both Roma and non-Roma knew those who – in spite of previous warnings – had repeatedly taken advantage of peasants' fields by pasturing their horses or harvesting potatoes without permission. These people were responsible for the con-sequences of their actions.[51] To say this is not to excuse those who set fire to the houses of Roma families. However, while the entire Hungarian community was not guilty of these offences, it might collectively blame the mob as a defensive strategy to protect individuals. Similarly police and courts must pursue and identify Roma offenders to prevent Roma adopting the same tactic.

This raises the question of how to protect communities from *internal threats*. What is the role of Roma activists, policy-makers and other involved experts in these situa-tions? Should we denounce offenders to the police? Although the authorities and police officers would say yes, a widespread moral code amongst Roma insists that to denounce your own people to the authorities is to betray them. While this might be a form of self-defence against collective retribution, it feeds the stereotype of Roma as uncooperative, hampers developing good relations between communities and impedes winning the trust of local authorities.

These Transylvanian conflicts present a challenge in raising questions about responsibilities within Roma communities. This involves finding defence-mechanisms to protect communities against wrongdoers amongst them and also strategies for human rights organisations other than simply denouncing Roma offenders to the police. But in doing so, are we blaming the victim?

---

[51] However also responsible were Roma families with children who spent their summer in the near-by forest after being forcibly evicted. See the subsequent report of Romani CRISS (referenced above).

Local knowledge and inter-ethnic violence in the 1990s

Similar kinds of local knowledge were being given to the Ethnic Roma Federation and to Romani CRISS when we were documenting cases of inter-ethnic violence in Romania during the early 1990s. In some localities non-Roma told us that they did not set fire to the houses of all local Roma but only of those they knew to be offenders. Twenty years later I am motivated to admit that amongst the Roma attacked, some had formidable criminal records. In the village of Mihai Kogalniceanu one Roma group were nicknamed 'Roma thieves' *(romi cori)* as a sub-ethnic identification. Stealing was an occupational niche for them and they were proud of their profession. Over three or four generations members of this lineage had been habitually arrested for theft in the village and surrounding area. In speaking about the Roma the local non-Roma tended to generalise but when it came to action, they burnt down all the houses belonging to this particular extended family and kept clear of the others. More or less the same pattern was repeated in other cases: local knowledge was not only expressed but also acted on when only certain houses were burnt down or destroyed – even if distinctions were not always too accurate and there were also collateral victims of violent mobs.

Sometimes our efforts to observe the law were opposed by Roma, especially by families whose members had criminal records. Rebuilding houses in accordance with legal regulations was also problematic. In one particular case we argued that our main goal was to restore the rule of law not to restore the houses *per se*. This, too, was resisted as it involved obtaining a court order based on a complaint against the offenders, which might bring reprisals against the complainants or their relatives. Others might also be provoked to inform the police about their accusers' previous crimes. The informal deal was that you keep silent about what happened to your house to keep others silent about your guilt.

At that time our main agenda was to protest about discrimination, so we claimed these pogroms targeted Roma communities in general, even though we noticed that mob violence was not directed against entire Roma communities in an undifferentiated way and were also told by local non-Roma and police that distinctions were made. However we did not want to publicise negative aspects in case it spread the idea that all Roma are criminals. Retrospectively I regret we did this, although at that historical moment it seemed wiser not to mention these kinds of local knowledge – after all almost everything seemed confused in Romania during the 1990s. These conflicts provoked mutually exclusive interpretations. On the one hand the media, police and local authorities reinforced the popular views of the majority, predominantly blaming the Gypsies. On the other Roma activists, backed up by international human rights organisations, framed their protest in terms of pogrom and discrimination while portraying Roma as victims.

The work of mediating and resolving these exclusive perspectives took place in the courts that passed judgement on who was guilty and deserved punishment.[52] Courts were not concerned with the substance of events. Their task was to proceed in accordance with the principles of European jurisprudence and their decisions can be seen as examples of a universal human rights paradigm applied in a legal context to local conflicts.[53] Concern for local knowledge remained in the background because mediation was primarily focused on administering truth and justice – as principles.

In the human rights world the dominant forms of action – *accusing, monitoring* and *ordering* – according to 'our' own concept of order – perpetuated cold war mentalities. In Roma organisations some human rights defenders cling rigidly to lofty principles making their practice inflexible. Roma activists tend to enclose themselves in a ghetto of politically correct discourse, which restricts their opportunities to make contact with realities 'out there'. Instead of becoming zealots in the defence of human rights, we should be finding more accommodating ways of proceeding as intermediaries. If we carry out in-depth investigations and make alliances, we can still be friends with Roma for this doesn't mean violating our moral code. For example, can we afford to challenge someone if we don't want to risk breaking off the whole dialogue?

Reconstruction of the social contract

Compared to the aftermath of the conflicts in the 1990s, the cases in Sânmartin and Sâncrăieni stimulated more complex debates with alternative approaches and different interpretations. It was easier to achieve understanding between the local majority and the Roma – by compromises rather than any expectation of absolute justice being done. Once the actors can reach an agreement by making a social contract, this also implies uncovering some of the more problematic aspects of Roma communities. Today such debates can be more relaxed than those the 1990s. We are in a more stable institutional environment, giving us the opportunity to re-examine our experience and disclose things in a way we couldn't do earlier. Detailed analysis of these realities provides a possible basis for forging alliances between organisations, activists and researchers.

---

[52] Decisions were made by the national and international courts in three cases of mob violence and interethnic conflict: on that in Hadareni in 2005, on those from Casinul Nou and Plăeşi de Sus in 2006 and on that in Boli din Vale in 2008 and 2009.

[53] These cases were also important for the development of legal culture in Romania, helping it adjust to the European code of juridical norms.

In cases such as the Transylvanian conflicts, a social contract should be established, based on trust between local actors. This means translating the concepts of universal principles into local terms to bring these closer to them. The role of Roma community organisers is to help shape the dynamics of relationships of people who will continue living together. Their social contract has to be based on mutual discussion and shared knowledge informing initiatives to be taken, making the role of community organiser redundant in future.

Roma organisers of human trafficking networks might be regarded as an extreme case requiring severe legal punishment since their behaviour damages the whole community. Apart from court judgements, community-based steps should be taken, sending early warning messages to offenders and so helping prevent such crimes. Restoration of customary law might be a way of achieving this – provided this is not done as merely a revival of Roma traditions but as an alternative to court procedures to strengthen the rules of co-habitation amongst Roma and non-Roma members of local communities.

The Pakiv experience and the documentation of gaps

The *Pakiv* European Roma Fund – which later on became the *Pakiv* European Network – was established in order to develop mutual trust, horizontal dialogue and active participation of Roma communities in decision-making processes that directly concerned their lives. The programme was supported by the World Bank and it had three main aims. The most apparent was to promote income-generating activities by providing micro-credit to local communities to fund small-scale enterprises. This initiative, offering an alternative to welfare dependency or migration, was based on the previous practice of the *Autonómia* Foundation in Hungary and Romani CRISS in Romania. The second was to develop an organisational culture combining modern democratic principles with traditional cultural patterns of Roma communities. The third was to train a new generation of potential Roma leaders to become community organisers, so that they could encourage social, political and economic initiatives in their own localities. After combining their theoretical knowledge with practical experience at grassroots level, they were to support similar projects of other community members. In this way *Pakiv* participants could eventually become politicians or officers as part of the Roma elite. The programme started in September 2000, with a year of leadership and management training for 21 young Roma from Bulgaria, Hungary, Romania and Slovakia. After this the new trainees prepared proposals for new programmes in their own countries.

Generally there was little sign of local authorities and public or private employers trying to provide job opportunities for local Roma communities. The same was true of Roma representatives, who devoted themselves to elections, seeking official posts or strengthening Roma national culture rather than concentrating on local community work. In situations where there were no available jobs, their speeches often became empty rhetoric about discrimination and empowerment. Any work offered to Roma was usually short-term training projects lasting ten to twelve months. As is often the case the only prospect afterwards was yet another short-term project and this cycle of repeated training did not lead to permanent employment. While employment-oriented programmes target individuals to enable them to compete for jobs on the labour market, the *Pakiv* programme focused on income generation, working with mutually supportive grass-roots Roma communities, families and small cooperatives. After helping clients survive at subsistence level, the next stage was to encourage profitable entrepreneurship – enabling them to repay loans, perhaps reinvest and even start paying taxes. A main *Pakiv* principle was that contributing to local budgets through taxes strengthened people's claim to citizenship.

The concept of *pakiv* (or *pativ*, *patiu* and *pativalo*) refers to 'trust', 'credibility' and 'respect' in the Romani language and so we adopted this for building bridges between the vernacular and organisational cultures of Roma. The local income generating projects were based on this attempt to work with the language and culture of grass-roots communities by transforming the idea of *pakiv* into a concept referring to actual responsibilities in the project.[54] *Pakiv* was taken as a principle to be applied in the work of community organisers entrusted with building local associations, which would continue to develop this language and corresponding practices.

Pakiv is not the only programme which uses Romani words in its name in targeting Roma communities.[55, 56] The adoption of such titles often represent an attempt to base these initiatives on the values and cultural practices of traditional Roma communities –

---

[54] The notion of *pakivalo* in a religious or Biblical context also refers to those who believe in the God of the Roma and follow religious rules.

[55] E.g. Roma associations adopt names such as *Phralipe*, *Pharile le Romengro*, *Amare Phrala* (from *phral* – brother) and the network of associations established by Marcel Courthiade in Poland, France, Albania and Romania is called *Romani Baxt* (Romani destiny). Several organizations have the word '*cris*' (court) in their title, such as the internal structure of the International Roma Union called *Kris Romano*, or *Romani CRISS*, which includes a play on words by referring to the quasi-judicial practice of traditional Roma communities, and more recently the Romanian League of the *Krisinitori*, established in June 2007.

[56] In Romania a peculiar outcome of the *Pakiv* programme was the appearance of organizations at the beginning of 2000s that included the *pakiv* concept in their names.

or to be more precise, to link NGOs, government projects and other broad policies to the codified set of traditional Roma cultural patterns known as *Romanipen*.[57]

Amongst these initiatives, *Pakiv* was probably one of the most ambitious in anchoring programmes and projects – prepared by both Roma and non-Roma experts – at grass-roots level in Roma communities. The standard organisational jargon of *bottom-up approach*, *capacity building*, and *empowerment* took on specific meanings by being connected to vernacular notions. These in turn could be turned into blueprints for organisational practices of civic associations. For instance the idea of solidarity in the world of civic associations has a conceptual equivalent in the Roma concept of *phralipe* (brotherhood), while the idea of transparency can be similarly identified with *pakivale* (trustworthy people).

The traditional meanings of *pakiv* are closely linked to the kinship system as they refer to marriage customs, bringing up children and observing family rituals. As with other codified forms of *Romanipen*, these are only valid amongst members of one's own group. In fact our goal was not to conserve these pre-modern features but to work with them as assets, on the one hand for building confidence in relation to mainstream society and on the other for developing democracy amongst Roma communities without undue external influences. The idea was to create a new understanding of *pakiv* which is related to Max Weber's notion of vocation *(beruf)* as a basic element of the capitalist ethic. In contrast to Communist attempts to assimilate Roma into the working class, our intention was to develop a measure of respect for distinctive cultural features. However this was only to the extent that these Roma features could contribute to social and economic adaptation instead of merely serving the interests of exoticism. This is what made the *Pakiv* approach and methodology different from that of other organisations.

Success or failure?

Did the *Pakiv* programme really fulfil its goals? Did we manage to create bridges or should our efforts be seen rather as indicators of the gap between the vernacular and organisational cultures of Roma? In my view the most significant lesson was that we are very much at the beginning of the task we intended to accomplish since the outcomes of the programme were controversial. The most outstanding failure was in the area of income-generating activities, since many of them failed within a year. Only

---

[57] In the case of Romania, these attempts characterise the work of ethnographers such as Delia Grigore, ideologists like Vasile Ionescu, NGOs such as *Amare Rromentza* or activists and cultural organizers such as Flori Motoi and Mihaela Zatreanu.

short-term financial support of 5,000-10,000 dollars was provided, although most enterprises needed more in order to plan for whole cycles of production and growth. A sewing workshop lasted only as long as financial support continued, while a beauty salon closed after the manager got married. In some other cases the loan was repaid from other funds, so instead of running the original business the entrepreneurs became involved in shifting money around. The *Pakiv* trainees were meant to return to their own localities to become local community organisers and start their own income-generating projects. Instead, most were soon drawn into the world of NGOs and official bodies. Even if successful, their links with grass-roots Roma communities or their own local groups became very weak.

However in other respects the programme could be considered to be successful. Although many of the trainees did not become community organisers, some became competent officials in the field of Roma policy-making. Some of the former trainees now work in the Roma Educational Fund; others became state-secretaries, managers of large-scale foundations or government officials for Roma affairs. This was largely due to the circumstances since administrative positions in governmental and non-governmental institutions became available for Roma professionals in the early 2000s. But officers in such bureaucracies gradually learn a language and procedures that detach them from the grass-roots. In other words, they became policy-makers *for* the Roma and not *of* the Roma. In our future debates participants should demonstrate whether they managed to use the concept of *pakiv* to connect vernacular and organisational cultures. Even if the *Pakiv* programme seems a failure in terms of its project specification for income-generating projects, it can be still considered a success as regards human capital development. What is more, it should be borne in mind that such projects failed in relation to the overambitious expectations at the outset.

My intention is not to give a final judgement on the overall failure or success of the *Pakiv* programme. Instead I want to offer constructive criticism and start formulating the terms of a debate about its aims and achievements. The debate should be continued by other participants as a next step for this is one of our duties. We were in charge of this programme and therefore it is our responsibility to reflect on our practices and carry out a critical self-assessment. If we manage to clarify these terms, it should lead to a wider public debate on Roma policies. One way to begin is to state the initial ideas and think about the gaps that emerged between them and the actual outcomes. My suggestion is that income-generating or employment training projects for Roma, which are financed by structural or regional development funds, should be stopped for a while. This is in order to have a moratorium and assess what is actually happening with these projects on the ground. Common wisdom suggests that they mostly collapse as soon as external funding is exhausted, either because there is no follow up or because their actual achievements cannot be measured properly. Documenting the gaps between Roma representatives with their jargon from handbooks or trainings, the requirements of funders and the life of grass-roots communities should be one of the first steps in the further development of Roma civil society and the organisational culture shared by Roma associations.

Final remarks on politics and activism

As this paper has argued, the idea of the Roma cultural nation can take different paths. One is that of separation by claiming rights to self-determination and sovereignty as did many other nations in struggles to establish their own independent states during the 19th and 20th centuries. The other path is to gain sovereignty as autonomous, self-governing municipalities, which nevertheless remain part of existing states and subject to their national governments. In the first option, Roma issues become the object of communitarian policy, where the EU has the principal competence – as with agricultural subsidies. In the second, Roma are primarily the responsibility of member states and the main role of the EU is to provide frameworks for the exchange of good practices, financial support and advice as well as ensuring the implementation of European anti-discrimination provisions and other laws on behalf of member states.

It is evident that Roma need to be dealt with as part of a European agenda, especially as regards migration, mobility and the fight against racism. However, making Roma into Europeans is not to encourage them to wander around Europe. The construction of Roma issues as a European concern should start at grass-roots level, based on their rights as citizens. Constructing the Roma nation assumes different dimensions if it is grounded on national and transnational networks of NGOs and local councils. In this case autonomous Roma municipalities could develop transnational networks through their mayors, local councillors and cultural clubs, providing the basic framework for a non-territorial Roma nation. However to maintain the balance between differing local contexts and the general perception of Roma as Europe's largest minority, the best compromise is to facilitate the exchange of good practices between local and regional authorities and nation states, so that these can gradually be accepted as guidelines.

The development of Roma civil society progresses by stages. Preferential educational quotas have resulted in increasing numbers of Roma professionals becoming qualified, even if their employment opportunities were not always evident. Some were recruited into national bureaucracies – often due to affirmative action; for others the rapidly expanding NGO world provided a labour market. Besides public and civic sectors, the private sector should now provide more job opportunities for Roma.

Nowadays, those employed by NGOs should become more like community organisers. This includes ensuring access to medical and school services, as well as teaching skills to foster self-reliance and self-organisation among Roma communities. In a world of funds and projects they should assist the development of grass-roots organisations, enabling them to win support for local projects by themselves in order to make their citizenship more meaningful. For a period of time the EU and member states will continue to provide subsidies for such initiatives as part of affirmative action but these projects will have to be taken over gradually by the beneficiaries. This is one of the responsibilities of the emerging Roma middle-class. Instead of remaining dependent on the generosity of donors and European funding, while pleading the case of other Roma as victims of racism and discrimination, their task is to cooperate with public service providers, policy-makers, businessmen and government officials in consolidating democratic practices. A sincere discussion on our shared concerns is one of the main conditions for making further alliances between the Roma and other segments of civil society.

I can foresee the emergence of a European-wide Roma culture: coherent, formalised, carried on by folk customs as well as by intellectual elites. These developments are similar to processes which led to mainstream national cultures. The bedrock of such a culture-building process would be the large and diverse Roma population across Europe, with members who have the confidence of secure citizenship as individuals in the states where they live. In addition to this, they should also have the possibility to choose between various options. These include the life of a Traveller pursuing traditional crafts; the trajectory associated with mobility into socially integrated and culturally diverse social environments or neighbourhoods, while seeking economically mainstream employment opportunities; or a sedentary life in large Roma communities which enjoy municipal services and various levels of self governance. Whatever path is chosen Roma should pay their taxes – just like any other European citizen.

INTEGRATION AND
THE POLITICISATION
OF ROMA IDENTITY

MARTIN KOVATS

Introduction

András Bíró has initiated this debate on the challenges facing 'Roma' people in general, and Roma activists in particular in regard to the 'future integration of this transnational community into a globalised world'. In this essay, I will respond by focussing on the relationship between Roma identity and politics, the nature and implications of the weaknesses of Roma as a new political identity.

There are two main reasons for concentrating on politics. First, though *'Cigány'*, 'Gypsies', *'Gitanos'*, etc., have been part of European societies and cultures for centuries, their explicit political meaning and significance have, historically, been very limited. Furthermore, overt Roma political activism is a very recent phenomenon but allows 'Roma' people to directly contribute to actual and discursive relations of power. Second, politics is important. It is the mechanism by which resources are allocated and thus is an essential medium for determining what opportunities are available for 'Roma' people (and others). In other words, we have two distinct, but related aspects of Roma integration; the 'integration' of Roma identity within mainstream politics, and the way political actions impact upon the socio-economic and cultural 'integration' of 'Roma' people in the societies in which they live.

This essay seeks to develop debate about the relationship between these two kinds of 'integration'. It argues that, as a new political identity, Roma has been relatively easy to integrate in mainstream politics, both intellectually and institutionally. However, this successful 'integration' has, on the whole, not led to the other kind of 'integration'. Indeed, the very emergence and expansion of Roma as an explicit political identity has had an ambiguous affect on the social and economic status of most 'Roma' people.

One thing is clear; the stakes are very high. Roma is a dynamic political phenomenon. The social and economic disadvantages of so many 'Roma' people are unacceptable and unsustainable. Unlike in the past, these disadvantages can no longer be (largely) ignored by mainstream society, but require action to be taken, most notably by states. However, 'solutions' to such objective problems, are complex, expensive and appear remote and idealistic in the current context. On top of these objective challenges there are profoundly aggravating subjective factors, multiple forms of fear and ignorance, prejudice and hatred. Mix these up with perceived demographic trends and the competitive (confrontational) nature of politics, and it is not implausible to think that the 'Roma issue' has the potential to dramatically destabilise several European countries and could involve human rights abuses on a massive scale.

In order to explain the coincidence of the institutional integration of Roma identity with the structural marginalisation of many 'Roma' people, the essay looks beyond the inevitable limitations of Roma as an emerging political lobby or constituency, and argues that the reality of 'Roma' people does not determine the political perception of Roma, which is actually a construct of the mainstream. This analysis raises the question of how and to what extent Roma identity can be a useful tool for improving the living standards and life chances of 'Roma' people.

Introduction to the Author

I will follow András Bíró's lead and introduce myself and my interest in the subject as this may aid appreciation of the content and conclusions of the essay. I am not a Rom. I can identify myself in a variety of ways, and for the purposes of this essay I am a political scientist. I came to the Roma issue through choice rather than necessity. In early 1990s Hungary, I was sceptical that the imposition of an economic model predicated on inequality and competition could establish political institutions and culture that would guarantee equality of opportunity. At a time when people were willing to talk about politics, I soon came to know to a number of Roma activists who described an emerging catastrophe neglected in mainstream political debate. It was obvious that the political significance of Roma was not just a flash in the post-communist pan but, would grow and grow in political significance, not just in Hungary but across Europe. I realised that we were witnessing the birth of a new form of politics, the critical factor in which was the explicit and irrevocable emergence of Roma people/activists into the public political arena.

I had to follow the story to see where Roma politics would lead, not in order to describe a fascinating new (political) tribe, but because just as 'Roma' people are part of humanity, so Roma politics is part of the political world. For me, the purpose and value of studying Roma politics is that it provides a vital perspective for understanding post-communist politics (and subsequent European integration). I have spent almost two decades trying to find ways to study and understand the Roma political phenomenon and theorise its political meaning. Looking back, I am pleased that my earliest intuition has proven correct. The Roma issue did not disappear with the consolidation of post-communist political systems, but has grown and evolved, rising up both domestic and European political agendas.

The Conventional Conception of Roma

Roma identity is a fact; it exists. It is used to refer to 'Roma' people. As a politicised identity this must have potentially profound implications for 'Roma' people and society in general. Therefore, in order to understand what those implications might be, we need to address the ontological question of who or even what does it refer to? It is recognised at the start that Roma identity means different things/refers to different people in different contexts and so this essay focuses on examining the meaning of Roma as a political identity on a wide scale, notably in terms of how it is used in a pan-European, universal sense.

How one conceives of Roma also has profound implications for how one explains the emergence of Roma as a political phenomenon and analyses the challenges Roma activists face in respect of 'integration'. In his essay, András Bíró adopts a conventional approach which, while acknowledging a degree of internal diversity, essentially considers Roma as a single and distinct population, a 'transnational community'. It is single because the constituent elements (people) of this 'community' can be legitimately (even necessarily) covered by a single label, i.e. 'Roma'. It is distinct in the sense that this population can be distinguished from all those who do not belong to this 'community', can be clearly defined as a sub-group within larger human populations (local, national, continental, global) – 'a unique socio-ethnic group spread all over the world'.

The assertion of distinctiveness sets up András Bíró's contention that (future) integration inevitably entails a 'price' in terms of the abandonment of (some) cultural characteristics. At a fundamental level this is inevitable as change, by definition, means that things which once were are no longer the same or even exist any more. In practice though, this debate focuses on the 'viability' of some essential 'Roma-ness'. Pushed to it furthest (though not its logical) conclusion, there is the implication that integration may entail the elimination of cultural difference and even of Roma themselves as a distinct entity, i.e. assimilation.

This conventional conceptualisation of Roma as a single and distinct people has very long cultural roots in Europe and has been developed over the last two hundred years by scholars and others active in Romani studies. However, the politicisation of Roma identity has taken this concept to a new level. It is no longer a rather abstract question who Roma are, but one with important implications for public policy, how resources are allocated and how social, economic, and cultural issues are discussed in many societies. Given that actual decisions are at stake that affect real people, the politicisation of Roma identity tends towards specifically identifying who is Roma, quantifying Roma in order to fix the identity as firmly as possible to objective criteria. In other words, the conventional perception of Roma, as articulated by András Bíró, is deepened and developed by the inherent needs of the politicised Roma discourse.

However, this does not mean that it 'proves' the accuracy of the conventional concept of the single and distinct Roma 'people', just that there is a new utility to that concept.

The Idea of Roma

How can we know whether this conventional conception of 'the Roma' is correct, if this 'Roma people' actually exists, whose reality we try to express when we talk about Roma? What is the evidence to support this view? What if the discourse of Roma people is not based on objective fact, but is a subjective product of the imagination? Clearly the discourse exists and is used every day. However, if it is not directly related to actual 'Roma' people, the implication is that the Roma political identity has meanings other than to express the realties of 'Roma' people.

Over the course of trying to understand the Roma political phenomenon, I have come to reject the conventional conception of Roma and move towards a completely different way of explaining Roma as a politicised identity. This does not mean that I do not recognise that there are real people who consider themselves and are considered by others to be 'Roma', but that the meaning of Roma, in the contemporary political context, is not a reflection of an objective reality (of Roma people), but is an ambiguous and malleable, even tendentious abstraction based on belief rather than fact.

An alternative to the conventional approach is necessary for an analysis that is better able to locate the Roma discourse within the wider political world and predominant ideology, and in order to explain the relationship between the relative ease of integrating Roma into mainstream political debate and the objective obstacles (and political decisions) that have prevented so many 'Roma' people from enjoying equality of opportunity and even basic rights, over the last twenty years.

Do we talk about Roma, in a political context, because there are people who posses some essential 'Roma' characteristic – just as women, Muslims, pensioners, etc., display some distinctive (defining) aspect the possession of which legitimately (and sensibly) allows the bearers to be categorised in a particular way? Or, do we apply the label Roma to people because they are considered to conform to a meaning of the word which has evolved over time and in different ways within European societies to distinguish some people in society from others. Is Roma identity an inclusive recognition of a real community of people, or a means for excluding/marginalising (traditionally marginalised) people from the mainstream?

Are people *essentially* Roma and so are called Roma, or is the label Roma applied to people because of its descriptive utility? To answer this question, and thus come closer to understanding the political meaning of Roma identity, it is necessary to see if there is any unique distinctive characteristic shared by those who are covered by the Roma discourse.

Knowledge Gaps

One problem in demonstrating the existence of some essential Roma-ness that defines and is congruent with the discourse is the incompleteness of available evidence. There are many reasons to explain this limitation. Historically, (but also today) there is the lack of recorded self-descriptions made by communities which, until recently, have lacked institutions and even literacy. Furthermore, the low social status of 'Roma' has meant, to put it crudely, that those with the capacity to describe and record have not felt it worthwhile to apply this knowledge to 'Roma' in a consistent and comprehensive manner. Even today, the Roma political discourse is dominated by literature produced by particular sources, 'interested parties', notably NGOs, governments and other policy making, managing or evaluating bodies and barely registers the very limited outputs of objective scholarship.

A further obstacle to the creation of a body of evidence which might demonstrate an essential coherence to Roma is the broad transnational spread of its supposed constituent communities. This means that (until recently) there have not been institutions whose interest and jurisdiction embraced all 'Roma'. Differences in perceptions of 'Roma' in different jurisdictions obstructs simple aggregation and also contributes to the considerable methodological problems inherent in designing and conducting comprehensive studies of all 'Roma'.

Recognising the limitations of available knowledge and comparable data is important as gaps mean that something significant (observation or interpretation) may yet be discovered. Nevertheless, there is still a lot of information about 'Roma' people, communities, circumstances, etc., it is helpful to briefly discuss some of the principle features of what is generally known and accepted about 'Roma' and the implications of this knowledge for the belief in an objective Roma essentialism.

Bases for Identity

There are a variety of means that are conventionally used as the basis for identifying distinct human groups, including:
  - Location
  - Citizenship
  - Institutional affiliation
  - Culture: Language, Religion, Practices
  - Profession/lifestyle
  - Community
  - Descent/origin (Race)
  - Self ascription

Location

Where people live (or have come from) is a very common way for identifying and defining human sub-groups, i.e. people from a particular village, town, region, country, continent, or geographical type – Londoner, northerner, Belgian, African, etc. Yet, Roma cannot be contained within any exclusive spatial entity, nor does the diffusion of 'Roma' people allow for any meaningful association with territory. There is no place exclusive to Roma, no place to which the Roma identity can be fixed and from there attached to people. Indeed, every significantly sized space where Roma people live is shared with (usually a majority of) people who are not included in the Roma discourse, i.e. not politically identified as Roma.

The idea of a Roma homeland (a 'Romanestan') is highly contentious. The traditional path of nation building envisages the nation/people claiming their own independent territory, their nation-state. But, for a tradition characterised by containment and exclusion, any 'Roma territory' is more likely to be a Bantustan, a reserve or theme park – more Gaza than Israel. In the new millennium, international Roma activists have responded to the sensitivity of the relationship between Roma and civic national identity by promoting the concept of a *politically represented nation* (see the International Romani Union's Declaration of a Nation), neither territorially bound nor a state. Nevertheless, this example of innovative political thinking does not help explain what Roma identity is, only what it might be.

The lack of a geographical basis for Roma identity has important implications both for the coherence of 'Roma' and practical integration, which effectively means how people (and identities) fit in with the economy, society and culture within which they live. However, politicised Roma identity itself explicitly seeks to transcend established geographical defined identities (to which 'Roma' people are always entitled). This is reinforced by the selective use of the argument that 'Roma' have no 'mother country', used in order to justify international intervention (and also to imply that states have less responsibility for their 'Roma' citizens). As such it displays an uncanny parallel with the traditional stereotype of the wandering nomad. While this 'transnationalism' might appear liberating to some, in a world still defined by nation-states it can also contribute to the marginalisation of 'Roma' people within their home countries.

Citizenship

In an age of states, citizenship provides one of the clearest bases for identifying people and distinguishing them from other people. In addition to being (practically) universal, there are clear procedures to explain how citizenship is obtained and its possession is objectively verifiable. Citizenship (civic identity) is also very important in respect of integration as it establishes opportunities for participating in decision making relevant to law/rights, entitlements and resource allocation.

Obviously, there is no Roma state and so there is no Roma citizenship. Almost all 'Roma' people have a citizenship, so the Roma discourse embraces many different citizenships. Furthermore, the citizenship that a 'Roma' person possesses is shared with many other people who are never considered to be Roma. Given this diversity and the importance of citizenship for integration, it is crucial to understand the relationship between Roma identity and civic identity. Does Roma identity strengthen, weaken or have no affect on citizenship? What conditions the relationship between the two?

Despite there being no Roma citizenship, an aspect of the politicisation of Roma identity has been initiatives that would provide Roma identity with some status or entitlements characteristic of a citizenship. For example, Roma passports or other 'identity' documents have been issued by Roma organisations to 'prove' the Roma identity of the bearer for official purposes (usually to support asylum claims). Entitlement to vote for a Roma self-government in Hungary is dependent on being on a separate Roma electoral register. The International Romani Union's Declaration of a Nation, while rejecting a Roma State, demands collective Roma representation in a post-state age of transnational governance. More recently, the European Roma and Travellers Forum has sought to explicitly disconnect Roma *national* identity from citizenship while demanding rights that transcend those of national citizenship (see European Roma and Travellers Forum Charter on the Rights of the Roma). However the relationship between Roma identity, civic status and entitlement evolves in the future, to date, there is no link between Roma and citizenship that can be used as a basis for Roma identity.

Institutional Affiliation

People can be identified on the basis of an institution to which they belong – a club or society, political party or church, etc. Often the institution itself provides the formal framework for a wider identity. In the case of Roma, there are no long-standing institutions that can be the basis of Roma identity – Roma is not a club.

However, there is an interesting relationship between Roma identity and Roma institutions, which is essentially linked to the process of politicisation. It is the Roma discourse which provides scope for Roma institutions that, in turn, perpetuate the discourse leading to further institutions, etc. Some people might feel that this is a logical and even desirable dynamic, raising the profile and capacity of 'Roma' people to promote their interests. The purpose of this essay is to question this assumption.

Cultural Characteristics

Alongside race, the most common way of expressing Roma distinctiveness is with reference to culture. In the modern age, the language of culture is more acceptable than that of race, and awareness of cultural 'difference' has relevant implications for policy and society. However, culture itself is a very broad category embracing many particular cultural traits, and boundaries are often not easy to delineate precisely. All human beings have culture, but also individuality, hence culture in any human group should be expected to display variety. At the same time, it is common for different 'groups' to share many cultural characteristics. Therefore, an essential basis for the existence of a culturally defined community requires identification of at least one characteristic that is shared by its members and which is also, to a significant extent, exclusive to its members.

Language

One of the most common cited of these cultural markers used as a basis for identity is language. In respect of the Roma discourse, reference is often made to Romani. However, Romani is NOT the language of 'Roma' people. The lack of a comprehensive, global (or even pan-European) survey of either languages spoken by 'Roma' people or of Romani itself means that there is an absence of accurate data about how many native Romani speakers there are and what languages 'Roma' speak. Nevertheless, the most widely quoted estimates of 1.5 to 2 million Romani speakers represents only 15-25% of the supposed 8-10 million strong Roma diaspora in Europe. In recent years a number of countries have allowed people to declare both Roma identity and whether Romani is their mother tongue, producing figures which support the view that Romani is only spoken by a minority of 'Roma'.

It is widely recognised that in some countries, such as Spain and the UK, there are no native Romani speakers (other than recent immigrants). Furthermore, Romani itself is characterised (as András Bíró notes) by dozens of dialects, many of which are mutually unintelligible. As the linguist Yaron Matras has observed, other than very young children there are no monolingual Romani speakers and 'Roma' people almost invariably speak at least one mainstream language. Therefore, language in general and Romani in particular cannot provide the basis for the Roma identified in the political discourse.

Religion

Religion is another cultural characteristic that is often used to define and distinguish human sub-groups (including those whose members often have little or nothing else in common). It has never been seriously argued that Roma share a common religion. Indeed, as András Bíró notes, (institutionalised) Roma spirituality is diverse and closely related to that of the wider, non-Roma population. There is no evidence at all to support András Bíró's supposition of an 'original... animistic religion'. The silence of the historical record on this matter does not itself disprove that there ever was some form of spirituality common to all 'Roma', however if such a thing ever existed it would appear to have no relevance to contemporary Roma identity.

Given the fundamental importance of religious belief and belonging in Europe over centuries, it would be incredible if this had no impact on 'Roma' people or identity. The historical record is filled with indications, both implicit and explicit, of perceptions of 'Roma' spiritual deviance or non-conformity – magic, curses, fortune telling, etc. This idea seems still to be very much alive today in the Romantic image of 'Roma' as 'free spirits', particularly useful in the entertainment industry. Would it be speculating too far to consider that in a secular Europe, a long standing perception of Roma spiritual 'difference' expresses itself in perceptions of Roma cultural 'difference' being at odds with (even a threat to) mainstream society? More basically, the fact that different 'Roma' people and communities follow different religions (and none) means that religion cannot be the basis for Roma identity.

Cultural practices – Marime, Romaniya/Criss

Though language and religion are the two cultural characteristics most commonly used as a basis for identity, the 'Roma'-related literature has long also referred to other particular cultural practices, notably those of purity/pollution and justice/self-regulation. Not being a cultural anthropologist, I have to confess to very limited knowledge in this area. Nevertheless, for any such cultural feature to be the basis of contemporary Roma identity, it would be necessary to show that the distinctive practice was common to those labelled Roma.

Purity practices do seem to be widespread, from the Balkans to the UK, and this is often explained as evidence of a shared cultural heritage. However, *marime* itself is never referred to as a basis for Roma identity, but only as a distinctive cultural practice. There may be two main reasons for this. First, many 'Roma' people/communities do not engage in any kind of purity (anti-pollution) ritual, it is not part of their culture (and such rituals may also differ considerably between communities). Second, such practices are conservative, even archaic and, to a significant degree, incompatible with a modern political discourse of 'integration'.

In this respect András Bíró is largely correct to argue that 'integration' probably means the abandonment of cultural forms from the 'pre-integration' age. However, it should also be recognised that such practices can be sustained if there is sufficient will within the community to preserve them. In part, this must depend on the meaning of the practice. Obviously, purity rituals are not unique to Roma, but are found, for example in Jewish and Muslim traditions. In Europe, Christianity has always contained elements of ritual purity (such as baptism). The anthropologist Fiona Bowie has argued that *marime* is an example of 'policing boundaries' between 'Roma' and non-Roma, which is not unusual among vulnerable groups. There is also evidence that these boundaries can also be between 'Roma'.

Self-regulation, communal law/justice also has a long pedigree in relation to 'Roma' stretching back to at least the Middle Ages. Today some communities still use communal methods for addressing issues within the community and there have even been attempts to have Romani 'law' recognised in mainstream legal systems. Of course this kind of communal self-regulation is not uncommon, though usually institutionalised, for example clubs and societies, religious courts, etc. It is also a feature of communities that have no recourse mainstream justice. Clearly communal justice can sit awkwardly with 'integration' and the mainstream 'rule of law', however, the key point is that it does not provide the basis of Roma identity in the political discourse. Roma is not the identity for people who ascribe to particular purity or judicial beliefs and practices.

Overall, there appears to be no cultural markers upon which Roma identity can be based. The problem is not that 'Roma' people do not have culture, evidently they do. Nor does it mean that there are no cultural characteristics distinctive to 'Roma' people, there obviously are (such as Romani). But this is not the same as saying that there is a Roma culture that defines (and identifies) Roma. It has been suggested that 'Roma' constitute a 'mosaic of culture'. However, without explanation of how the different component parts fit together the image does not help identify anything essential about Roma. On the contrary, it supports the alternative hypothesis that Roma is 'in the eye of the beholder'.

Occupation, Lifestyle

Occupation and lifestyle are objective characteristics, which are often used as the basis for identifying human sub-groups, e.g. farmer, pensioner, sailor, athlete, etc. Obviously, Roma is not a profession or a job. Nevertheless, there is a strong connection between the identity and an economically derived lifestyle. The most important of these is the association between Roma and an itinerant lifestyle, commercial nomadism or a peripatetic labour force. The historical basis to this association is discussed below, but for now it is sufficient to point out that only a tiny minority of 'Roma' today engage in some form of itinerant lifestyle. In his essay Nicolae Gheorghe refers to the use of *'nomadi'* to categorise 'Roma' migrants in Italy. The nomadic image can be seen to have wider influence as a metaphor expressing a perception of Roma as disconnected from land and from the mainstream in general. András Bíró specifically refers to the lack of farming traditions among Roma and consequent importance of the service sector, however, it equally well manifests itself in respect of contemporary mass unemployment and welfare dependency.

Just as is the case with cultural practices, among 'Roma' there are distinctive lifestyles and economic characteristics. However it is hard to see any objective connection (in terms of lifestyle/occupation) between, say a wealthy UK Traveller, a *Kalderash* cleaner in Romania and an unemployed Slovak Rom. Any such connection is in the mind of the observer. Furthermore, all these distinctive characteristics are not exclusive to 'Roma' but are, to a greater or lesser extent, shared with people who are not considered Roma, including an itinerant lifestyle. More generally, the huge diversity of 'Roma' people and their economic conditions mean that there is no possibility that occupation or lifestyle can provide a basis for Roma identity.

Nevertheless, the politicised Roma discourse has contributed to a close association between Roma and lifestyle/occupation. This reflects not the circumstances of all 'Roma' people, but mainstream institutional interests. The need to direct some kind of social policy towards Roma communities has led to the conceptualisation of Roma as a group subject to poverty and exclusion, as distinct from an ethnic/culturally defined 'people'. However, this observation anticipates the later discussion of how it is not 'Roma' people themselves that define the Roma discourse, but mainstream interests.

Race – origin/descent

As noted above, a key component of the conventional conception of Roma is the notion of shared, distinctive racial characteristics derived from a belief in a common origin outside of Europe. It is recognised that many 'Roma', especially in Central and South East Europe, appear physiologically distinct from their (non-Roma) compatriots. At the same time, it is also true that many people who are labelled Roma (and some who even identify themselves as such) look no different from indigenous 'Caucasian' Europeans. Similarly, there are many people, in Central and South East Europe with relatively dark skins and 'Roma-like' appearance, but who are not considered 'Roma'.

In other words, unlike 'racial' identities such Black, Asian, etc., physiognomy does not provide an essential shared characteristic of 'Roma'. This is supported by genetic analysis that demonstrates the diverse biological heritage of 'Roma' today. The argument that 'Roma looking' *non-Roma* are actually descendants of people who were once Roma, i.e. they have become assimilated and lost their 'original' identity, does not support a racial Roma thesis, but serves to underline the fact that racial identity is a construct reflecting economic, social and cultural factors. Despite many people having a firm belief that there is clear distinction between 'dark Roma' and 'white non-Roma', in reality such a distinction is only partial and selective and 'Roma looking' cannot provide an objective basis for Roma identity.

Self-ascription

The final characteristic that needs to be considered as a possible basis for the Roma of the Roma discourse is self-ascription – how people identify themselves. At first this might seem fundamentally subjective, however whether one identifies as something or does not is a fact – you either do or you don't. In an age of individualism, it seems that the most ethically acceptable approach to take is to consider as Roma those people who identify themselves as such.

However, there is a problem – how can we know what someone thinks about their identity? Clearly this 'thought' needs to be transmitted and, for most purposes, be recorded so others can experience the 'thought'. If this were the basis for the Roma identity of the public discourse, Roma would refer to those who identified themselves as *Roma*. This is not much of a problem in respect of Roma political activism, where those involved invariably declare their identity, however, it is far less clear-cut in terms of the wider discourse about other people.

The conventional method for defining the boundaries of a self-ascribed identity is to record how many people identify with a particular identity in a census, though surveys or other forms of recording (such as voluntary equal opportunities monitoring) are also used, usually in a particular context. In the Roma issue, the most comprehensive surveys of self-identity are national censuses. However, not only do most European states not specifically include Roma in their census, even where they do the number of people identifying as 'Roma' is invariably rejected as an 'understatement' and not reflective of the 'real' number of Roma.

The matter is further complicated by the fact that the word Roma itself is both a communal identity and a generic label, which individuals who accept a 'Roma' label may not necessarily identify with. It might be possible to aggregate the number of people who call themselves Sinti, *Cigány*, *Lovari*, Roma, Gypsy, etc., but that wouldn't tell us how many of them also accepted Roma identity. In other words there is both a lack of comprehensive and consistent recording of Roma self-identity and a rejection of the data when people actually do identify themselves as 'Roma'. This means that the Roma of the Roma discourse does not refer to those people who have demonstrated that they identify as Roma or even 'Roma'. On the contrary, it explicitly rejects recorded self-ascription as the basis of Roma identity.

Nevertheless, a necessary object of Roma activism is to encourage more people to identify as Roma. It is likely that the politicisation of Roma identity over the last twenty years has increased the number of people who consider themselves to be Roma than would have otherwise done so. In the future, even more people may do so, even the many millions who are conventionally estimated in the political discourse. However, at present there is no evidence that this may be the case, meaning that the 8-10 million 'Roma' of the discourse exist only because society has decided how many 'Roma' there are, not because that many people have declared themselves to be Roma.

Empirical evidence – conclusion

Noting that Roma is a highly heterogeneous 'group' is nothing new. However, the purpose of the above discussion has been to relate this diversity to the politicised discourse of Roma identity. The discourse implies a coordination of political activity based on the assumption that 'the Roma' are a single and distinct group. Yet, this brief review of what is known about 'Roma' people in relation to conventional bases for identifying human sub-groups, shows that there is no single, objective characteristic shared by all – no Roma land or citizenship, institutional or cultural markers, physical features or even (self)identity. Indeed, it is possible that there might not be a single such characteristic shared by even a majority of supposed 'Roma'. Furthermore, all potentially definitive characteristics are not exclusive to 'Roma' but are shared, to a greater or lesser extent, by people who are excluded from the Roma discourse and identity.

Of course this not to say that there are no people who consider themselves to be Roma, or that such people do not have any cultural or racial characteristics or that they do not share these characteristics with other people (who also identify as Roma). The point is that if there is no characteristic common to all, how can Roma be a single group to which a single identity can be authoritatively applied? If all pertinent characteristics are also, to some extent, shared with 'non-Roma' how can 'Roma' be distinguished from 'non-Roma' by what is, by definition, an exclusive identity?

The 'problem' of heterogeneity has been a fundamental challenge for Roma political activism, particularly the wider you go, and notably at a European level. The fragmentation, diffusion and diversity among 'Roma' is a major obstacle to coherent political activity. There are also important implications in respect of how mainstream politics and society understand and address 'Roma' people, their circumstances and policy needs. As Nicolae Gheorghe acknowledges, it is not hard to see that one of the effects of the Roma discourse is likely to be a tendency to simplify complexity, promote stereotypes and thus undermine the effectiveness of policy actions.

One response to the problem of who is Roma has been formulated by the European Roma and Traveller Forum, whose Charter for Roma defines a Roma as someone who 'avows oneself to the common cultural heritage of the *Romanipe*'. This means that someone is Roma who believes in 'the Roma' and certain associated characteristics or values. At one level this definition clearly does not fit with the dominant political discourse of Roma, which is not based on Roma self-consciousness. But, ironically, it also expresses a fundamental truth, namely that the discourse is driven by the wide-spread belief that there is a real Roma people out there – even though objectively and empirically there is no clear idea of who or what it might be.

Another effect of the lack of clear objective markers to identify 'Roma', is the importance that becomes attached to the idea of a common historical origin. Indeed, contemporary diversity can be seen as the 'proof' of the common origin, expressing the divergent cultural evolution of communities over time and place. Though a shared past does not resolve today's difficulties in respect of identity defined politics, the historical record may at least be able to present an intellectual justification for labeling communities as Roma.

Historical Argument

While the need to believe in a common Roma past is important for claiming a legitimate coherence for the diverse reality of 'Roma' people today, it also facilitates the integration of Roma identity into mainstream political discourse. Perhaps the greatest single issue related to Roma is discrimination. The claim to a common origin enables Roma to be perceived as a racial group, or at least one similar to groups, such as African Americans, and so as part of the universal struggle for civil rights. Of course, civil rights struggles are not limited to ethnic/racial groups, but the implicitly racial discourse of common Indian origin aligns Roma with a particular political tradition. Another tradition it plays into is the European nationalist one. With its displacement from an original homeland, migration (*völkerwanderung*) and the preservation of culture, the Roma national narrative is similar to that of other 'nations'. This provides the Roma discourse with a credibility to make claims for political autonomy of some degree, if not territory.

Nevertheless, attractive as the narrative may be, there is still the question of to what extent it reflects all the known facts, or is a product of imagination (if so, whose?). The question of 'origins' has accompanied 'Roma' from earliest times. For the last 200 or more years the linguistically based case for medieval Indian origins has become widely accepted. Yet, it is not just a question of identifying a particular event in the past, but also how that event relates to the present, i.e. knowing what happened in the centuries between.

Knowledge Gaps

If there are large gaps in our knowledge about 'Roma' people today, these are immeasurably greater in respect of the past, particularly the further back one goes. There are almost no records produced by 'Roma' people themselves. The older historical record largely amounts to legal and governmental documents, presenting a more or less 'official' representation of 'Roma'. References to 'Roma' are not common, though concentrated archival research and subsequent scholarship will certainly provide a far clearer, evidence-based picture about the past of 'Roma' people than exists today.

Apart from the limitations of the written record, the reconstruction of an authentic Roma past is also greatly constrained by a lack of the kinds of material remains, which are conventionally (and increasingly) used to expand our knowledge of the past, especially of the lives of the non-literate multitude. There is no material evidence for the Roma origin in India or anywhere else, no Ur founding city or region that can be reliably linked to 'Roma' or at least Romani. There is no material trail out of India and across Europe. There are no characteristic architectural styles preserved in the landscape. There are no characteristic field systems or other alterations to the environment. This is not surprising for a community so strongly characterised by itinerancy and temporary settlement.

Though often associated with metal working and even though some communities have been known explicitly by their trade, there don't seem to be distinctive craft products by which 'Roma' can be identified. As non-elite people, 'Roma' did not mint coins. Though some place names refer to *Cigány*, not many in Central Europe seem to derive from 'Roma'. Indeed, the name '*Cigány*' itself would probably imply that mainstream society had determined the label. In other words, there is dearth of non-literary evidence that might help identify a Roma origin and to reconstruct a 'Roma past', and the written record itself is extremely limited and distorted by its sources.

Language

This lack of physical evidence means that, unusually, the key piece of evidence in the Roma national narrative is the Romani language and its mixed vocabulary with a strong Sankrit derived element. Today many (though an unknown number) of people speak Romani, but this is not a single standardised language, but one composed of many different dialects, some more widely spoken than others. Dialects mix the vocabulary and grammar of other languages with Romani words and even the core Romani vocabulary is not common to all dialects. As a link between past and present, Romani is not strong as so many 'Roma' people do not speak any dialect of it. It is argued that non-speakers have 'forgotten' their 'original' language. While there has certainly been 'language loss' in recent times (and on-going) there is very little evidence either of who spoke Romani (and what kind) and what 'Roma' people of the time or the ancestors of today's Roma actually spoke. Indeed, the idea that some people have 'lost' Romani recently might indicate that linguistic change could have occurred in the past too, thus making Romani an even less reliable tool for revealing the supposed shared Roma past.

More fundamentally, language and people are not the same. People learn languages, can speak several languages, can change their principal language and the language used within a family or community can change over time. Language changes are often seen in relation to power relations – nation-building, conquest, etc. As there has never been a Roma (Romani speaking) state the survival of Romani can be seen as a representing successful resistance to hegemonic languages. However, there simply isn't the evidence to know the social factors that have conditioned the evolution of Romani – how many people 'joined' the Romani speaking community, how many left, when and why. Linguistic history can provide evidence about social relationships in the past, but cannot reconstruct these relationships. Even if we had a good historical record by which the evolution of Romani could be traced, it would remain a history of a language, not necessarily of a 'people'.

Unsurprisingly the evidence of Romani itself is far from unambiguous and has been interpreted in many ways over the last two centuries. Differences of opinion between scholars is not itself a problem and some analyses are going to be better (more defensible) than others. The core of Romani implies that there was a community which developed it. However, where that community emerged, from whom and why is something which can only be reliably identified with the help of other, non-linguistic, evidence (which is absent). Furthermore, Romani can be a part of a hypothesis of what happened to that community, but it cannot reconstruct either the history of that original community or the histories of those communities that speak a form of Romani today. It certainly can't, by itself, prove an unbroken social link between the two.

Genetics

The assumption that Romani implies an original community to create the language appears to be supported by genetic studies, such as Gresham *et al.* (2001). This looked at genetic markers (haplotypes) in 14 Roma communities, most from Bulgaria. The research found both male and female lineages common to the groups studied, indicating a degree of common ancestry. Furthermore, these markers were associated with Asia (if not specifically India). However, there were also many other lineages shared between two or more populations, some of which were 'Asian', while many others were characteristic of Europe, the Middle East and even North Africa.

Genetic studies on 'Roma' have not yet become representative and tend to be of families, a single or just few of the huge number of communities that are labelled Roma today. Comprehensive genetic analysis would provide a wealth of information about how individuals and communities relate not only to each other, but also to 'non-Roma' populations. As discussed above, though many 'Roma' today appear 'non-European', there are also many Roma who do not. It would be no surprise if further genetic research demonstrated that 'Roma' have multiple genetic heritages and cannot be exclusively confined to ancestors who 'came out of India' a thousand years ago.

The historical record

The historical record does not help in pinpointing the community which Romani and genetic studies imply existed in the past, though many candidates have been proposed over the years. However, written information about communities that can more reliably be linked with today's 'Roma' first appears in Byzantine sources. As noted above, the historical record about 'Roma' is limited overall, but is also characterised by being the product of observers of 'Roma' rather than records of 'Roma' people themselves. Low status and methodological challenges also mean that 'Roma history' has received little specialist attention. A further problem is that the lack of other, corroborative, evidence means that attempts to reconstruct 'Roma history' are heavily dependent on the identity itself, i.e. searching for references to *Cigány*, Gypsies, etc.

Historical sources show how an identity (derived from an Athinganoi identity) spreads from Byzantium through the Balkans and across Transylvania and into Central Europe. For centuries this identity is applied to people who appear in official records usually as subjects of authorities, taxpayers, servants, slaves. There are good grounds for seeing a relationship between the manifestation of 'Roma' in Central and South-East Europe and immigration – the need to allocate 'new' people to a place in the feudal order. However, it is anachronistic to believe that people perceived others in the same way as we do to day (such as ethnic minorities). Furthermore, once an identity emerges, it does not necessarily keep the same meaning over the centuries and across different countries, and regimes. Therefore, as Nicolae Gheorghe discusses in relation to Romania *robi*, even though contemporary accounts sometimes refer to 'Roma' as a people or a group, it is clear that there was a strong, though varying link between 'Roma' identity and formal social, legal and economic status.

In western Europe, the Gypsy tradition begins with a notable immigration, the arrival of large itinerant communities in the early fifteenth century. However, these initial 'Gypsies' were more a sensation that established the exotic image of the Gypsy in the west than the genealogical ancestors to the region's later/contemporary Gypsy populations. By the sixteenth and seventeenth centuries, when Gypsies are regularly referred to, they are not incorporated into a feudal structure, but exist more outside of the law, subject to harassment and punishment. Though there has long been (and continuing) migration from eastern to western Europe, the powerful association between Gypsy and a nomadic lifestyle has led observers, both past and present, to see Gypsy communities as indigenous rather than 'Roma' migrants.

'Roma' history is a field which deserves much greater attention, which will create many important insights into how European societies have developed. Though the record in essentially biased, i.e. a record of how others have perceived 'Roma', it does show that the way mainstream society has considered 'Roma' has had a centuries-old, powerful influence on the identity of these communities – *Cigány* and Gypsy. Whether today's politicised Roma identity is so different will be discussed shortly. The historical record also shows that different economic, legal and political environments affect the activities, composition and identity of 'Roma' communities. What the historical data doesn't demonstrate is a coherent history of a 'Roma 'people', in the conventional terms of a conquest/occupation, a regime/dynasty, institutions or culture.

Historical argument conclusion

There are immense challenges inherent in trying to accurately reconstruct the history of small, non-literate, non-elite communities over many centuries across the whole of Europe (and beyond), which have not been met yet. Obviously people living today and their communities have historical roots, which could be identified, including how they have fitted in with the wider social environment. There could also be the history of the putative original community that developed Romani, and even a history of Romani itself. It would not only be interesting, but also a contribution to wider understanding of countries, Europe and humanity if these could be known, as well as how they relate to each other.

However, the basic problem is a lack of information. There are points of evidence that need to be taken into account, but how this is done leaves plenty of scope for creativity. Just as contemporary diversity requires the universal Roma discourse to simplify the concept of 'Roma', so the sparseness of data about the past tends towards a simplified historical narrative. For more than two centuries, the Romantic narrative of an Indian people has been popular. For emergent Roma political consciousness and activity a narrative of the past (to explain the existence of the present) is an existential need. It would appear that in the case of Roma, it is the present that defines the past.

Roma Identity – a Mainstream Construction

The purpose of the two previous sections was to look at 'Roma' today and in the past as part of answering the question of who is the Roma of the Roma political discourse. Neither the past, nor present diversity, or even self-consciousness would appear to require the collation of these different populations into a single category. Indeed, on the face of it, the evidence would justify not putting them under a single label. Of course there are many people who are self-consciously Roma, and this number is growing. But, the Roma discourse is not confined to those people, but encompasses many millions of people who can be identified against no objective criteria.

So, if we are not compelled by evidence to consider 'Roma' as a single and distinct group, why do we do so in the political discourse of Roma? The answer would seem to lie in factors outside of the actual existence and characteristics of 'Roma' people. We can take a clue from the historical record, in which 'Roma' identities have been defined and applied by mainstream society, particularly by officials.

Accepting that Roma identity is a construction is quite conventional. In his essay, Nicolae Gheorghe argues that Roma identity 'is actually an ideological construct and does not signify any cultural homogeneity. It is mainly an administrative term serving policy-making requirements'. Therefore, we need to look at the motivation of wider society for constructing the contemporary Roma political discourse, the advantages it provides in enabling society (and its leaders) to explain the particular circumstances of 'Roma' people (and thus allowing society to explain itself) by identifying particular people and communities in a certain (collective) way. Furthermore, the (cultural, political, legal) weakness of the people subject to the identity/discourse allows for a discourse to be driven by not by who 'Roma' people are, but by how others perceive 'Roma', i.e. mainstream society identifies and defines the Roma of the political discourse.

The external definition of Roma is implied in the not uncommon idea that Roma is a legitimate subject for policy due to accumulated disadvantages created by wider society. According to this view (which is expressed, for example, by the EU), 'Roma' identity can be used as a focus of social policy as it can be used to embrace communities that have a long history of exclusion. Other commentators have argued that a Roma focused political approach is required by the prejudice and discrimination faced by Roma people, i.e. Roma is that who is subject to prejudice and discrimination by others who perceive them as 'Roma'. What both arguments have in common is seeing 'Roma' identity not in intrinsic terms but in a reactive way, with the politicisation of Roma identity as a necessary response to mainstream prejudice and marginalisation of a particular section of society.

Looking at the role of the mainstream in defining Roma helps to explain why the identity is applied to such diverse populations. It is not that Roma identity has been created by Roma on the basis of shared characteristics, but that Roma is more a rebranding of the traditional generic identities which, historically, have been attached to a wide range of different communities. This means that Roma has inherited all the baggage of these traditional identities and that the mainstream's idea of the Gypsy continues to be applied to people, but in an increasingly politicised discourse.

Does this matter? The answer has to be: Yes! Politicisation changes the nature of the more general discourse about 'the Roma'. Previously, mainstream society could imagine 'the Roma' in a largely abstract way, as a socio-cultural phenomenon, though this also had implications for how 'Roma' people were treated in society and by authorities. Politicisation makes an explicit link between Roma identity and the allocation of public resources (which are essential in modern society) and political management/control (not just of 'Roma' but of society as a whole). Crucially, the discourse does not exist as the only possible identity of 'Roma' people, who all have other identities that are more directly linked to political and legal entitlement and opportunity, notably citizenship. In other words, the politicisation of Roma identity is a conscious choice by mainstream political actors for mediating political debate and decisions.

Roma Identity and Activism

So far this essay has approached the question of how Roma identity has been (politically) integrated while 'Roma' people have not, through a discussion of where the identity comes from. It has been argued that Roma identity is not a reflection of the characteristics of 'Roma' people, but is the latest form of a centuries-old process of mainstream state/society constructing and applying an identity to particular, peripheral communities – primarily in order to explain their marginal existence and why they are not treated the same way as other members of society. The following section looks more specifically at Roma political activism in light of this analysis of the meaning of Roma identity.

Time of the Gypsies

The rise of Roma up political agendas can be seen as a welcome, if belated, recognition of the existence and needs of an historically excluded ethnic group. After centuries, European societies are finally coming to terms with their Roma minorities in order to overcome injustice, prejudice and discrimination. A key element of this new age is the emergence of explicit Roma political activism, Roma people finally participating in the public debate about 'themselves'. This sense of optimism is enhanced by the wider political and ideological context, which advocates inclusion.

There have been many occasions in the past when 'Roma' has been a big political issue and the subject of policies, often punitive, so the fact that Europe today would be addressing Roma issues is not surprising. What is different though is Roma political consciousness and activity. Roma politics allows 'Roma' people and their issues to be debated in public, puting Roma on the political agenda. Roma politics has played an important role in the creation of a variety of political initiatives, most of which formally seek to improve the lives of Roma people. Furthermore, Roma politics is primarily a post-communist phenomenon so appears as a product of democratisation. It also coincides with European integration and the establishment of political structures encompassing this 'European minority'.

The convergence of these systemic changes gives the appearance that this could be the 'time of the Gypsies'. Despite the huge problems of poverty and discrimination and the limitations of nascent Roma politics, the occasion has arisen to begin to address past and present wrongs. To achieve this is a matter of time and persistence. The right system is in place which will deliver, eventually. Contemporary, globalising/ transnational neo-liberal democracy is a superior system to those of the past, e.g. nation-states, state socialism, the proof of which is this more engaged and progressive approach towards 'Roma'.

This perspective on the Roma political phenomenon is clearly more than just about Roma identity and activism, but is an implicit endorsement of an ideological and institutional system, and its associated political culture. Unsurprisingly, there is strong tendency for the Roma political discourse and Roma political activists to conform to the ideological framework of the political system. Activists must believe that their actions will make a difference through the system, lobbying will lead to better policy/political actions. Thus, Roma is easily (enthusiastically) integrated into the political system.

Ethnic trap

'Time of the Gypsies' is not the only way to understand the Roma political phenomenon. First, the theory effectively (if not necessarily) accepts and promotes the idea that there really is a single and distinct 'Roma people', as implied by the discourse. This supposition creates the objectivity upon which the politics can develop. However, as we have seen, there is no objective basis to the belief in the pan-European 'Roma' people. Second, despite twenty years (particularly the last decade) of Roma being integrated into political debate and systems, there is widespread dissatisfaction and disappointment with the degree to which this has failed to achieve greater equality and justice.

How can we explain the apparent disconnect between the politicisation of Roma identity (with its accompanying features of Roma activists and organisations, public debate and political commitments, Roma policy guidelines, frameworks and hundred of millions allocated to Roma programmes, not to mention the promotion of cultural identity and laws against discrimination) with the depth of poverty and exclusion, the persistence (strengthening) of prejudice and exclusion? Is it just taking time for the 'right system' to deliver or is this 'unanticipated' outcome the necessary and inevitable result of actual power relations? If so, what does that imply for Roma political activism?

To answer this we have to look at the main features of the mainstream political system in relation to 'Roma' in terms of its actual determining forces, rather than an idealised one. Despite its antecedents, the politicisation of Roma identity is fundamentally a post-communist phenomenon. The post-communist period is characterised by the abandonment of an ideological and political system focussed on the full inclusion of all workers and national unity (of course, there were exceptions over time and place). It was replaced by a system which does not guarantee employment, promotes competition and inequality. The economic system is based on profit maximisation and labour markets restructured in favour of those with greatest market skills. At the same time, pluralist political systems have favoured those profit-oriented interests (global as well as national) in the competition for public resources, resulting in severe pressures on public services on which the newly poor/unemployed are increasingly dependent (the rich can purchase their own services and get the best out of public provision).

The unsurprising result has been the recreation of structural poverty and unemployment, notably amongst the less skilled (profitable) workers, and the reduction in their welfare and access to quality public services. The poor have lost out in terms of priorities, with scarce resources targeted at those who can better encourage investment and profit. One example of this is the switch of investment to higher education rather than pre-school or vocational education. For many 'Roma', dependence on the state has increased at the same time as the state's inability (unwillingness) to provide for them. The state has to manage the poor, not to help them overcome their exclusion, but to minimise its obligations so it can continue to support more profitable sections of society. It is hard to see how this basic dynamic is going to change in the foreseeable future.

According to this analysis, state policies are primarily aimed at managing/containing Roma exclusion, rather than overcoming it. The Roma discourse provides several advantages in achieving such an aim. Focusing on Roma identity distinguishes 'Roma' people and their issues from the majority of society. It also allows politicians and authorities to play on long-standing prejudices towards Roma (including those prevalent amongst officials) that Roma are a particularly problematic and difficult group to deal with. Creating an ethnic policy concept that does not fit well with the thematic structures of government means that Roma policy is not practically integrated into policy processes. More obviously, the ambiguity over who is Roma means that Roma policies are hard to quantify, either in terms of what is needed and what is achieved.

There is also a structural problem of particular importance in terms of Roma – the lack of clear links between central and local authorities. This disconnect allows central authorities, such as governments or international organisations, to make inclusive statements, which are then ignored or inadequately implemented at local level. Overall, Roma policy is characterised by low expectations and lack of accountability, fundamentally because of the social and political weakness of the now politically isolated objects of the policy. Instead, authorities have found it easier to promote Roma cultural 'differences and separate political representation, civil organisations, Roma experts and advisors. In this way, the formal integration of Roma individuals/organisations and identity into mainstream politics can be achieved at the expense of the integration of 'Roma' people into the mainstream economy and society.

Implications for activists

If the Roma discourse is essentially a mainstream construct for managing and marginalising (the political needs/demands of) 'Roma' people, Roma activism itself is part of the process of exclusion, not least by providing an apparent legitimacy to state actions. This situation leaves activists with three main options if they are to avoid being an integral part of the problem.

The first of these options is to simply abandon Roma identity politics and to politicise on a non-ethnic basis. This would prevent activists from unwittingly endorsing exclusionary processes and allow them to focus their political activity firmly on objective needs and circumstances rather than a subjective and problematic identity. This is an option for some individuals who would prefer to be politically engaged within a mainstream party, or at least on the basis of a mainstream identity (such as national citizenship) so as not to have their politics defined by Roma identity and all the baggage that comes with it. In a sense this can be seen as the politicised version of what 'Roma' people have done throughout the centuries, downplaying a 'Roma' identity in order to try and achieve more within the mainstream (social mobility) – assimilating into the mainstream (identity).

However, the wholesale abandonment of Roma identity politics is not likely to happen as there are too many factors driving it. The objective conditions of dependency on policy will last for a long time, making 'Roma' people subject to state actions. Furthermore, the utility to states and more powerful political forces for addressing policy needs through the ethnic prism will also remain for the foreseeable future. There will continue to be Roma projects and programmes, budgets and policies, all of which perpetuate the politicised identity. The on-going drive for societal and political management in the context of widespread antipathy towards and lack of solidarity with 'Roma', means the politicisation of Roma identity will remain functional as a way of keeping 'Roma' people and their issues separated from the mainstream, weak and marginalised.

Just as importantly, the emergence of Roma political consciousness and activism is existentially bound up with the politicisation of Roma identity – that is what it is. It seems improbable that those participating in this historical process will simply walk away and either give up politics altogether (because the need to be politically engaged still remains) or resign from the 'privileged' status the identity gives to their participation in public life. Finally, the combination of the needs of both mainstream political actors and Roma activists will continue to support funding and status for explicit Roma political organisations and institutions, whether these are state bodies or in the NGO sector.

Roma Nationalism

However, continuing to play the game according to the rules defined by the mainstream means that Roma activism becomes part of the problem, legitimising the ways states respond to exclusionary tendencies that effectively reinforce the marginalisation of so many 'Roma' people, particularly the poorest and most vulnerable. The solution would seem to lie in Roma politics developing so it becomes less reactive and better able to define the Roma discourse itself and so exercise greater influence over political decisions. Unfortunately, this will be very difficult due to the profound structural weaknesses of Roma as a political community/interest group, including diversity, diffusion, dependency and fear, lack of own resources or labour power, unpopularity (prejudice and discrimination) lack of social capital, low levels of education, lack of political traditions or democratic mass membership organisations.

The question is how can Roma politics develop much greater 'political weight' by which it can have greater impact on the wider political world? Inevitably, the most obvious path to go down is to intensify Roma as a political constituency through the spread of Roma political consciousness and the strengthening of Roma political activity through greater unity among 'Roma' people leading to better Roma mobilisation. This can be seen as a nationalist approach as it is a political strategy based upon increasing power by bringing together (unifying) and politically coordinating the (putative) Roma nation/people.

However, nationalism is by its very nature exclusive. Though it can appear to address the interests of the 'nation'/people, it offers nothing to those who are not part of that 'people'. In respect of 'Roma', this is highly problematic. Politics is always a competitive struggle and there is already a strong (and growing) perception that the political interests of 'Roma' are not shared, but are even antagonistic to those of 'non-Roma', e.g. resources allocated 'Roma' could be used 'better' elsewhere. Furthermore, as weak, unpopular minority populations any greater mobilisation of 'Roma' can relatively easily be 'outmobilised' by 'non-Roma', (not least through use of the law, police, etc.).

Nevertheless, politics is about power, not consensus (which is just a means of achieving power). Clearly, 'Roma' have the potential to undertake political actions, which can force a response on the part of the authorities or society. Potentially, 'Roma' could represent a significant electoral bloc, though this has not materialised to date. Instead, there is a widespread perception that 'Roma' votes are often bought and manipulated by mainstream parties. 'Roma' people could engage in mass civil rights activities such as marches or hunger strikes, riots and even terrorism, all of which would require the state and society to confront the issues they raise.

Regardless of whether one accepts the large population estimates at face value or not, in some states 'Roma' have the potential to cause serious disruption and pose severe problems for governments, even making society ungovernable unless their demands are met. However, confrontation may just lead to greater oppression allowing states (with popular support) to suppress a problematic political movement rather than make concessions to it. Roma nationalism may be an excuse for further institutionalising the exclusion of 'Roma' people.

Politics of Shared Interests

The structural (political) weaknesses of 'Roma' means that Roma nationalism seeks to create political strength through the unification of an essentially incoherent imagined community with the potential to be disastrously confrontational. So how can Roma activists achieve the necessary increase in 'political weight' so as to be better able to define the political discourse? Nicolae Gheorghe implies, with his distinction between ethnic nationalism and civic rights, the answer lies in looking for allies not primarily among other 'Roma', but amongst other (non-Roma) people in their political environment, including individuals, community organisations, trade unions, political parties, etc. If Roma activists are able to engage in political activity that embraces a far wider range of people and bodies than exists just within the (notional) 'Roma community', there is a chance of creating a force which must be contended with and reduces the risk of being marginalised by traditional anti-Roma prejudices.

Roma politics posits the idea of a common interest among people based on their being Roma. However, 'Roma' people have many other interests, which are, to a greater or lesser extent, distinct from any Roma identity they might have (or which is applied to them). These interests might be to do with better public services or employment opportunities, support for a party or an ideology, community needs or environmental concerns, holding the corrupt and incompetent to account, the structure and governance of the economy, realigning power relations at local, national, even international levels, etc.

Engaging in non-ethnic (identity) politics does not mean the abandonment of 'Roma' identity, but it does entail being able to successfully articulate how that identity fits in with the non-ethnic agenda. This means activists have to be able to think through and explain their politics carefully, rather than stay in an ethnic comfort zone where these matters are assumed. Political solidarity requires Roma activists not simply to work with 'non-Roma' who sympathise with their Roma-focussed agenda, i.e. what 'non-Roma' can offer 'Roma', but also what 'Roma' activists/people can contribute to the agenda/movements of others. It is through the process of shared political struggle that people reach new levels of mutual understanding and respect and overcome fear and prejudice.

Of course, these 'alliances' with 'non-Roma' have defined Roma politics from the start. States have constructed Roma organisations to legitimise their policies and manage expectations, political parties have used Roma politicians to secure votes and NGOs need Roma to attract attention and funding. These mainstream bodies have created a pathway for Roma activists to which they have naturally gravitated as they offer opportunities, but the intrinsic weakness of these activists and their dependence on their sponsors, means that their 'promotion' has been at the 'price' of sacrificing the interests of (most) 'Roma' people. A good example is the enthusiasm for Roma on the part of liberal ideologues and politicians. While liberals are preternaturally sympathetic to questions of ethnic/cultural diversity and oppose explicit racism, they are also advocates of the (neo)liberal market economy and the small state, both of which have proved immensely damaging to so many 'Roma' people (and others), particularly in post-communist states, and has led to the deepening of both objective and subjective marginalisation of 'Roma'.

Instead of becoming tools in someone else's game (which is fundamentally antithetical to the interests of most 'Roma' people), Roma activists could seek to forge alliances with those with whom they have shared interests such as a more equal society in which all people (and not just those privileged by wealth and connections) can fulfil their potential through enjoyment of the benefits and protections available in modern society. This kind of politics is much more difficult to construct and sustain than simply accepting patronage and following funding, requiring clarity of thought and action to be able to create and work successfully in alliance with others. It also requires there to be partners among 'non-Roma' with whom Roma activists can work. This has proved a major problem due to the traditional divide between 'Roma' and 'non-Roma' and the weakness of 'civil society' in many states.

The novelty and dynamism of emergent Roma politics means that it will evolve in many different directions in the years to come, including the three approaches discussed above, and others not mentioned. Because the circumstances of 'Roma' people mean political engagement (of some kind) is inevitable, activists are compelled to explore different methods to find out what works and what doesn't. So far the weakness of Roma identity politics has resulted in that politics being ignored or co-opted, and uninfluential. In the future, new opportunities for political alliances will open up, some of which will enable 'Roma' people to work with their fellow citizens to achieve mutually beneficial goals in a way that actually improves the living conditions and life chances of 'Roma' people (and others) and which creates solidarity between 'Roma' and 'non-Roma' on the basis of common interests. Now and in the future, the key factor is how wider society understands and relates to 'Roma' politically. Thus, it is not 'Roma' but the mainstream which determines not only who Roma are, but also who they can be.

Conclusion

In his essay, András Bíró discussed characteristics of 'Roma' people and the implication of these for integration. Though the capacity (including perceptions and culture) of real 'Roma' people is an essential aspect of any discussion of social and economic integration, it is not the only one of relevance to the Roma debate. This chapter has sought to open up one of these other aspects by questioning what is meant, in the political discourse, by 'Roma'. The Roma discourse is defined by Roma identity and so questions of integration have to take account what it means. In doing so, the chapter has focussed on two aspects of integration – the discursive/institutional integration of Roma identity into mainstream political processes and the impact of this integration on the socio-economic integration of 'Roma' people.

Roma identity is also an essential aspect of Roma political activism and so its meaning needs to be considered by Roma activists. While it is entirely reasonable to see the relative failure of Roma activism to improve the living conditions and life chances of many 'Roma' people as resulting from its novelty and various structural limitations, activists also need to consider the identity as whole. This chapter has argued that the identity is fundamentally a construct not of 'Roma', but of the mainstream and that this is just part of the more general dominant influence of the mainstream over 'Roma' people. Furthermore, at this time, the power relations that define the mainstream are not conducive to the socio-economic integration of excluded 'Roma' people. But, because 'Roma' people in general, and Roma activists in particular, can't be ignored, the Roma political discourse has emerged as a means of finding a place for Roma (identity) within political structures, but which does not upset mainstream interests.

The implication is that Roma activists are, to some degree, part of the problem of Roma exclusion. Of course, activists have to believe they are trying to create a better world, which includes the abolition of poverty, exclusion, prejudice and discrimination. However, while this is relatively easy to conceive, it is altogether much harder to achieve. The chapter raises the question of whether, in the current economic and political climate, Roma identity politics can be a progressive force and suggests that it can only be so if it develops away from a focus on Roma identity and orientates its activity on finding common ground with non-Roma, and thus qualifies the political use of Roma identity.

WORKSHOP DEBATES

THE AIM OF THE WORKSHOP

ANDRÁS BÍRÓ

The main purpose of this whole endeavour has been to stimulate dialogue between activists, intellectuals and commentators. Encouraging this dialogue has been in the forefront of the initiators' minds from the very start. For this reason it was decided to extend the discussion beyond the initial debate between the authors of the three essays through the medium of print as far as possible. Consequently a number of activists and intellectuals were invited to offer a short response to the essays in preparation for fuller discussion at a follow-up workshop. Brief extracts from these comments are included as text boxes accompanying the edited transcript of the workshop proceedings.

Roma and non-Roma with similar interests in developing the current level of discourse surrounding Roma took part in a workshop held near Bucharest in the autumn of 2011. The first day allowed participants to clarify points with the authors and engage in preliminary discussions, while the second day's proceedings – which were recorded and subsequently transcribed – were devoted to more focused debate on what had been identified as key topics.

The structure of this chapter is organized into eight sections, each of which concerns a single topic although certain overlaps in content are unavoidable. The views expressed by speakers during this second day have been edited and inevitably shortened in order to make them more accessible to the reader. Also, in some cases, remarks have been repositioned to present more coherent coverage of specific themes and issues.

In the same spirit a final chapter reflects on the workshop discussions and opens the floor to further expressions of opinion and viewpoints.

This collective effort has never been considered as an 'answer' to the urgent and challenging questions now facing Roma throughout Europe. Nevertheless it was intended to provoke a critical – and self-critical – attempt to analyse some of the underlying causes and inherent obstacles surrounding the historic emergence of this old actor in recent decades as a new, undeniably highly visible presence on the European scene. The answers, if any simple answers exist, will be given hopefully by the new generation of activists who approach the situation of each and every Roma living in the European community by regarding them as equal citizens of their countries and of the EU.

DEMOS OR ETHNOS

Two dilemmas

Kristóf Szombati: In discussing this topic I think we are faced by two dilemmas. The first involves a more practical issue – ethnic politics. The immediate question is: Do we need Roma parties that represent the Roma cause? Or would other means help Roma activists more in their work at local and national level?

The second dilemma is broader in scope: What is Roma activists' vision of Roma identity and the future for their people? Two very different proposals are put forward. One is that Roma should strive for inclusive citizenship in the nation states that actually exist, and which, according to current global dynamics, will continue to exist for the foreseeable future. The other is a more a cultural conception of the Roma as a European nation or people. While I don't think that these aims are mutually contradictory – at least at the ontological level – they do require priorities to be debated as regards which political strategy should be adopted. Perhaps we should start with the more concrete matter and then move on to the wider question.

Ethnic or civic politics: a false dichotomy?

Kristóf Szombati: One of the main arguments in favour of establishing Roma ethnic parties has been that Roma have specific concerns such as discrimination by the majority which could not be opposed effectively without focusing on ethnicity. Unrelated local initiatives of Roma activists require reciprocal support of the kind generated by ethnic solidarity. However there are also serious counter arguments and I was among those making these. Firstly, is basing political identity on ethnicity too narrow an approach? It can be argued that factors other than ethnicity and discrimination – for example class – are also hindering Roma integration. Then there is the problem that ethnic parties make building alliances with potential allies far more difficult.

Iulius Rostas: Recently we organised a debate with doctoral students from the National School of Political Science and Public Administration in Bucharest. This was to discuss *ethnos* and *demos* – as Nicolae Gheorghe had expressed it in his text[1] – and the

---

[1] The distinction between *ethnos* and *demos* had originally been drawn by the sociologist E.K. Francis. Nicolae Gheorghe acknowledged his book on ethnic relations, which reconstructed sociology from the point of view of ethnicity, as a formative influence on his own approach.

representation of these in the public sphere by ethnic and mainstream civic parties. To help decide which option was preferable a local Roma politician, Gruia Bumba, was asked about his experience in the 2008 elections of standing as a candidate for a mainstream party in a mixed district but with a significant Roma presence. We asked him whether he should have played the Roma card to win votes. He answer was: 'Look, people are very pragmatic. They're concerned about concrete issues in their neighbourhood and lives. They don't care about symbols.' He added that as it was a constituency with a mixed population it would have been risky – even dangerous – to have gone around saying 'Hey, Roma! Vote for me because I'm a Roma.' 'But you might have been an elected if you'd done that', we said. He is someone who knows the culture and speaks Romani but who is interested in local neighbourhood issues that are not necessarily connected to ethnicity. The point is that politics gets pragmatic and transcends the ethnic divide in marginalised communities, which are more appropriately described as vulnerable communities since marginalisation has to do with power. In such situations politics becomes very materialistic and ethnic symbols are disregarded.

A further debate on this topic involved about a dozen Roma activists, where all concerned declared their personal preference for ethnic parties – but offered different reasons. The main argument was that the discrimination issue is limited to Roma and that an ethnic party is more effective in mobilising Roma voters. Nevertheless the Vice-President of *Partida Romilor* – the electoral organisation of Romanian Roma – said: 'Look, our experience is that we entered into coalitions with mainstream parties at local level and we included Roma candidates in their lists. So it's necessary to be flexible and compromise, taking into account various factors like financial resources and local issues.' Other Roma electoral candidates, including Costel Berkus, were also wary of asking people to vote for them because they were Roma and thought this a risky tactic.

Željko Jovanović: There's the same dilemma in politics as in NGOs. Most Roma politicians approach parties as individuals and claim an unspecified level of support among Roma voters. Then they ask: 'Are you going to give me an electoral slot?' That's not the way to go about it; politics doesn't work like that. Roma can't just expect parties to reserve seats for them. Instead you need to become a member of the party, support its programme, share its values, work for it, strengthen your constituency within the party and in that way get a place on its list.

We don't necessarily have to make an unconditional choice – *either* ethnic politics *or* civic politics. Nor should we make decisions based on fear – for example worrying that adopting ethnic politics might be harmful. Both options can be used. Politics is about persuasion at election time and many factors come into play in making a choice. In Serbian elections our communication with the media concentrated on general issues such as education and employment to avoid creating ethnic tension but we also mentioned the situation of Roma. However, when electioneering in Roma communities, we had to use a celebrated folk singer to gather an audience and then we talked about discrimination.

This is all relevant to identity because discrimination arises from the non-Roma perceptions of Roma. I think politicians are much smarter than us. We deliberate in abstract terms about what's better. But politicians concentrate on practicalities, because that's what brings in votes. So it's not a case of either/or. For instance, people create a dichotomy between minority rights and human rights. But minority rights are also human rights. You're not either a citizen or a minority. You can be both. There are obvious overlaps there. So I don't think we need to discuss this issue in terms of dichotomies.

András Bíró: To a certain extent I'm responsible for provoking this topic because I introduced it into my paper in rather an abrupt manner – perhaps too hastily. This is too important an issue to be treated as cursorily as I did. We know the kind of dangers that can arise from excessively insisting on the ethnic aspect. At the time I had in mind the model of the Hungarian Roma party but that is really another discourse, another historical development, another group. I was only trying to say that this is a possible way of achieving a political presence, within a context of citizenship

Martin Kovats: Nevertheless, concrete tactical decisions have to be made at election time whether or not to use the ethnic launch pad for mobilisation. My question to activists is: What methodology do you use in order to decide which choice you are going to make in any particular context? These judgements also raise questions of accountability and about how you evaluate whether good or bad choices have been made – with evident implications for future action.

My further query is related to judgements made in certain Central and East European (CEE) countries where there is a strong association between the majority national identity and citizenship, Hungary being the obvious example. How do activists choose to make politicised use of ethnic identity in such particularly nation state-centric contexts? This refers back to the point in András Bíró's paper about using identity as a means of strengthening citizenship.

Roma identity and power

Iulius Rostas: I think the whole debate about Romani identity is closely connected to power and I commented that the three core texts had little to say about power – either within the Roma community or in relation to others, including the political system.

When we talk about Romani identity we are referring to three key components bound up in a hegemonic relationship.

The first component, the *țigan*, is an identity imposed by others on the people we refer to as Roma, whilst the second so-called 'traditional' identity is a legitimation of a way of life, claimed mainly by Roma who speak Romani and observe *Romanipen* customs. These people devised various survival strategies, referred to in the core texts, which still appear to be effective to a certain extent. Finally there is the Roma political project – a quite new identity constructed by Roma intellectuals with the aim of renegotiating the social contract between Roma and non-Roma.

> Categories of analysis and those of mobilisation are not necessarily the same and might even contradict each other. For example, defining an entire urban area as a 'ghetto' or its inhabitants as an 'underclass' on behalf of experts can be a factor in itself that contributes to the fragmentation of these spaces and communities. Strategies of interpretation based on such concepts tend to reproduce exclusion on an analytic level as they represent the social worlds of the marginalised as being separate and fully excluded from the more respectable domains of society. To put it differently, while intervention projects are supposed to serve the aim of 'integration' or 'community building', in practice they do little more than contribute to the processes by which inhabitants of stigmatised areas internalise the stigma and then direct it towards others in their respective environments.
>
> *Gergő Pulay*

In debates about Roma marginality, the real issue is not poverty but power and the way Roma perceive their role in society – how they relate to the political system and to other people – but little research has been carried out on Roma perceptions of their own role. Without a fundamental identity shift to feeling proud of being Roma, no change can occur in Roma communities. As long as Roma internalise the stigmatised identity of *țigan*, they will continue to suffer psychological complexes as their subordination and victimhood are embodied and reinforced in this discourse.

Concerning the process of improving the relationship between Roma and wider society, I prefer the term 'accommodation' – in the sense of negotiation with others – to 'integration', since both sides would have to make certain concessions. Certain sensitive issues for Roma communities would need to be clarified, such as condoning under-age marriage, begging and theft from *gadje* [non-Roma]. Indeed, Nicolae Gheorghe argues that it is impossible to campaign for human rights and at the same time observe *pakiva* law since this is essentially a matter of loyalty to the clan, which traditionalists argue takes precedence over ethical principles. Here there is a direct clash of loyalties. Therefore the concepts of traditional *pakiva* law and *Romanipen* would need to be re-examined involving non-Roma as well as Roma activists.

As regards whether ethnic or civic political activism is more effective, I think that the attempt by Nicolae Gheorghe and other Romanian Roma activists in the early 1990s to reconstruct Roma identity in civil society was misplaced, since power is intimately bound up with politics. You have to campaign in the political arena to fight for power and that's why I believe an ethnically-based organisation is preferable for empowering Roma. How can you construct Roma as a political project? For me the topic of Roma is a political issue, raising basic questions about social arrangements, the social contract and the type of culture within societies.

Reinterpretation of Romanipen

Kristóf Szombati: I prefer to speak from a much broader perspective, basing my remarks on twenty years of Roma activism. Over this period I have noticed that the impact of this activism *on* Roma identity has brought about certain changes. One is how Roma see their identity in that we are now trying not to reconstruct but to reinterpret this, since Roma groups differed widely as a result of having lived in isolation from each other. Another is the effect of activism on the mainstream population.

Speaking personally I never dreamt that there are two to five million Roma in Turkey or two million Roma in Romania. Through activism, I met different Roma groups which led me to recognise that the *Romanipen* is not defined solely by my own values and traditions. Consequently I began to accept the values of others. This long process of self-realisation among Roma has been aided by the support of external donors. Adopting the term *Roma* has been an important step in escaping from the stigmatising 'gypsy' identity but this still persists and is still the name most commonly used by non-Roma. When someone asks: 'Who are these people? Roma?' the usual answer is: 'No, they're gypsies.' We need a reinterpretation of *Romanipen*, especially within Roma groups and involving activists throughout Europe. This is because usage of the names Gitanos and Sinti causes confusion. While these people recognise that they are part of the broader Romani community, they still prefer to be called by their own distinctive names – because they are proud of them.

Using these names has advantages. Widely varying conditions mean that a single, universal approach to political organisation is not possible. Roma activists can choose one or the other option, depending on the context. In 2007, at an OSF-supported Balkan conference in Macedonia, participants discussed whether a mainstream or an ethnic strategy was better. Although each has its pros and cons in my opinion organising on a civic basis is far more common and much more effective.

This produces better results for Roma issues than political activism because ethnic Roma political parties, having entered the system thanks to the opportunities provided by civil society, are now misusing their position and serving mainstream interests in the context of political rivalry. As was attempted in Romania with talks between Nicolae Gheorghe's civic group and the Roma Party leader Nicolae Păun,[2] we have to clarify matters with Roma politicians to try and build new political elites in order to continue protecting and promoting Roma interests.

My personal preference is for Roma politicians to stand for mainstream parties because the level of debate and the practice of democracy within the Roma population is low, almost non-existent. There is no real democracy, just manipulation of their own people by the more skilled or powerful Roma. Consequently, although advancing Romani interests within the mainstream is a tougher and longer process, it is ultimately more fulfilling. But we can't reconstruct Roma identity as easily as Nicolae Gheorghe proposes. I'm opposed to this. Instead we have to reinterpret our identity by our behaviour in civil society, which should be accepted by us and then by non-Roma.

> Power, money, fame are all much stronger incentives than Roma values to those involved in the Roma movement. This needs to be the basic presumption we start with and the main mistake in Nicolae Gheorghe's arguments and in his past in my view. We do not need Roma values at the core of the Roma movement but simply some values that will prevent Roma activists to be motivated just by power, money and fame.
>
> *Valeriu Nicolae*

Roma as a cultural nation without territory

Martin Kovats: In not just this discussion, but in many other discussions and conversations I've had with Roma activists about Roma politics – it's all about Roma and all inward looking. It's about this or that community or activist or group or meeting that said this, that or the other. What is missing is any expression of political theory and how you actually understand the political world. I don't even hear debates linking up with what's going on outside this room in the wider world. I'd like to ask activists: Why is that? Why do you not have a discourse that actually relates to the wider world outside? I think this is absolutely vital because, apart from a few outsiders like me who have got some weird personal interest in you and your lives, you don't offer anything

---

[2] See the following debate.

to the millions of other people out there who aren't particularly interested. They will only engage with you if you engage with them on *their* conceptual terms.

> My short period as an organiser suggests that the Roma activists who have achieved the most for their communities tend to be those who have sought to go outside the experience of their own people in order to find experience of the majority which allows them to get their ideas across. This is not something that all Roma activists – not to say leaders – understand. Some have failed to grasp two basic tenets: That communication with others takes place when they understand what you are trying to convey to them. And that people only understand things in terms of their own experience. Sadly, of course, the majority is less and less willing to listen to Roma voices. But there are circumstances – as when it feels concerned or threatened – which still provide opportunities for meaningful and effective communication. It is in the utmost interest of Roma activists to seize on these moments.
>
> *Kristóf Szombati*

Nicolae Gheorghe: I appeal to you – help us to develop our thinking about relations between the nation and the state. When opting for the path of civic activism in the 1990s the embryonic theoretical thinking behind this decision had been the process of separation of church and state – with the Peace of Westphalia after the religious wars in Europe – and the analogous problem of how to separate the nation from the state. Given the situation that Roma are geographically dispersed it is possible in theory to construct a Roma nation that is not connected with territory and the state, unlike the modern combination of nation and state that has emerged in European history. Instead, this would be a kind of post-modern construction. I'd like to have a discussion about how it might be possible to be a nation, politically, but without a territory and a nation state. Indeed, that challenge was the core agenda of the first World Romani Congress.

> The creation of Roma as a political construct can be viewed as a post-modern, late nation-building process. Nicolae Gheorghe and Andrzej Mirga hinted at this in their 1997 article – *The Roma in the Twenty-first Century*. Despite the non-territorial character of such a Roma 'nation', the ever-globalising world and the EU enlargement process provide at least the possibility for uniting significant numbers of Roma as a trans-national people within the borders of the European Union. If the international community considers reconciliation of ex-Yugoslav peoples in the Western Balkans, why would it not be possible to talk about Roma within EU borders?
>
> *Cristi Mihalache*

Željko Jovanović: Alternatively we could look at other countries' experience of creating a state peacefully. **Nicolae Gheorghe:** Breivik[3] said in his pamphlet that the solution to the Roma problem is to create a Roma national state. **András Bíró:** So the nationalist extreme right is supporting you? **Nicolae Gheorghe:** No. This isn't my preferred option. **András Bíró:** I know it's not your option, but politically they're together with you. Is that what you want? Is it? **Nicolae Gheorghe:** No, no, no. But unless progress is made in articulating a theory about the construction of Roma as a political people – in the medieval sense of an *ethnos*, not in the modern sense, then the idea of a territorial nation state of Roma will be imposed by extremists – at least rhetorically, even if not in practice. **András Bíró:** This train of thought is pointless since in any case no suitable territory exists. Equally futile is the desire to create a postmodern cultural nation when the concept of nation is deeply rooted, historically, in the territory where the nation was formed.

   Nicolae Gheorghe: The nation state will eventually disappear over a century or two. **András Bíró:** Wishes based merely on wishes are empty. **Martin Kovats:** This is my point. The whole issue hasn't been properly thought through and sufficiently theorised.

Nicolae Gheorghe: You know that a Romani passport was issued by the sixth Congress of the International Romani Union. It's called the *Romano L'il*, or Roma Passport in English. This was catalogued with a code at the same office where national passports are registered in Geneva and functioned as an IRU membership card – just like the ID for a Communist Party member. However some Roma regarded this document as equivalent to a national passport, claiming it was valid for travel abroad and offered IRU protection to the bearer. So you see how people are manipulating this. **András Bíró:** But migrants want such a document. Business is business. **Nicolae Gheorghe:** Of course, but if you're playing politics this often means dealing in ambiguities and fantasies rather than in clear-cut, well-defined issues and perfectly constructed theories. In this case there are activists playing with the chimera of a Roma national state. **András Bíró:** Playing with concepts in this way runs the risk of encouraging national governments to renege on their responsibilities to their Roma citizens. For instance, Hungarian extremists are currently talking of criminality but this could soon slide into a discourse about territory and a demand for Roma to be expelled from Hungary. They'll say: 'Go somewhere else! Leave us alone!'

---

[3] Anders Breivik, a Norwegian, far-right extremist, carried out a terrorist attack in July 2011, killing 77 people – mainly teenagers. His manifesto denounced multiculturalism and advocated the deportation of all Muslims, among others, from Europe.

Nicolae Gheorghe: I'd like to refer back to my short pamphlet about the myth of Roma nomadism, which has been circulated to participants.[4] This argued that solving the problem of Roma migrants was not the responsibility of Roma, nor of the EU, but of Romania. European citizenship at its current fragile stage of development doesn't offer a viable solution and instead Roma citizenship of their own countries should be stressed. Consequently the role of the European Union should be to provide the framework and back-up to strengthen local and national citizenship in order to improve conditions for Roma. This means Europe coming into the Roma village, not the Roma village going to Europe. Using this approach *Romanipen* and Roma culture can be accommodated within a civic framework. Supporting Roma communities and strengthening their solidarity is the only way to keep them in their villages and avoid mass emigration. Majority populations feel threatened by arrival of Roma migrants. This isn't fantasy or media stereotyping. They really feel threatened!

András Bíró: I'd like to be down-to-earth now to put things in perspective. Only the recent increase in Roma migration from Romania and Bulgaria to Western Europe has placed Roma high on the political agenda. Before that Roma migration was negligible in comparison with global migration from Africa and Asia and elsewhere. Consequently Roma issues had not attracted much attention. In my opinion we've neglected this matter of numbers and their respective impact on Roma issues – both in East and in the West.

Apart from the difference in comparative size of Roma populations in Eastern and Western Europe, the significance of their dissimilar historical experience is often overlooked. While it is undoubtedly true that Roma have suffered discrimination wherever they lived, the experience and effects of forced integration by CEE state socialist regimes is unknown among Roma in the West. Also, when talking of activism and Roma consciousness, this is complex enough to deal with in a CEE context without broadening the discussion to include Western countries as well. For example, in Spain with its relatively large Roma population, where there have been long-term national and regional policies in place to improve the living conditions of Roma, these problems have been virtually resolved unlike in the East. Furthermore, questions of identity are very different in Southern Italy or England than in Macedonia or Hungary.

Therefore it is essential to respect the historical borderline between the two parts of Europe and concentrate primarily on the huge social and political problems that will determine developments in CEE countries. While Roma issues such as strengthening their identity and furthering their acceptance will not affect the shape of French so-

---

[4] Gheorghe, Nicolae (2010) The myth of the Roma 'nomad': and how a 'European Approach' to the Roma issue already exists (ed. Rupert Wolfe Murray).

ciety, they will have a profound influence on the future of Macedonia and Hungary. So let's get things into proportion and face up to reality by prioritising investment in the extremely scarce resources available in terms of Roma political will and people.

TRADITIONAL VERSUS MODERN

Political arrangements in Romania – resulting tensions

Nicolae Gheorghe: In my text, there's a specific paragraph on *ethnos* contrasted with *demos* but I totally agree they have to be linked. Nevertheless these appear as separate in Romania, both methodologically and in the way the Roma movement is evolving. This is due to the specific peculiarities of the Romanian constitution, which proclaims Romania as a national state but offers national minorities reserved parliamentary seats in compensation. Therefore, even if they don't reach the threshold in elections, Roma – as well as the other eighteen or nineteen national minorities or associations representing them – each have a guaranteed seat in the Romanian Parliament. Amongst these the most effective and disciplined is the Hungarian Party. For the past twenty years the seat for Roma has been held by the Roma Party, which obtained the highest number of votes in competition with other Roma associations. In fact, the Roma Party is actually registered as an association like any other NGO but it acts just like a political party.

I am opposed to Romania being defined as a national state – preferring a separation of citizenship and nationality – but at present Article One of the Constitution rules out such a change, for the time being at least, and we have to accept the world we are living in. So in 1990 our association decided to work within the Romanian institutional framework to construct Roma as a national minority. Our goal was to try and reconstruct ethnicity within the space of citizenship by means of civic associations, using the tools of democratic and civic mobilisation. But there was no desire to return to ethnicity as a romantic *Volksgeist*.

This organisation which I founded – the Ethnic Association of Roma and predecessor to the current Romani CRISS – was like a federation of local associations which made their own decisions about activities such as festivals and sporting events. The idea was that you are what you are – in this case Roma – because you *wish* to be Roma and associate with others to promote specific aims. But for twenty years Roma people in Romania have been living with this dichotomy and tension between the Roma Party and the civic sector. Consequently Romania is probably one of the countries where this dichotomy has been most clearly articulated and recognised amongst activists.

Earlier, in 1996, I had drawn up a written agreement with the leader of the Roma Party, Nicolae Păun, confirming that their party would represent Roma as a national minority in Parliament while our civic association would concentrate on projects, programmes, education initiatives and mobilisation for social activities. This worked for a time since instead of competing and arguing with each other, both partners had mutually agreed roles. However, things became more complicated in the 2000s when some Roma from civic associations began campaigning for the reserved parliamentary seat with the aim of replacing the Roma Party. So the Party retaliated by starting to implement civic projects. Nowadays the relationship between the two organisations is rather confused and we are hoping to renegotiate the agreement to take account of the current situation. But the root problem remains the clause in the Constitution which, by reserving just one parliamentary seat for an estimated half million to a million Roma, has effectively blocked their political mobilisation over the past twenty years. Instead of organising a mainstream political party and fighting for votes like any other party, Roma have been diverted into competing for that single seat.

Kristóf Szombati: But could you explain about the tension you spoke of earlier?
Nicolae Gheorghe: The tension is caused by the Roma Party's strategy for winning votes by saying: 'You're Roma, so vote for us. If you don't vote for us, you're not a real Roma. If you're a real Roma, then you vote for the Roma Party.' We disagree replying: 'Yes, we're Roma and we can vote for whatever party we wish – on ideological grounds, not for ethnic reasons.' Costel Berkus is an outstanding Roma activist, but he stood as a candidate for the Social Democratic Party and Gruja was included on the Liberal Party list. Both are Roma but they have different political views. And this is something that you can cultivate with others in the semi-private space of ethnicity, which is an extension of the family – a putative family.

So that's what underlies the tension. It's because we Romanian Roma are arguing amongst ourselves once again over politics. But only yesterday I called Nicolae Păun and offered to back his proposal for a parliamentary bill against begging. We're on good terms, not only personally but politically too, and can agree on specific measures when we have a common political interest.

At the same time a gap has widened in Romania between modernising Roma – who uphold European values and universal human rights – and traditional Roma – who still maintain clan and tribal structures, retain their marriage and pollution rituals, kinship bonds and feasts and who follow *Romani kris* [Romani law and judgements]. These Roma have now established an Association of Traditional Roma, which intends to compete for the reserved parliamentary seat. They believe that those of us who have adopted a civic approach – and even a democrat like Nicolae Păun – are somehow contributing to the assimilation of Roma. They brand us as assimilationists for advocating greater integration and mainstreaming of Roma in society, for wanting better educational achievement, for seeking the prevention of under-age marriage, the abolition of ritual displays of virginity and abandonment of other traditional practices. Consequently debates between traditionalists and modernisers are often heated and sometimes very personal.

Some of those of us denounced as assimilationists – for being political Roma but not cultural Roma, since we don't follow the clan rules – have recently been discussing how we can try to reconstruct ethnicity in the associations. How can we reconstruct traditional values like *Romanipen* [Romani way of life] or *pakiv* – encompassing trust, honour, etc. – and find equivalents in civic organisational language, using terms such as 'bottom-up', 'transparency', and 'accountability'? We haven't found a solution yet and this still represents a gap. Even in the Pakiv organisation we didn't try hard enough to find everyday Romani-language equivalents of the organisational language we use in our reports and projects. This was something we criticised ourselves for. So I think a question for activists remains: How can we reconstruct ethnicity with civic means – as part of civil society and democracy – not in romantic, conservative and sometimes reactionary terms? I'm not ashamed to say that some elements of Romani culture are reactionary and in conflict with democratic principles.

Comparisons with Hungary and former Yugoslavia

András Bíró: There are analogous situations elsewhere to the case of Romania, where the dominant majority 'national' population and its close relationship to the state, as embodied in the constitution, limits the extent of genuine full citizenship for people of other ethnicities. I'd just like to explain the corresponding Hungarian box of tricks. In both the previous Hungarian constitution and its very recent replacement, there is provision for the voluntary representation of thirteen minorities – twelve national and one ethnic. Although the original plan was not implemented an illusory system of self-governance was substituted, conveying an impression of substance but in practice delegating minimal powers. This model even allowed non-Roma to vote for Roma self-governments, although this glaring anomaly was later corrected. This strategy was a trick to emasculate potential Roma mobilisation by offering formal autonomy but in effect gaining state control of the Roma movement.

Nadir Redzepi: I think that the Romanian system with reserved seats is very similar to arrangements for minority representation in the Western Balkans, although individual countries differ in the models adopted. The difficult situation after the Yugoslav wars in the late 1990s and early 2000s meant that Roma needed to struggle even to achieve reserved seats. We believed that would at least give us an opportunity to compete.

Otherwise we wouldn't have stood for election. At the time this strategy was accepted as a necessary step but in retrospect we can see it was a mistake.

I feel that the previous discussion of elections treated Roma identity too crudely. It's far more complex and a whole range of factors has to be taken into consideration – not just folklore, family values, early marriages and such matters. Roma identities differ significantly depending on whether they are rural or urban and on which religion they follow. The fact that dissimilar Roma communities interpret distinct elements of any identity in their own way poses problems for both political and civic activists. Also Roma communities react and behave differently to mainstream communities. But while the Romanian electoral system seems to result in a polarised 'ethnic versus civic' debate about Roma, Serbia presents a less coherent and more nuanced picture. Let me give a very prosaic example from electioneering experience where we had to take two major Roma groups into account – the Orthodox and the Machvaya. We heard earlier of presenting a political programme in Romania to the mainstream media in terms of general issues, while a folk singer had been needed to attract a Roma audience. But in Serbia it wasn't even possible to use the same musicians for these two different Roma groups.

In electoral campaigning among Roma it is too simplistic to talk about an 'ethnic agenda' as such, since Roma communities can have very different priorities. In some countries the focus was on migration and elsewhere on gender. When Roma activists in Serbia were asked last week about which policies they wanted add to those already included in the Decade of Roma Inclusion, the twenty or so around the table were almost unanimous that cultural issues were most important – like introducing the Romani language into schools. But these were only the second or third priority for Macedonian Roma.

Another difficulty is that the language used by Roma political campaigners and civic activists in debating how to engage in identity politics or advocacy is impracticable when talking about ethnic identity or *Romanipen* with the masses. This mismatch is due to the situation where Roma are without a state of their own and are currently politically marginalised. But if Roma were to play the ethnic card to gain access to existing power structures, then they might be able to use mainstream institutions to reinterpret or reconstruct Roma identity for the masses.

Political roles of Romani culture

Remus Anghel: Isn't there a clear distinction between structural assimilation and cultural assimilation? The meaning of structural assimilation includes having proper jobs, like the majority population. On the other hand if there is a shared Roma culture with early marriage and other elements and even though particular groups have different understanding and interpretation of this culture, this might change through negotiations. This Roma culture has nothing to do with assimilation. People may say: We are Roma, we are very well integrated and we have nothing against being different from the majority. Consequently Roma identity is no barrier to structural assimilation. A debate among Roma might confirm that Roma culture is not opposed to integrating with other people.

Nicolae Gheorghe: But it is, these days. When Nicolae Păun announced that he intended to propose a parliamentary bill to criminalise begging, the Union of Traditional Roma immediately denounced him as a traitor to the Roma. It declared that he would be summoned to the Romani Kris and condemned as *marime* [polluted] with no right to represent Roma any longer. So this is a clear clash between civic and ethnic values – with Romani culture being used as a weapon.

Another example of this comes from the 1981 Third World Congress of the International Roma Union (IRU) in Göttingen. The current IRU President was Ján Cibula, a Roma physician from Slovakia but at that time living in Zurich. Sinti delegates declared: 'We can't remain in the same room as a medical doctor, as he is, by definition, polluted.' So they resigned from the IRU and Cibula was not re-elected as President and subsequently suffered from depression. Here again the culture was used as a weapon to eliminate a competitor.

More recently a crime involving a young Polish Roma made the headlines when he fatally stabbed a young Belgian in a Brussels metro station in order to steal his mobile phone. The perpetrator fled to Poland where he was eventually arrested in the home of an aunt who had concealed him. When the police asked her why she hadn't reported him, her answer was: 'I couldn't do that. It would be against our Roma rules'.

Also, if you go to a child protection agency or even to the police to complain about someone who is trafficking children, then you are breaching the code of the traditional Roma. So, sometimes these cases are hard to deal with. In 2004 for the first time I had the courage to raise the issue of trafficking in public debate, which prompted some people to talk about the decline in traditional values. Sometimes young women and girls – some as young as thirteen – are trafficked abroad on the pretext that they are travelling to their wedding, using early marriage among traditional Roma as a cover story. In reality, their destination is the sex market.

It was a very heated debate and continued for three days. One young Moldovan Roma had argued passionately: 'We have abandoned our tents and nomadism, so the only traditional value we have left is the virginity of brides at their marriage. If that is taken away, there will be nothing left to distinguish us from everybody else.' So I brought in a white handkerchief with paint on it and hung it next to a Roma flag and said: 'Let's choose. Which is our symbol of identity? Is it the flag or the virginity handkerchief?' It's a dilemma, but sometimes we have to make choices.

Jennifer Tanaka: If we're talking about constructing a culture, it's simply not true that Roma always support each other. In both Romania and Hungary, there are Roma saying: 'It's never happened before but we do have problems of theft within our own community.' Roma stealing from Roma! And what about moneylenders?! How does that fit in with *pakiv* and *Romanipen* within Roma communities?

> Self-ascription, both as a right or as a duty, should be seen as directly linked to the idea of Romani identity. The term 'identity' in this case assumes a vague significa-tion and it is based on a perceptive and emotional link more than a set of prescriptive elements and values. The terms 'characteristics' and 'values' picked to identify 'exclusive' Romani traits, such as language, culture, music, a history of discrimina-tion, etc. might also be ambiguous and lead to a general stereotyped view of Roma (which I call the Romani 'box'). If generalized and applied as labels, these might even become a limitation and restrict individuals both in their sense of identity (e.g. 'Am I an a-typical Rom?') or their will to self-ascribe (e.g. 'Do I adhere to a set of values and characteristics and do I want to publicly affirm that I also embrace traits that neither I or my family possess?').
>
> *Elisabetta Vivaldi*

At a study workshop Ian Hancock talked about some of the very core traditions maintained by the Kalderash living in the United States, explaining that these people are more isolated than in Romania. His listeners – a group of twenty-five young European Roma – looked at each other in amazement at what they heard. Although these customs lie the heart of a certain tradition, in my opinion Romani culture as well as Roma identity is a continuum. This began with core traditional values and close-knit communities but now extends across the spectrum to someone who is perhaps highly educated and is learning the Romani language but is fully integrated and yet also proud to be Romani, wanting to engage in promoting Romani rights and identity. People like this have joined the Roma Access Programme. Therefore identity should be viewed as a continuum. How Romani identity is dealt with along that continuum is also relevant to the tasks of building civic and ethnic consciousness. This means we can't just generalise.

Željko Jovanović: We all talk about Roma values in general but these vary from com-munity to community. When I joined the Open Society Institute, everyone spoke about OSI values. Hearing this I read through an OSI manual but found no mention of them. So then I went to an OSI documentation centre but my search there produced the same result. Six years later I happened to pick up a book by George Soros and on page 200 and something, I discovered the sentence: 'I never wanted to provide a list of values. I leave open societies and communities to decide their own values.' So our discussion reminded me of Soros' view that there should be a constructive context in which values can compete – but in a way that avoids confrontation and armed conflict.

So the task is to create an environment in which differing traditional communities can retain their authenticity in the way they wish. But in present-day societies such a context does not exist where we can not only debate values but promote them through public institutions and where Roma who disagree with the outcome can create their own values. Unfortunately Roma are unable to control these structures.

Nicolae Gheorghe: You mean Roma activists. But take the case of Roma churches. Adventist Roma have relinquished some of their values and customs in order to accommodate the ritual of the Adventist church.

Salomeea Romanescu: In my view the significance of multiple identities has been neglected. As an individual I can be proud of being a Roma, a Romanian citizen and a European at the same time. Feeling close to Romani values doesn't mean not admiring and accepting the EU principle of integration, which aims to bring people together in a collaborative framework to avoid hostile competition and ultimately war. I can also recognise Romani values within European values. However, not all Romani values are good and certain other values are missing which we need to introduce into our culture. The same is true of *gadjikane*[5] values. Therefore we need to select and accommodate to live in peace but this will require negotiation. **Nicolae Gheorghe:** What do we have to give up? As Željko Jovanović said, if we want to reach an accommodation, we have to make a trade-off. What part of Romani culture as we understand it now, of *Romanipen*, should we give up? What are we willing to negotiate? **Salomeea Romanescu:** Yes, we need to analyse that. We shouldn't improvise…

I argue that that modern Roma identity should be built on renovating certain widespread traditional values that are shared by most (or even all) Roma groups such as respect for family and elders, regard for nature and the super-natural, etc. Modern societies (not only Roma but also *gadje*) need such values and actively seek them. Therefore Roma should not abandon but transform their traditional values. In this way the example of building contemporary Native American identity (in the USA, Canada and Latin America) could be used as an inspirational model.

Dejan Kolev

---

[5] Non-Roma.

Roma in private but not in public

Martin Kovats: I don't think my earlier question really got answered. I think there's a fundamental issue that activism needs to confront, which is how do you deal with people who are Roma in private but don't want to be Roma in public? This raises ethical as well as political and strategic issues. If activists incorporate such people in their public discourse – including them in reports, as numbers, as part of the Roma population and describing their situations – then they are affecting how these people are understood in public, and therefore potentially how they are treated in public too.

But if certain communities don't affirm Roma identity because they don't want to come out in public, then identifying them in this way is talking about people with a free hit, basically, with no accountability. You're affecting how they're treated, but you're not being accountable to the people you're talking about. If I wanted to be a bit provocative, I'd say this is rather like outing someone. It's as if someone might be happily homosexual at home but is then exposed by having their face plastered all over the Web or a newspaper with a caption saying: 'This person is gay'. If they don't want their gay identity to be public, this raises huge ethical problems. So how do activists deal with this dilemma? What have you done so far to think through this problem?

Nadir Redzepi: Activists call them 'seasonal Roma' and we try to convince them they should become permanent Roma. **Martin Kovats:** But you're still talking about them without their participation and permission. **Nadir Redzepi:** But we do recognise each other as Roma. These people don't join in and it's not easy to persuade them to become more involved in Roma issues.

Jennifer Tanaka: I just want to link this debate on private and public identities to one of the topics we haven't discussed yet – discrimination and citizenship. We've described Roma as the largest minority in Europe, socially disadvantaged, suffering intolerance and structural discrimination, or using similar terms in the arguments that we've developed. And over the years we've been successful in gaining a certain amount of recognition of this situation. But the issue, which came up much earlier in the discussion, was to what extent have we been effective in combating discrimination and including the movement in this activity. Or is this approach no longer effective?

So one of my questions is that if people are Roma at home and finding their way successfully in their own lives – yet we're still counting them as part of the ten million Roma in Europe – are we offering them an alternative discourse? Did our previous debates on political identity, civic identity, civic consciousness and related matters refer to these people's situation? Or are we only offering them the chance to be part of the minority suffering the most discrimination in Europe, which is the object of social inclusion policies and the recipient of structural funds.

What we tried to do in the beginning was to raise awareness of these inequalities and social injustices. But as a result we've now also created language that has been adopted by institutions, governments and in some cases the mass media, about firstly, an extremely socially disadvantaged group and secondly, a social structure facing discrimination right across the board. So maybe these developments are part of the problem of this dichotomy, for acknowledgement of certain family traditions, children being proud of their parents and grandparents and similar things all takes place predominantly in the private sphere. Talking with young people reveals that their heroes are actually within their families. These are good role models of people who have escaped from their restrictive circumstances. However, in the public sphere, the discourse is entirely about disadvantaged groups. So perhaps the tension between private and public is related to the question of what it means to be Roma.

Martin Kovats: In public. **Jennifer Tanaka:** Yes, in public.

Ioana Vrabiescu: This is a good point, because we, as Roma, cannot ask everyone to come out and be Roma in public. That's why activists and public figures serve as role models for others. The process of moving from the current established view of a marginalised and victimised ethnic group to an acceptance by wider society that Roma should not suffer discrimination will inevitably take time. As already mentioned, this is comparable to the situation of homosexuals where all gays can't be asked to publicly state their sexual orientation and then be told that in future they won't suffer discrimination.

Željko Jovanović: Over the years, we have seen many Roma take advantage of opportunities provided by affirmative action and donor support, such as jobs or capacity-building for a career. Afterwards, some of them became ashamed of their identity and avoided involvement in Roma issues. I think the problem has several layers and recently read a book about Jewish emancipation during the nineteenth century when a similar phenomenon existed. According to this study there had been various patterns and strategies of emancipation in individual countries and so perhaps, in terms of the Roma movement, different strategies might be needed for dealing with the challenges that Roma face in all twenty-seven EU member states. In my opinion people sometimes weigh up potential rewards and penalties when making decisions about being Roma at home and in public, or about taking the benefits of being Roma but afterwards not being Roma. They think about what they might gain from declaring their identity and what they might lose.

One approach would be for Roma to declare their identity within a society without discrimination. But we don't believe such a society exists. Another strategy would be to provide structured opportunities to bring back those who have left the Roma community but nevertheless want to demonstrate loyalty and voice demands on behalf of the community. New initiatives were introduced along those lines targeting Roma who had derived benefits from OSI in terms of their private careers, in order to recruit them for the Roma movement. So although they had left the community, we suggested that they should speak out on its behalf. This was an attempt to create common bonds based on language and history without reference to the issue of cultural values.

In our experience of activists, the younger generation rejects the idea of having to choose between ethnic identity and citizenship. Some of those who attended mainstream schools and attained a secondary school diploma or even a university degree have made friends with non-Roma fellow students and don't want to give up either of their identities. They need to be both Roma and citizens. The problem is that society doesn't really accept the concept of dual or multiple identities, of being both Serb and Roma, or both Romanian and Roma. This can also cause problems among children from mixed marriages where one parent is Roma.

> Martin Kovats' paper argues that Roma identity politics can only be 'progressive' if it develops away from a focus on Roma identity and finds common ground with non-Roma. I do not understand why he sees Roma identity and the establishment of common ground with non-Roma as mutually exclusive.
>
> *Gwendolyn Albert*

For most Roma who have left the community there are no structured opportunities for returning. Neither education not the media provide any encouragement to remain Roma – quite the opposite. But for those who we can recruit into the movement, in terms of politicising their identity as Roma, we can take further action and maybe save those generations. By means of a chain reaction, they might then try to influence the system, the politics and policies, in order to encourage others to adopt Roma identity. But that identity would be complemented by citizenship since, as I've said, younger generations don't want to choose between the two.

Two further problems are bound up with the concept of identity. To speak about identity – in the singular – rather than about Roma identit*ies*, limits the options within the Roma community. Furthermore, even to speak about **Roma** identit*ies* – in the plural – excludes those who want to assume an identity as a citizen as well. Therefore a different type of discussion is needed to clarify these issues.

Iulius Rostas: I have already spoken about the three components of Roma identity – *ţigan*, traditional Roma and the constructed Roma – and schematically these can be conceptualised as three concentric circles. The innermost circle consists of traditional Roma, because the boundaries of their community are very strictly prescribed, requiring members to speak *Romanes*[6] and comply with *Romanipen*. Nevertheless traditional Roma sometimes assert that the Roma community is ten million-strong, which – given their own very restrictive membership criteria – is a complete contradiction. Politically constructed Roma form a larger circle since the boundaries for inclusion are more flexible. Here, speaking *Romanes* is not essential but there is an expectation of intelligence or rather political awareness. Finally, the largest circle is that of *ţigan* – an identity imposed by outsiders entirely on the basis of their perceptions of skin colour, how people dress and speak, where they live and so on.

However certain groups have been ignored such as successful Roma who are assimilating, such as star footballers and TV personalities, who haven't declared their ethnic identity because they don't want to be associated with Roma. But activists haven't tried to understand why they behave in that way, though it was obvious that – as successful performers – they have made rational decisions on the grounds that their image is important and would be harmed by being associated with criminals and social problem cases. Consequently these successful Roma end up on the outer edge of the largest circle although they are well-connected and possess know-how and might possibly provide financial resources for the Roma movement if offered symbolic incentives. This is something activists have failed to do.

In fact, Roma activists don't have a vision of Roma emancipation. For many activists everything that happened to them was due to the fact that they were Roma. They think: I failed that exam or I didn't get that job because I'm a Roma. Yet while identity plays a significant role in some contexts, in others it is completely absent. If I go out to a disco in the evening, I don't go as a Roma. I go as a person – to have fun. But for a significant number of Roma, activism became a path to emancipation and even a kind of therapy: 'I've dealt successfully with my complexes about being *ţigan*, about being Roma, and now here I am in the public arena, proudly over-communicating my ethnic identity.' However, there's another route to emancipation. Some people, who can't deal with these sorts of complexes or face up to them in a different way, want to distance themselves from Roma. For them this is emancipation through atomisation – by detaching themselves from their group, saying to themselves that now they are urbanised they don't want to visit their relatives in their home village or associate with Roma.

Yet it's very important to examine how the various elements of Roma identity impact on different Roma groups in order to gain a better understanding of how

---

[6] In the Romani language (but literally, in the Romani manner).

identity functions in the public sphere. For instance the socially constructed Roma identity, as a political project, is totally irrelevant for some Roma communities, such as the Gábors. They don't care about such things since they're successful. They've found their economic niche and don't depend on strengthening their identity. Others – musicians like the Lăutari – openly reject this new identity since it actually threatens their livelihood. If you advertise Roma music, almost no-one will come to your concert because wider public knows about Gypsy music – not Roma music. For them, 'Gypsy' or *ţigan* is a brand which they market.

GENDER ISSUES

Roma identity: a gender perspective

Ioana Vrabiescu: I'd like to start by offering a simple challenge to everyone here. How can a gender perspective be incorporated into Nicolae Gheorghe's account of constructing Roma identity. How precisely can Roma identity be related to women? The most common stereotype of Roma women is of the way they are treated but what is their place in such an explanation? It may sound naïve to speak in this way but I haven't heard anyone mention this topic. Perhaps it's because we're afraid of emasculating the Roma, since the masculine principle is at the core of the Roma identity. But when constructing a Roma identity, we shouldn't avoid taking a gender perspective into account.

Nicolae Gheorghe: So you're saying that none of our core papers explicitly address this issue and that the intersection of gender, class and race is not sufficiently developed in our texts, or doesn't appear at all. Your paper and that of Salomeea Romanescu both suggest you feel that by the very fact that you are female, you are writing from a Roma woman's perspective. But I reject the assumption that because someone is a woman or a man they automatically adopt a female or male perspective. My aim is to think as a human being, not as a man. Of course I accept your right to your perspective and want everyone to accept your challenge – but as thinkers and as colleagues who try to introduce a gender perspective or feminist perspective in our discourse. And that's why I very much welcome contributions to the text from you which are the product of minds – of your minds.

Ioana Vrabiescu: It doesn't matter who is contributing to the construction of Roma identity but they should adopt a gender perspective and take account of gender roles. But where are the gender roles in the discussion of identity in the texts?

Christian Petry: Could you give a few examples of where you think the core texts are biased in omitting a gender perspective?

> A gender analysis would stress the inequalities between women and men in socialist society and the enforcement process of another genderised system. Even describing the post-socialist period, [András Bíró's] vision about Roma women activists is a melancholic, romantic one, and has no evident understanding of feminist Roma thinkers. The post-socialist order (in Romania) consists of the 'processes of social differentiation and the underlying cultural mechanisms that produce and legitimize the newly constituted hierarchies' (Vincze), including new gender discrimination. That's why more attention needs to be paid to Roma thinkers, especially when they argue about Roma activism and activists.
>
> *Ioana Vrabiescu*

Ioana Vrabiescu: Well, in the discussion of Roma assimilation during the Communist era in Romania. At that point it should have been said that young women factory workers were at the same time also working in the home.

Nadir Redzepi: I've often been criticised for not being sufficiently gender-sensitive. However most Roma issues relate to the entire Roma population, which includes both men and women. Therefore a gender perspective is inappropriate in such cases. Within the Romani movement it is women's organisations that insist on introducing gender but understood as a women's issue, although it should involve both sexes. Consequently we've never been invited to discuss the relationship between Roma men and Roma women. These organisations tackled difficult issues on their own, putting the blame partly on Roma traditions and partly on socio-economic and other factors. Their analysis was reasonable enough but they always operated independently and never approached the overall Roma movement in order to act together. And that's the reason why the Roma women's movement has lagged behind and now finds itself in a disadvantaged position.

I have always tried to convince these Roma women that they're a very important part of the whole Roma movement, particularly in their crucial role as the first educators of our children. A recently published study of children aged ten showed that Roma children see themselves as inferior and having a lower status. This is the opposite of other ethnic groups who regard themselves as better than the rest. This problem arises from how Romani women bring up their children. We should have this kind of debate but, apart from these two ladies, I don't see any Romani women activists present here. Did we invite them?

Ioana Vrabiescu: This is exactly my point. While it's true that you have to be a woman in order to talk about Roma women, a gender perspective, above all, involves women, men and their relations in the community. So, whenever you analyse or want to talk about identity, you have to take into account gender roles in the community. If you ignore a gender perspective, you are simply ignoring women and gender roles. You are assuming that everything is understood but nothing is understood when we're talking about identity.

Nadir Redzepi: No, it's not true that we ignore a gender perspective because our work is directed at both sexes. Far more girls than boys take part in some of our activities. **Ioana Vrabiescu:** No, that's not what I'm getting at – it's a question of how you talk about identity. If you ignore gender, assuming that gender roles are well-known, you can easily be accused of adopting stereotypes. You said 'Roma women are the educators of our children', but why shouldn't Roma women and men, too, be the educators of Roma children? This shouldn't be taken for granted.

    Nadir Redzepi: I said 'the first educators'. **Ioana Vrabiescu:** Yes, but that's a statement not an analysis.

Gender perspective and accessible discourse

Iulius Rostas: I'd like to make a related point that fellow Romani women activists often introduce a gender perspective by presenting issues using abstract, intellectualised forms of discourse that don't make much sense to ordinary people in Roma communities. A more accessible approach would be to start with examples of taking the point of view of Romani women and their roles in the community. These don't need to be traditional roles. In fact these roles were transformed in very different contexts. I base my remarks on observation of a few Roma families in Romania and what happened after they moved to Spain.

    In Romania the women were not valued, in the sense that whatever work they did – in and around the house or for neighbours in order to buy food – was not regarded as work. Only the men were seen as providing money and they were all-powerful, deciding everything. When these families moved to Spain, conditions were different – particularly now with the crisis, when the men lost their jobs. So, instead the women became the breadwinners – but they were still expected to do the housework. Another case involved the sensitive issue of domestic violence. This was widespread in Romania, where men smacked their wives as a matter of course and other people ignored this, minding their own business. But in Spain when there were such incidents the police arrived and even arrested Roma husbands, causing consternation among the Roma who couldn't understand how such a thing could happen.

Will Guy: I, too, saw an example of sudden change in women's roles when doing research among Travellers in Scotland. Traveller women were never allowed to drive – because their husbands were afraid they'd go off and have affairs with other men. But when the men began losing their licenses because of convictions for drunken driving, they had to ask the women to drive. This reversed the power situation within the family – not completely, but it made a tremendous difference.

Iulius Rostas: Examples like these not only make underlying issues more readily intelligible but encourage Roma to accept different roles for Romani individuals – both men and women – in relation to the state and officials and among themselves. They also raised the question: How can Romani women and men be redefined in more equal terms? They also make it clear that if the goal is Roma integration in mainstream society, it would be impossible to have just Roma men and *gadje* sitting at the negotiating table. Romani women should have their seats as full negotiators too. This is how I see a gender perspective being incorporated on Romani issues.

Frameworks for discussing hierarchies

Christian Petry: Can I remind everyone that discussion should relate to the core texts. So far, only one example – about the Communist era – has been given of the texts lacking a gender perspective. The problem of the debate at present is that we are confronted by a solid wall with no door or window to let us escape. The immediate question is this: Where does the lack of gender-sensitive language falsify what has been written in the texts? **Ioana Vrabiescu:** My answer is that the texts simply address a uniform Romani culture or people and therefore perpetuate inequalities by not revealing the various structures of discrimination, including that of gender roles.

Nicolae Gheorghe: In view of such criticism I would like to add a paragraph to the section on Romani culture in my paper to clarify my position. Earlier I had been very impressed by the PhD thesis of Elisabeth Tauber, which reviewed the entire sociological and anthropological literature about Roma. Her study adopted the approach of the French sociologist Louis Dumont, who studied the caste systems in India and compared these with western societies, which – in theory at least – are organised on the egalitarian principle. Dumont categorised these ideal types respectively as *homo hierarchicus* as opposed to *homo egalitarius*. Following this model, Elisabeth Tauber argued, that – based on their beliefs about what is pure and what is polluted – Roma society and mentality are hierarchical, dividing God and mankind, the old and the young, men and women. From this point of view traditional Roma society is completely at odds with the egalitarian model of European society.

This analysis, based on rigorous research, told me a lot about Romani social organisation. As my paper explains, efforts to reinvent the Romani *bulibașă* [traditional local leader], Romani *vajda* [chief] and Romani *krisatori* [judge] attempt to bring back figures from a highly hierarchical culture into present-day democratic societies. Although Roma often celebrate such initiatives as maintaining tradition, authenticity and culture, this is a contradiction. Likewise I hope that, in relation to gender, we will challenge this hierarchical model of organisation. I cannot challenge the concept of God in traditional Romani culture but I *can* challenge the hierarchical relationship between man and woman in everyday life and in Roma society and also the consequences of this hierarchy. So I agree with all our colleagues who keep drawing attention to patriarchy, authoritarianism and the subordination of women. However I think that in the future the relevant evidence and criticism should be put into a framework like that of Elisabeth Tauber, although of course this is not the only possible framework.

A Roma spring? Potential for a cultural revolution

Nicolae Gheorghe: I would like, at some stage, to see a revolution in Roma society towards democracy. András Bíró asked: 'How can we build democracy within *single* Roma communities – or even within Roma families?' This can only come about by changing hierarchical patterns – including gender roles – which are deeply embedded in a society that we otherwise describe as marginalised, excluded and discriminated against. This contradiction needs to be recognised more clearly in the discussion.

Perhaps a gender-aware approach, or a feminist approach, will be a way of promoting change. In Italy, it was the women who started to denounce the mafia leading to a much broader struggle against them. I hope that, at some point, there will be some courageous Roma women who will denounce our Roma mafiosi – the traffickers, those who exploit men, women and children. We're waiting for such a rebellion by these women, who are harshly, brutally and savagely exploited, both by men *and* by women.

I partly agree that we need new, appropriate language to talk about issues and also to each other. However we need to be careful with sensitive topics like crime and early marriage because extremist right-wing parties, or an unsophisticated mayor, can exploit these to serve their own interests. I think we need to choose the correct way to speak about such matters and to know what we want to achieve when we talk frankly, leaving aside an ethnic context.

Béla Rácz

There are mothers-in-law who exploit young women. This is done not only by men. We have spoken about young girls who are victims of early marriage but we should also be aware that young Roma boys are victims of this practice too. If a ten or eleven year-old boy fails to manage an erection during the wedding night and therefore is unable to penetrate the hymen and prove the bride's virginity, he becomes a complete outcast. He is traumatised by his father and by the whole family – because he cannot do a man's job – and the resulting psychological damage can last for the rest of his life. I personally know of such cases. Consequently doctors exist who administer injections to stimulate chemically-induced erections. Of course, girls are far more frequently victims of the custom of early marriage. Therefore a balanced gender perspective should also include discussion of such practices. I agree with Nadir that as activists, whether men or women, we have a common interest in the democratisation of Roma societies, in promoting equal relations and a humanistic approach to both girls and boys.

Christian Petry: Thank you, Nicolae. You are hoping for a Roma Spring, and Nadir Redzepi is saying that it's already happening.

But if we talk of discrimination, then gender stereotyping of Roma women is a very good example of this. If young, they are portrayed as beautiful and if old, as witches. Here anti-gypsyism looks very different depending on whether it involves women or men. Roma themselves also practice discrimination based on stereotypes, as in the case of Sinti brides required to conform to traditional customs. There are instances of young Sinti women who have to conceal the fact they are university graduates in order to appear eligible to marry a Sinti husband. Therefore inequalities need to be identified.

Ioana Vrabiescu: If people wonder why prominent Roma don't openly admit their identity, for Roma women this is much harder. Since women are already discriminated against in mainstream society, Roma women have a further threshold to cross in order to speak out in public. This is not, therefore, a matter of discrimination in Roma communities. However, since mainstream society discriminates against women, Roma will just copy that model and discriminate against their own women. Therefore when talking about the construction of Roma identity, it is first necessary to take account of the position of Roma women, because it mirrors the situation in wider society. It is not possible just to say that Roma society is traditionally hierarchical since that has already been imposed from the outside. Racism is already gendered because mainstream society is already gendered. All those who copy that model are doubly discriminating against their women.

That's why the texts, when they don't take the gender aspect into account and simply address a uniform Roma culture or people, are just discriminating in a different way. Therefore they perpetuate inequalities by not revealing the various structures of discrimination, including that of gender roles. This is the structure through which discrimination multiplies in our minds and, of course, in politics. It's important how you construct a discourse of identity, in order to have a political effect afterwards.

András Bíró: I'll start with this well-known old Arab saying: 'You wake up. You beat your wife. If you don't know why, she knows.' This is the classic macho culture which in particular dominated pre-modern structures. However I disagree that the Roma minority model is an imitation of the majority model. They exist in parallel, so there was no need for imitation since they have always coexisted. While such attitudes and behaviour can still be found among Bulgarian, Romanian and Hungarian and other Roma, my twenty years experience of working with Roma has revealed an a-democratic, really pre-modern, macho power structure among them.

This is a controversial topic because it is regarded as part of 'Roma culture' and even celebrated as such. For this reason non-Roma are often afraid to criticise as in the example of a film on the Vlach community in Hungary, made by a non-Roma activist, which let the Vlach women speak for themselves. When a woman university graduate emphasised very clearly that the male is the important person, there was no comment or criticism by the film-makers. So building civic consciousness and status from an ethnic basis opens up the question of the connection between modern values of citizenship based on human rights – an egalitarian concept – and the traditional Roma way of dealing with women. Therefore it is crucial to link the gender equality issue with citizenship, as well as with ethnic identity.

Roma women's role in dealing with institutions

Jennifer Tanaka: I, too, think there's confusion between women's rights and a gender perspective. When we discuss citizenship-building, one thing that could be added from a gender perspective is looking at certain roles. This might be fruitful since Roma women were often the people who dealt with the institutions such as schools and local authorities. And when we speak about a gender perspective, this is not about women's roles *per se* but about examining different roles and how it would be possible to build on those roles. Therefore in considering citizenship and identity and organising communities at the local level, it should be recognised that we gain access through the women.

Will Guy: We're meant to be thinking about what implications all these issues have for activists. Therefore I very much support Jennifer Tanaka's position on this. Based on my own experience of Roma projects in several countries – it is now women who most commonly interact with civil authorities and by these means they are gaining new power in changing the circumstances of their families and communities. This is most clearly evident in Spain where women are seen as the core of the family, holding everything together. NGO practitioners in Spain recommend that projects are likely to work better if the women are approached and involved. This is valid for projects aimed at improving family health – perhaps a rather stereotypical example – but also for employment, where some projects encourage women to work outside the home. Because of the difficult economic situation nowadays, prospects for Roma women are improving in comparison with those of their menfolk. This means women will play a more important part in future – inevitably, because of changing circumstances.

László Fosztó: I'd like to compare male and female Roma activists acting as mediators in dealing with civil authorities and institutions. Male activists tend to take a more visible public role but the women are very different and probably have much more influence on communities than the men speaking in parliament or in Traveller and Roma forums.

András Bíró: My experience from working with Roma NGOs is that women in positions of responsibility usually take their jobs more seriously than men and work more conscientiously. And I'm not talking about just one case. When Roma women overcome the obstacles and become leaders – and even mayors of which there is one instance in Hungary – they take more responsibility than their male counterparts. The capacity of women for caring, not present in males, means they become more democratic leaders than men. This very positive dynamic perhaps represents a strategic point for developing Roma activism. Therefore the training and career development of activists should take gender into account as a constructive and liberating factor.

CITIZENSHIP FOR ROMA: COMBATING DISCRIMINATION

A Europe-wide perspective

Nicolae Gheorghe: A leitmotif of our two days of debate has been how to move beyond limiting concepts of identity. In earlier discussion these were likened to concentric circles but Elisabetta Vivaldi preferred the metaphor of boxes as better conveying the constraining nature of such identities and posing the question of how to escape their limitations. But the previous focus on 'Roma activists in Central and Eastern Europe' – not only at our conference but in the discourse over the past twenty years –

is one such confining box. I would prefer a wider perspective taking account of Roma activists throughout Europe.

Juan Ramírez Heredia in Spain, Dominique Steinberger in France and Romani Rose in Germany are examples of Roma activists and politicians who have adopted different approaches to those of their Central and East European counterparts. Dominique Steinberger, with a republican concept of citizenship, has no doubts about his status as a French citizen while also being a Rom. Similarly Romani Rose is a *deutscher Bürger*, a German citizen, and his *Zentralrat Deutscher Sinti und Roma* [Central Council of German Sinti and Roma] receives support from the German state. He can be both Sinti and German because the concept of citizenship in Germany is constructed differently than in Romania or Hungary, where citizenship and ethnicity are fused. Likewise the Gitanos of Andalusía feel they are Andalusians, with a strong local identity of which they are very proud. They affirm that they are Gitanos, a *pueblo* [people] in Spain, and are Spanish citizens but also are part of the Roma people in Europe. At the same time they are recognised by other Spaniards as genuine Andalusians.

While Martin Kovats regards the lack of a common religion, the limited use of the Romani language, the diversity of Romani dialects, the scattered location of Roma, the nonexistence of a homeland, the multitude of citizenships shared by Roma, and other aspects of diversity, these elements might be seen from another perspective as helping the process of identity construction. For example, the fact that Roma are multilingual, multi-religious, multicultural, possessing multiple identities (in the sense that they are Roma but also Hungarians, Romanians, Bulgarians, Spaniards, etc.), could be also valued in an intellectual project to construct Roma identity. One reason for such a project might be the fact that nowadays – to non-Roma – Romani identity has incorporated a significant aspect of 'Gypsyness'.

Iulius Rostas

Differing levels of identification are involved and consequently it is important to examine the various ways citizenship is constructed in different countries. To enable people to be both Roma and Romanian it will be necessary to arrive at some kind of citizenship as in the United States, where it is possible to be a 'hyphenated American'. So, in Central and Eastern Europe, people could be 'Macedonian-Roma' or 'Romanian-Roma', with the citizenship as the stronger identity and the element after the hyphen as the weaker one.

There is a reason why previous discourse has concentrated exclusively on Central and Eastern Europe, which is that for political reasons the EU wanted to treat Roma issues as a problem restricted to candidate countries and new Member States. Yet Roma activists have been accused of being complicit in this interpretation since they have benefited from it by being able to promote their own interests. They gained resources, so it was also a matter of funding. However there is a risk that if this predominant focus on Roma in Central and Eastern Europe is maintained, Roma activists will fall into their own trap. They need to broaden their restrictive conception of Roma to include Sinti and Gitanos and Zingari and also take account of the experience of groups in Western Europe. This widening of perspectives should not just be in territorial terms but also across generations.

Livia Plaks: The explanation why we and others concentrated on Central and Eastern Europe was that we were responding to the wave of violence sweeping across the region after the collapse of Communist rule when Roma were very much the target.

Nicolae Gheorghe: Nevertheless our perspectives should be broadened by prioritising discourse on citizenship since Roma are better protected by strong citizenship than by strong ethnic identities. This is maybe where I differ from Iulius Rostas and others. In my opinion Roma activists could make a positive contribution to consolidating democratic institutions, civic society and society as a whole and not only for the sake of their own identity. Over the past three years it has become clearer to me that if I would like to protect myself or my children, it would not be as Roma *per se*. Those who want close-knit security and protection should stay part of the clan. But for integration, or even assimilation, strong citizenship rights are needed but not necessarily strong identity. Ethnic identity is something personal and private – like religious belief. For this, and other reasons, I have argued against the favoured approach of other activists – to 'Europeanise' Roma issues with an official structure in Brussels, headed by a dedicated Commissioner for Roma Affairs. In my view Roma are the responsibility of the state of which they are citizens.

Ethical considerations

Martin Kovats: The remark about ethnic identity as something personal harks back to our earlier discussion about people who are Roma in private but don't want to be Roma in public. Given the activists' goal of trying to build the Roma political movement, it is very understandable that they should seek publicly to emancipate people as Roma, whether they like it or not, including people who don't want to be Roma in public. But we need to examine underlying ethical issues.

Also there is potential ambiguity in strengthening citizenship. While citizenship can be discussed in terms of rights, regardless of identity, the question of 'civic identity' remains. When discussing how the Roma movement could assert citizenship – are activists doing that as Roma, or are they supporting people who might be Roma to assert their civic identity, which is not Roma? How do activists see the interplay between asserting the Roma identity and asserting the civic identity, and what are the implications for practical citizenship rights? These questions might be answered by empirical research but some kind of theoretical framework is required to understand what is meant by citizenship in any particular context. Without such a framework activists can't be sure they are doing the right thing in order to achieve what is actually quite a clearly articulated aim, namely strengthening the citizenship of certain people.

Ethnic and civic nationalism

Christian Petry: We are not discussing discrimination enough, particularly given the rising level of anti-Gypsyism and discrimination in *all* European countries. Discrimination was played down when Brussels asked all Member States to develop Roma integration strategies. Although combating discrimination is one of the basic principles for Roma policy, some countries have declared that this should not be given high priority. So it has become just a minor part of their strategy.

At the same time it is important to realise that the EU has not developed a strategy of its own but has just put forward ideas. Member States have been told to develop strategies but they have failed to do this. The issues of discrimination and citizenship are necessarily linked – and not by chance

Livia Plaks: Speaking as a practitioner I want to remind those present of some practical realities. I met recently with some twenty high-level Romanian politicians of cabinet rank and when I asked them about their ideas for Roma integration, the shocking response was silence apart from a couple of brief remarks. The only comment that might be seen as in any way remotely 'positive' was: 'Let Brussels develop a strategy and then we'll take it from there. We will get the funds and we'll do what Brussels tells us to do.' When I pointed out that these people were *their* citizens, the response was a flat denial: 'No, they are citizens of Europe. They're not really our citizens. This is a European problem. It's not this country's problem.'

Given such attitudes it is essential that Roma should keep emphasising their rights as *bona fide* citizens as one of the most important issues to be tackled. But how can the difference between Roma communities and the majority be reduced? As a parallel case in point I am one of those people with multiple identities. One of these identities is

Jewish, which often attracts the label of 'cosmopolitan' – meaning that such people are unreliable and unpatriotic and can never be counted as real citizens.[7]

Željko Jovanović: We only raise this dichotomy between identity and citizenship when discussing the case of Roma but the citizenship of majority populations contains a strong ethnic element.[8] Romanians in Romania and Hungarians in Hungary have all the instruments of power to impose their ethnicity. Consequently, even when there are colour-blind policies, their application is not colour-blind. Therefore an emphasis on minority rights is useful precisely for the purpose of achieving fully-fledged citizenship.

Julius Rostas: I agree that the ethnic identity of the majority prevails. CEE countries are nation states of the majority ethnic group, often defined as such by their constitutions, which prevents them being truly multi-national.[9] Furthermore, whatever general policies are introduced affect minorities disproportionately. Educational policies are an example where structural issues have a huge effect on Roma – like segregation, where being Roma means access to lower-quality education or limited access to education in general. Moreover, engaging in activism implies challenging the allocation and distribution of resources and power in society. That is not a private matter anymore but a very political issue.

Will Guy: Spain represents a positive example where the gap between Roma identity and citizenship has been bridged to a far greater extent than in CEE countries. Historically Spain was an anomaly in Western Europe since, as in the CEE region, Roma had been forcibly settled by the state in past centuries. Perhaps as a result of early settlement, especially in Andalucía, specific Roma cultural elements and occupations – most notably flamenco and bullfighting – have permeated Spanish society to become part of wider Spanish identity. This has occurred nowhere else to such a degree.

Other positive lessons from Spain are the effects of political and societal change following emergence from totalitarian rule. After the death of Franco the Spanish state

---

[7] Jewish communities – spread in a diaspora like Roma – were seen as incapable of loyalty to the states in which they lived and were suspected instead of allegiance to international Jewry. For example Jewish politicians in post-Communist Poland were accused of being 'cosmopolitans' – and therefore untrustworthy – in contrast to 'real Poles'.

[8] Relevant here is Kymlicka's argument that the majority ethnic group is always dominant, refuting the spurious dichotomy where Western European states are seen as characterised by ethnically neutral 'civic nationalism' (viz. France) as opposed to the 'ethnic nationalism' of CEE states (Kymlicka, Will (2000) 'Nation-building and minority rights: comparing West and East', *Journal of Ethnic and Migration Studies* 26, 2:183-212, April).

[9] The Czech Republic was cited as a counter-example.

rejected the legacy of his regime and became more liberal, as is evident from the strengthened position of women in comparison with other Southern European countries. Positive policies have included a new approach to Roma issues with support for the Fundación Secretariado Gitano – one of the most effective Roma NGOs in Europe – and eagerness to use EU funding to improve the situation of Roma. Consequently when Spanish activists were asked recently in an EU survey about educational segregation, they almost had difficulty in understanding the question. The eventual response was that since Roma mostly lived among the majority population, they naturally attended local schools alongside their non-Roma neighbours. In Spain positive political developments in general and EU membership have also benefited Roma but sadly regime change in former Communist countries had diametrically opposite outcomes.

Citizenship and language at the local level

Nicolae Gheorghe: The danger of emphasising discrimination without at the same time recognising the importance of linking this issue with citizenship is that Roma might portray themselves as perpetual victims. But talking of victimisation does not mean diminishing the fight against discrimination. The current task for activists is to find a way to construct citizenship so that it will be more meaningful for those who belong to coherent ethnic groups and have a strong ethnic identity. This does not only apply to Roma for people can be part of a strong Hungarian community and yet still be Romanian citizens. Indeed some members of the Hungarian elite in Romania are adept in manipulating this concept.

A further problem is how to convey the concepts in this discourse when talking with people at grass-roots level in the Romani language. For example how can we talk to somebody about citizenship using the vernacular language of Kalderash. One project has been exploring whether the concept 'them' could be utilised in this way. In Romani, 'miro them' means something like 'my folk' in English. It implies identification with a larger group than the family. From it, the broader abstract noun 'themu-nipen' was constructed as a way of moving towards something like the idea of citizenship. The aim was to get inside the minds of Romani speakers and imagine how they would express the abstract ideas that were used in activists' discussions. Through 'their them', people belong to something broader that was indicative of citizenship.

Bearing in mind earlier criticism that the local community shouldn't be idealised, I think nevertheless that the best place to bring these elements together is at the local level. However to achieve this it would be necessary to reconstruct, theoretically and politically, what the local community should be, so that Roma would form a constituent part, as in Spain. I have been working on the pakiva themunipe project prior to the conference and while it is too small a project for such big ideas, it does represent a way of moving from reflection to action via projects. In addition a glossary of organisational language has been explored together with the Pakiv European Fund. Therefore the hope is that in the near future some key words, themes and expressions from these two projects could be presented. These would try to convey messages of ethnicity and citizenship in Romani language that is not that of the clan. Rather it would be the Romani language of active people in the community, not only of activists.

Jennifer Tanaka: Another challenge is that even for majority communities in countries such as Hungary and Romania the concept of citizenship or of a social contract between individuals and the state is relatively weak and abstract. So, although these concepts are being translated into Romani language for Roma, raising these issues actually addresses a broader constituency.

> Instead of concentrating on ethnic mobilisation, Nicolae Gheorghe suggests Roma NGOs might work towards creating the *demos*. He indicates the smaller units of social life – local communities and self-governing local authorities – which could be entirely based on Roma organised in a local *democracy* rather than simply mobilised ethnically. His examples seem to be of more or less homogenous Romani settlements but, as I understand it, these local democracies must include people with Romani and other ethnic backgrounds. This idea is compatible with the idea of local communities and local political representation, which need to be understood as a common interest of all the people sharing a location and its resources.
>
> *László Fosztó*

László Fosztó: The sense of citizenship can be very ethnicised – at least in Hungary – and implies a linkage to the state that is very local, via mayors, local councillors, local policemen and the like – because at that level they are the state. However it is at the local level that most abuse and discrimination occurs. Therefore I very much agree with the argument in Nicolae Gheorghe's paper emphasising the importance of the *demos* since twenty years of attempting to reinforce ethnicity in various countries has not managed to mobilise Roma, for example to form an effective party. But perhaps I sense a disagreement here between Nicolae Gheorghe and András Bíró.

András Bíró: There's no disagreement since my discourse concerns broader issues than political parties. People are discriminated against on ethnic grounds and this may become the glue holding them together in an ethnic consciousness based on citizenship, which might find political expression. But first of all comes a socio-political movement – a process – that may or may not lead to a party or an organisation. However I don't have any template for this.

Jennifer Tanaka: It will only be possible to begin to articulate answers on how to speak and implement action on issues such as the relationship between citizenship and national identity when the right questions can be formulated. However the whole issue of discourse, although touched on, has not been sufficiently explored yet.

RELATIONS WITH THE MAINSTREAM

What is meant by 'mainstream'?

Željko Jovanović: I'd like us to reflect on whatever the word 'mainstream' might mean to you when thinking about activism and the mainstream context – whether this context is social, political or economic.

Martin Kovats: In my paper, and whenever I'm writing about the issue of Roma politics, I use the term 'mainstream' to mean everything outside the Roma box. I know that by having a monolithic concept of 'mainstream' creates problems but I'm trying to establish the dichotomy between the Roma and the rest of the world for my own analytical purposes.

Željko Jovanović: But if you say 'everything outside the Roma box', does that mean outside the Roma ethnic community or the Roma ethnic movement or Roma ethnic issues? **Martin Kovats:** What I'm looking at is the political interface between 'Roma' as a label and the institutions that Roma are interfacing with – whether it's ministries, local society, NGOs or whatever.

Nicolae Gheorghe: Your paper provoked many comments and criticisms. I admired its analytical sharpness and it reminded me of the philosopher Immanuel Kant in seeking out a Roma identity and then problematising it. Your paper is intriguing and challenging for many readers and so, speaking frankly as a friend, I should say that some people are not happy with your paper. You draw a distinction between Roma as a political elite and ordinary Roma 'down there'. But those in the first category, who have managed to integrate into the establishment and are successful in putting the Roma issue onto the agenda, we are part of the mainstream, aren't we?

Martin Kovats: No, because when I talk about 'Roma', I'm not talking about Roma as a people. I'm talking about 'Roma' as a label used in public discourse, whether by Roma people entering the public arena and associating the word with certain claims or organisations or by mainstream society using the word in a policy document or analysis. So I'm using 'Roma' as an abstract term. **Nicolae Gheorghe:** But that's actually part of the mainstream, isn't it? **Martin Kovats:** It's now part of the public world.

Engaging with mainstream society

Željko Jovanović: We held consultation meetings with Roma NGOs focusing on three topics in relation to the overall strategy for engaging with mainstream society. These were Roma and their empowerment, policy-makers and advocacy and challenging negative attitudes in the mainstream population. However the only result was an exchange of practices by NGOs promoting cultural identity, and to a limited extent the monitoring of media attitudes to Roma. No-one offered any ideas about how to build relationships either with mainstream political bodies and political activists or with the majority population in general. Some NGOs misunderstood the question and said they dealt with mainstream attitudes by employing non-Roma in their organisations. This revealed a lack of ideas about how to enter into meaningful dialogue with the majority population about mainstream issues.

> In contemplating potential approaches for community organizing among Roma in CEE region, I would have a slightly different approach than that of Nicolae Gheorghe, which seems to focus on building partnerships with local authorities and also facilitating (peaceful) co-existence with other non-Roma. I believe that when community organising is practiced successfully then it should ultimately challenge and change local power dynamics. It should challenge the decisions of local authorities and elected representatives – non-Roma and Roma – and hold them accountable for their decisions and actions. I believe that if we do not, then we cannot ultimately change the status quo, which until now has not produced any real breakthrough, but has resulted in furthering the interests of certain Roma and non-Roma alike.
>
> *Jennifer Tanaka*

Nicolae Gheorghe: In the case of Romani CRISS and a number of associations in Romania, we explicitly identified ourselves as being the civil society component of the Roma movement, which also included ethnic parties, electoral representation and other elements. We also presented ourselves as the Roma component within mainstream civil society, enabling us to mount joint actions with a number of associations located at various structural levels. This was a means of mainstreaming our Roma associations by complying with the accepted practices of civil society and offered a way of developing an organisational identity.

Christian Petry: I'd also like to draw our attention to key nodal points at the interface between Roma and mainstream society. There are 25 Roma mayors. All mayors deal with health, education, water and everything that concerns the majority population. They're responsible for their entire community, not just the Roma. Furthermore, we have many Roma journalists who, as journalists, are not restricted to commenting on Roma issues but also write about the world in general. Why don't we talk to them too? Getting out of the box means talking to those people who perform roles in mainstream society.

András Bíró: Self-segregation is one of the sicknesses of the Roma movement. Roma needed to choose like-minded *gadjo* organisations with whom alliances could be built instead of passively being chosen. The success of the black liberation movement in the United States would have been impossible without the support of churches and white liberals – however they should be termed. As a consequence of long-established segregation and enduring discrimination, Roma have developed a powerful victim mentality which prevents them making positive decisions to ally themselves with one group or another at advantageous opportunities. Instead they allow themselves, at best, to be chosen by others as in the marketplace. Perhaps Roma might want to collaborate with church organisations but, if so, this should be on their own terms and not those of others.

Livia Plaks: Over the years the goal – or even *obsession* – of our NGO[10] has been precisely to bring in mainstream society, so that both sides could listen to each other, and to see if there could be positive results by changing some people's minds. I'd like to think that we have succeeded, because it has involved a whole range of civil partners. Naturally there has been greater success with non-extremist elements but even some of the extremist groups ended up attending meetings on a regular basis – and some people's minds have been changed. So, in my opinion, maintaining regular dialogue with mainstream parties and mainstream society should be an integral part of Roma culture and politics.

Željko Jovanović: Yes, but what are the key issues we should discuss with them?

---

[10] Project on Ethnic Relations (PER) <http://www.per-usa.org/>

Livia Plaks: The main purpose of these meetings was to improve Roma political participation. We tried to persuade mainstream political parties to include Roma on their tickets or else to work together in alliances where there were Roma parties. Nevertheless it wasn't easy. It was very hard to get the politicians to sit down with the Roma. For their part, many Roma displayed an inferiority complex, although there were some notable exceptions. Frankly speaking, the result was often very one-sided meetings. Even when several government ministers were seated at the table, for example in Romania, the Roma representatives were unable to respond in a way that led to meaningful discussions. Consequently the ministers didn't come to the next meeting.

We worked very hard in Romania and Slovakia to try and persuade mainstream parties to sit down with Roma politicians telling them: 'It'll work for you. You will gain Roma votes.' Well, guess what? Very few Roma voted. So afterwards the mainstream parties said: 'Well, it wasn't worth it. We hardly got any extra votes.'

Nadir Redzepi: You shouldn't raise expectations that the mainstream will allow Roma to influence the outcome of elections. **András Bíró:** Then we have to take it.

Nadir Redzepi: We should send a clear message to the activists that as long as they naïvely remain timid and undemanding in seeking their rights, Roma will never achieve effective political leverage. But in any case the majority would never allow Roma to exercise political power. Civil society is under the control of the mainstream.

Željko Jovanović: If we appreciate the benefits of local-level dialogue with the mainstream, what areas should we target in view of our limited human resources?

Christian Petry: Other areas of potential common interest – apart from votes – are education and public order. Educational desegregation has been a prominent issue for the Roma movement but this has had destabilising effects. Mainstream educationalists demand quality and so pushing for desegregation has been one way of trying to ensure that Roma children have access to the same educational standards as the majority. However high quality education can be achieved in other ways. As regards the issue of criminality, I've never read of Roma or Sinti asking for Roma or Sinti police to be trained in community relations, although Turkish and other minorities want this.

András Bíró: Now we're discussing how we could influence the policies and understanding of the mainstream political power structure in relation to the Roma. Political parties are potentially interested in Roma in order to gain votes both at local and national level. Consequently a Roma movement with a strong constituency could exert power. On policing, very serious efforts have been made by the Hungarian Ministry of the Interior to recruit Roma police officers. However the initiative has been hampered by the unwillingness of Roma to apply because they thought this disloyal or unethical but perhaps the local and national Roma movements could encourage this. Nowadays in Hungary there's an association of Roma policemen.

Martin Kovats: And in the Czech Republic too.

Dialogue with right-wing extremists?

Željko Jovanović: We've talked about ways of engaging with the mainstream including dialogue with other political movements or parties on issues that interest us. But does this extend to discussions with right-wing extremists such as *Jobbik*?

Nicolae Gheorghe: For a number of years now some of us have been in contact with the *Noua Dreaptă* [New Right] party in Romania. The idea had been to discuss with the people who were talking about the *ţigani* and using malicious stereotypes of Roma to better understand their point of view. As yet we haven't approached the extreme right, because we don't have something like *Jobbik* in Romania – for the time being at least, thank God. But there are similar extremist parties elsewhere – like *Ataka* in Bulgaria and Slota's party in Slovakia.

Nadir Redzepi: I'll have to discuss this hypothetically, because I could never be in a room with illegal groups that are outside the system and organising parallel structures.
Željko Jovanović: *Jobbik* is in the system. **Livia Plaks:** Very much in the system.

Nadir Redzepi: We should debate with them to challenge *their* idea that Roma are the main problem confronting society. Since the non-Roma majority monopolise political power and legal authority, these parties are simply lying when they try to convince their constituents that Roma are to blame for financial and economic problems. This is a completely biased and fascist approach. Instead we should talk openly about problems of *their* endemic corruption and the mistakes of *their* politicians rather than concentrating on the Roma, who are only a minor factor. They're trying to solve the Roma issue but on the basis of their ideas but they can't solve problems like Roma criminality without us – without the Roma.

Željko Jovanović: So if I understood you correctly, you're saying that even if we sit down at the table with them, we need to present facts, to challenge the assumptions underlying their political ideologies, and to provide alternative solutions for social problems, as opposed to the ones that they suggest.

Iulius Rostas: To be honest I've discussed Roma criminality with *Jobbik* although liberals would refuse to do this, seeing it as politically incorrect. Why not discuss it? Yet, as a Roma activist, I feel uncomfortable if asked by mainstream politicians and officials to offer a blanket solution to Roma issues such as educational and housing segregation since situations vary in different localities. In some places the priority might be education but elsewhere it could be health or housing conditions. So why should I impose my point of view on the life of those people? I would not feel comfortable about providing such a message.

Nicolae Gheorghe argued in his paper that controversial or criminal(ised) enterprises such as begging, forced marriage, and human trafficking have become grist to ultra-right mills because of Romani silence on these issues. I applaud all efforts to eradicate all practices that violate human rights; however, I dispute the notion that Romani silence is to blame for these issues being exploited by the ultra-right. The ultra-right in Europe is not interested in dialogue with the objects of their contempt, and operates on a level that is 99% fantasy. In the Czech Republic, for example, completely groundless rumors are regularly spread at local and national level of Roma receiving some sort of special advantages, usually financial, that simply do not exist. Granted, begging, forced marriage, and human trafficking are not myths, but the ultra-right would never be interested in what Romani people have to say about these topics or anything else – and they are not serious interlocutors on any topic to do with human rights in any event, by virtue of their own inhumane and racist politics.

Gwendolyn Albert

Another problem is that Roma activists are often inconsistent about such issues and fail to build alliances with potential mainstream collaborators. On the specific issue of educational segregation, sometimes the anti-segregation discourse in education was constructed in such an exclusivist way that activists alienated potential allies. For example, they failed to join forces with NGOs campaigning for children with disabilities. Everybody has an interest in transforming the education system to make it more inclusive but the Roma anti-segregation activists concentrated on just the Roma aspect of inclusion.

Cooperation at local and national level

Željko Jovanović: I think this last point supports the view that Christian Petry has been advocating over the past two days – that talks should take place at local level – where Roma activists and those on the liberal left and even on the far right probably know each other as individuals. This should help smooth the process of negotiation and avoid the heated political clashes so frequent at national level.[11]

Nicolae Gheorghe: I agree about the importance of discussions at local level but think we should also consider the connection between Roma and the national interests of states. Indeed, the reason why Livia Plaks and PER were successful in placing Roma on the national agenda, was that during the period when Central European countries and Romania and Bulgaria were about to join the EU, the link between Roma and national concerns was clearer. After accession Roma issues decreased in priority because this link was no longer evident – except perhaps in relation to Serbia and the western Balkans. I think there is now a new opportunity to discuss Roma issues with mainstream parties and top officials in Romania and Bulgaria. These countries regard entry to the Schengen area as in their national interest but Roma are seen as an obstacle to achieving this aim. This link has been made explicit and stated publicly both by the Romanian President and Minister of Foreign Affairs and the Roma issue is once more at the top of the political agenda.

Yesterday, Iulius Rostas mentioned the memorandum of the Ministry of Foreign Affairs, in which the issue of Roma was explicitly worded in terms of the interests of Romanian diplomacy. Livia Plaks mentioned that, according to some top Romanian officials, the Roma issue is a European issue rather than a Romanian one. That is one issue to discuss: how much national and how much European identity, and what are the positions of Roma activists and parties on this issue? Some Roma parties and individuals are arguing that the Roma issue is a purely European one. Salomeea Romanescu stated that very clearly. I would defend the opposing point of view that Roma are primarily a national issue.

Martin Kovats: I endorse what has been said about the importance of the local level and agree that mainstream interest in Roma issues grows and diminishes at different times. I would suggest that we are increasingly moving into a period when there is more and more mainstream interest, whether local or national, in trying to engage in and deal with Roma issues, simply because of the sheer dysfunctionality that is creating economic, social and political problems. One of your existential functions as a Roma movement is precisely to present Roma issues to the mainstream and show that it's in their interests to engage with you as a Roma movement. The question is: *How* does the mainstream, whether local or national, actually deal with it?

It strikes me that, particularly in Hungary but also more broadly in this region, there's a lack of confidence in the ability to find the right method for dealing with

---

[11] This point was made strongly on the section on local knowledge in Nicolae Gheorghe's paper.

whatever problem is being tackled in relation to Roma. We had all these programmes and we can argue about whether they were well planned or whatever. But the outcome was a perception that these things really didn't work and that the democratic way of addressing problems had not met the need of the majority population to resolve them. Consequently it was these policy and practical failures which created space for the emergence of a new discourse from the mainstream: 'Well, what we actually need is a heavy-handed dictator to put those dysfunctional Roma people back in their box.'

What this means is that, regardless of how bleak the situation may be now, all Roma-related initiatives have to be successful enough for the mainstream interest to think that it has at least benefited from doing them. For example, those local authorities that are already interested in trying to engage in Roma issues may take an initiative. If such initiatives are successful, then the mayors who are more ambivalent can be pulled into the enthusiastic camp and we can isolate those authorities and mainstream interests that are just hostile.

Dialogue with the mainstream: who, what and where?

Željko Jovanović: Several explanations could be given why Roma communication with the mainstream has been very weak. These include Roma self-segregation and inferiority complexes as well as inconsistency in their articulation of choices when discussing the different options for resolving complex problems. There is mutual acceptance that an interface with majority society exists but this boundary needs to be approached differently than before because society has changed since the 1990s when we started the whole Roma movement.

This raises the question: *Who* is entitled to talk with the mainstream as Roma representatives? Nicolae Gheorghe stated that in Romania the Roma NGO sector had interpreted itself as the Roma component of the mainstream NGO sector and the civic component of the Roma movement. But András Bíró suggested that those with constituencies and votes had the legitimacy to be communicators between the so-called Roma movement and the mainstream.

Then, even if the interface is approached by both sides, *what* do we talk about? Among the main topics suggested have been political participation, how mainstream parties understand and promote the inclusion of Roma within the structures of political parties and electoral politics and the highly sensitive subject of criminality. The importance of utilising both mainstream and Roma-specific channels for funding Roma initiatives has been emphasised.

As to *where* the talking should happen, we still have a blurred understanding of the relative advantages of local-level negotiations – practical discussions about matters such as sewerage and water pipes or dialogue about the national interests of the state. These involve different incentives – Schengen membership as opposed to tangible local services. We should probably – and I'm using this word as a provocation – *instruct* our activists to concentrate on both the local and national level in dialogue with the mainstream. In such discussions citizenship and issues concerning the whole of society should be emphasised for this is the message we care about and think the most relevant and productive.

Nicolae Gheorghe: Who are the activists you would like to instruct?

Željko Jovanović: The activists who will read the book.

INTEGRATION

EU and donor funding and their effects

Željko Jovanović: The previous discussion on relations with the mainstream has already raised the issue of majority perceptions of apparently lavishly funded Roma projects producing no discernible benefits in greater Roma integration.

Nadir Redzepi: And it's a mystery where the money goes.

András Bíró: In spite of the best intentions, funding from foreign private donors for Roma issues – including the tens of millions of dollars spent by the Open Society Institute (OSI) – was handled irresponsibly, naively and unprofessionally. I don't know what proportion of these funds went to the Roma civil sector, the NGOs, but personally I am extremely critical of the prostitution that has gone on. However funding from the EU and governments is quite a different matter.

The problems arose from the absence of criteria or monitoring in what essentially amounted to a traditional donor-client relationship. I would have supposed an organisation calling itself the 'Open Society' would have developed and implemented more effective procedures than simply repeating the 'do-gooder' Western tradition of giving money to the poor but as a result objectives have not been reached. Frankly speaking, I hope my words may reach the ears of those distributing funds to make them understand that being generous is not enough. Money can be extremely corrupting unless sufficient checks and balances are in place to require full democratic accountability from recipient NGOs, with relevant paperwork on specific expenditure, and not just general bureaucratic reports. The key question is: 'Do you have the paperwork to prove you've used the money appropriately, or not?'

Will Guy: Money from Europe was said to be very different but in my experience of evaluating EU-funded Roma projects, many of these were also very inefficient. They were frequently inadequately monitored and insufficient attention was paid to their real impact, both by national governments and the European Commission, leading to repetition of similarly flawed projects. Consequently the same mistakes were made over and over again.

Željko Jovanović: The more money there is, the greater the bureaucracy.

Martin Kovats: I have a feeling that certain Roma programmes contributed to the devaluing of the citizenship of Roma people. This came about because the activities were often provided not by national governments but by outside bodies which were additional or tangential to the state. Moreover, in providing funding, external donors have a means of enforcing their own ideological and institutional interests on the way the Roma movement develops, which may or may not be in the interests of the Roma movement as a whole, or indeed relevant to it.

Iulius Rostas: I think it's very relevant to put this discussion in the book, because we hold Roma activists and Roma organisations accountable – but we have to assess the responsibility of donors too. Donors have an important role in setting the agenda of Roma NGOs. Basically, the majority of Roma NGOs are accountable to their donors, not to communities. So it's very important to have this discussion. I've suggested that the OSI would be doing a great job if it organised a meeting to bring together critics of its Roma work. **Željko Jovanović:** We're thinking about how to do that.

Christian Petry: I must say I feel very uneasy about this discussion. We are making sweeping generalisations about donors but what do we know about the Pestalozzi Foundation and others and what they're doing? In fact this meeting has been paid for by private donors. What might come out of it will be paid for by private donors. So, do you know all the foundations that are active in the area?

Željko Jovanović: But we can specify the role of George Soros within Roma activism. **András Bíró:** We should broaden the scope to discuss not just the Roma movement and George Soros but donors and donors' techniques, in which Soros has an important role. **Željko Jovanović:** But we don't know about other donors.

Iulius Rostas: That's not the case. I think we have to examine several indicators. Let's see how many Roma are on their Boards and whether their procedures are transparent. For example, does the Pestalozzi Foundation have a strategy on Roma? Those kinds of details are posted on the Internet. Also have they consulted with Roma? Somehow,

I was lucky, because I worked in the OSI and with the European Commission on this, and I got to work with a lot of NGOs in the EU-funded civil society programme. In this way I got to know the work of several foundations, at least in Romania. Consequently I can say that nobody else, including the OSI, was as open and transparent about making public their criteria for awarding projects, about their strategies and how they consulted. We could talk about it at least at this level.

> Lack of communication between Roma NGOs in Romania has sometimes led to absurd – nevertheless extremely dangerous – situations:
> a) organisations implementing projects in the same community with the same target group and previously unaware of each other's activities have not tried to cooperate;
> b) NGOs have only concentrated on a single EU financial instrument – the Sectorial Operational Programme Human Resource Development – without seeking funding from the European Regional Development Fund or Cohesion Fund (currently we don't know of any projects financed from these sources that are targeted at Roma communities);
> c) NGOs have no underlying strategy for the sustainability of project activities which often means that the entire development process ceases when external financing comes to an end.
>
> *Gelu Duminica*

Nicolae Gheorghe: In a paper by Margaret Matache and David Mark, they write: 'In terms of accountability, transparency, efficiency and inclusiveness, we may say that these matters are not yet explicitly on the NGOs' agenda or that they are in an early stage of being considered.' The paper specifically mentions the donors' policies and their effects on NGOs. Jennifer Tanaka also discusses this in relation to the policy of the European Commission.

Salomeea Romanescu: We also ought to talk about other social projects, which never respond to the real needs of the community. This is because NGOs just want to serve the interests of the donors or international institutions or governments, and so it's a struggle to respond to the needs of the community. If we want to be honest with these people and make a difference, we have to ask them what their needs are and give money to meet them – such as housing and jobs. **Nicolae Gheorghe:** This is already being done by private foundations, the European Commission and governments in many places. **Salomeea Romanescu:** I'm talking about European funds, because they are a separate matter. The European Social Fund gives money for developing competences rather than for providing jobs. So we're wasting the European Union's money and hence its citizens' money. This is our budget, so we should also be asking for money to improve the situation of the Roma – not through general mainstream funding but specifically targeted to be sure Roma get something.

The price of integration

Nicolae Gheorghe: The situation is far too diverse and complex for us to discuss here and now in the short time available. We need much better evidence to support what we say. It was suggested that a matrix with columns could be drawn up to show the dimensions of integration and indicate the price to be paid for each dimension.

Christian Petry: This is exactly what we have to do. There is an important issue with experience of this kind but we can't solve it now. We'll flag it up as a specific project to be tackled in future. But can I ask if everyone is happy to leave this as it is? Can you live with a book expressing this conflict without analysing and commenting on it? **Željko Jovanović:** Yes and no. If the book acts as a provocation, then it's good. But if András Bíró is trying to establish a dogma – although I don't believe he is – then we can't live with it.

András Bíró: What I'm trying to say is this: After we have analysed the situation are we able to find a clear answer? Let's take a concrete example: Should we defend Roma cultural values on gender, just because they're Roma values? These are the 'costs' I'm talking about. Is the Roma movement ready to accept the fundamental values of human rights, given the conflict between human rights and certain Roma traditions? A further topic I haven't yet addressed is this: What price should be paid by the majority in return for the effort made by the Roma, if some meeting point were possible in future? It's a huge topic. **Nicolae Gheorghe:** We did cover this earlier to some extent, although not explicitly, for example when we talked about civil society. This was part of the trade-off.

> I am not trying to reaffirm yet again Roma as victims of the gadzikane system; I just want to remind you that such a system will not put Roma integration into practice because it is too preoccupied with its own priorities and has no feelings of sympathy or social solidarity for a different one. I do not naively anticipate that *gadzikane* systems should be changed because of the Roma, but I do expect and insist that *gadze* respect their own laws, moral values and ethical principles about protecting weaker groups in society.
>
> *Nadir Redzepi*

Christian Petry: In Europe now the whole discussion about integration is heading in the direction of inclusiveness plus management of diversity – not so much assimilation and integration. That is, somehow, over and done with. The most interesting cities I have seen, like Stuttgart, simply include discussion about the integration of Roma in their inclusion discourse. This means you ask whether society is integrated rather than blaming the victims by asking if they are integrating. Originally, 'integration' was a sociological term describing the quality of a society. Then it became a word to describe the willingness of people to integrate. That has now changed again. This is why 'inclusion' has become such an important concept – particularly the combination of 'inclusion' and 'diversity management'.

András Bíró: I have the impression that diversity management, that is multiculturalism, has lost much of its momentum in the last five to six years. It has almost disappeared. **Christian Petry:** Not in the big companies. That's where it's making a comeback. **Martin Kovats:** I'd love us to have a discussion about what 'multiculturalism' means from the perspective of the Roma movement. But that might be a next step for later.

EUROPE'S CRISIS: ROMA MIGRATION

The significance of migration

Remus Anghel: There's a lot of confusion about the burning issue of Roma migration – particularly to Italy and France – which has sparked off heated political rows in recent years. But not a lot of hard information is available. One of the key issues is the criminalisation of Roma, and we need to address this. Also we need to ask questions like: What are the criteria for the comparisons we have to make? Should we deal with Roma migration on its own, or should we understand it in terms of wider structures?

Nicolae Gheorghe: If Roma now feature prominently on the European agenda, this is because of migration. It's for no other reason. It's not because of their poverty or the discrimination they suffer. It's entirely due to the fact that politicians are worried about Roma migration. **Iulius Rostas:** I totally agree that this is the only reason why the European Union reacted. Migration triggered policies towards Roma at the European level. Yet the EU framework strategy doesn't cover this issue. That's the irony of it. Roma were put on the agenda because of migration, but migration isn't dealt with in the strategy.

Is debating migration worthwhile?

Martin Kovats: You mentioned confusion and a problematisation of Roma migration. But do you mean that it's the mainstream or the authorities that are problematising it? Are there objective problems with certain types of migration that might be associated with Roma? Is it a discursive, artificial problematisation or are there objective problems that need to be addressed? Or does the Roma movement problematise certain aspects of Roma migration in order to attract attention to itself?

I find such discussions frustrating, because they are speculative. This is a real issue with real implications for how we understand why people move, the circumstances they move to, their behaviours there, how society reacts to them and how the state reacts to them. I think it's quite obvious that we are at a point in Italy and France where, if mainstream politicians want to make an issue out of Roma migration, they can. That should open up an interesting debate about why that touches buttons. But we also have many instances where states don't make an issue of Roma migration. So we need to move beyond opinion and thoughts and start working out some reality of what is going on. We need to choose one or two aspects of this whole discourse and really try to find some truth in it, rather than just talk, talk, talk, which is what we seem to do far too often.

Remus Anghel: As I said, one of the problems is that there is little research on Roma migration. **Martin Kovats:** Well, if we don't know what we're talking about, then maybe we shouldn't be talking about it. I thought the point of this exercise was to really demonstrate that there were good-quality ideas amongst Roma activists, rather than that there are a lot of things that Roma activists can talk about.

Roma migration to Italy and manipulation of the term 'nomads'

Remus Anghel: We do know something about migration to Italy and the way Italian legal structures deal with Roma. **Željko Jovanović:** Do Italians take the same approach to each migrant group? **Remus Anghel:** Yes they do in general, although the category of 'nomads' is applied to the Roma. Italian laws on nomadism were framed with reference mainly to Italian Roma. Since then new migrants to Italy basically entered the same structures of opportunities. Ethnic Romanians had migrated to Italy some years earlier than Romanian Roma, which is one of the reasons why the former were better integrated since they had managed to secure better economic niches.

The way in which the migration evolved in Italy involved different phases, starting from the moment when people arrived there without any support and adapting over time. Both ethnic Romanians and Romanian Roma lived in tents to start with, in awful conditions, and then they lived communally in flats. So the process was like a ladder upwards as these people adapted to the market. Local residents saw these people living in tents and usually said: 'OK. It's just Romanians, or just Roma, staying there.' But in fact what was happening was a kind of upward mobility. New migrants came in and took the places of those who had moved on. It was this larger phenomenon that led to criminal activity or the trafficking, which tends to happen within any new group of migrants. But perhaps the Roma became more obvious in this respect because they were more visible, they came later and they were poorer.

> Nicolae Gheorghe compares Roma with Roma but is this valid? Is it correct to compare Roma from Italy and Yugoslavia to those from Romania? Why should we not compare Roma from Romania to ethnic Romanians, as this makes sense? Romanians 'too' slept in *campi nomadi*, they too migrated irregularly, they too were trafficked on various occasions. And they, too, are Romanian citizens and also are often considered to be a problem in Italy. Why are these two groups not comparable? Are we not going to learn more by comparing them?
>
> *Remus Anghel*

Nowadays the situation of Roma is very varied and includes both traditional and non-traditional groups. Many non-traditional Roma look very like Romanians, so if Roma migration is described as problematic and marginal in itself, this is largely a misrepresentation of the actual situation. Undoubtedly there are some objective problems arising from migration of Eastern Europeans to Italy since this sometimes involves trafficking – not only among the Roma but also among ethnic Romanians as well. All donors and all governments want to solve this issue and criminalise this type of migration, saying it has to be dealt with. But if Roma migration is considered in isolation, without any comparisons, attention will be disproportionately focused on the criminal aspects of this phenomenon.

Željko Jovanović: Can you tell us why this category of 'nomads' is imposed on Roma in the camps? After all, they don't move around. Or do they move from camp to camp?
Remus Anghel: Yes, some do move from camp to camp, although they are also integrating. But we have to understand this in the context of Italian integration policy. Most of the migrants living in Italy today were irregular migrants and the state didn't intervene to regulate this migration. Consequently many people living in camps were

classified under the legal definition that had existed before for the Italian Roma. Now when other groups arrive, it's easier for the authorities just to say: 'All right, they're Roma, so they're like the others.' But in fact, they're not. They are not nomads, they're migrants, which is something quite different. **András Bíró:** But the Italian term applied to Roma migrants is *nomadi*. **Remus Anghel:** Yes, it's a stereotype. **Nicolae Gheorghe:** It's not only a stereotype since laws are involved at regional level. It's not just stereotyping by the wider population or in the media. There are laws and regulations about nomadism.

Elisabetta Vivaldi: The main problem in Italy today is the 2008 Nomad Emergency Decree which made, and is still making, a serious impact on Roma people. Many, mostly settled Roma from former Yugoslavia were living with their families in camps but after 2008 most of the big camps were dismantled and moved to the outskirts of cities. If the name 'Nomad Emergency Decree' is analysed, it can be seen that the concept 'nomad' really did not fit the population in question. Likewise the word 'emergency' implies a sudden, abnormal situation, which was not the case. Finally the term 'decree' suggests a duly adopted legal instrument applying to every individual. In fact, however, this *ad hoc* improvised measure was created only for Roma.

Italian Roma have been living alongside other Italians since the fifteenth century but do not have the status of an ethnic minority. It is debatable whether or not they are assimilated, because they remember their origins. But perhaps are playing with their identity or simply complying with the law. However there is nothing in the Italian constitution requiring people to affirm their ethnicity. For example, if you have mixed Chinese-Italian parentage, you don't need to declare this and your documents simply record that you are an Italian citizen.

Migration became an extremely sensitive issue around the 1990s when the Yugoslav wars drove many people to flee abroad. Although Roma were not the only refugees, the difference is that after twenty years many Roma from former Yugoslavia are still living in the camps. Indeed a whole generation has grown up in the camps and faces a major legal problem. A large number of Italian-born Roma, many of whom are now adults and have children of their own, are stateless. They are eligible for Italian citizenship when they reach the age of 18 but have to satisfy the necessary conditions, including a requirement that they are stateless. An official document is needed to confirm this but this is often hard to obtain. Without such proof many young people become stuck in the camps. As recently as September 2011 the Council of Europe's Human Rights Commissioner, Thomas Hammarberg, drew Italy's attention to the problem of stateless Roma from former Yugoslavia.

Living in the camps is hardly an ideal situation for citizenship applicants trying to pursue an independent life since they have to continue negotiating with the relevant authorities and also organisations, whose workers are usually non-Roma. Moreover the projects developed around the 'semi-legal' camps are often barely permissable and, in addition, there might be frequent funding intermittency. Even if public institutions invest in organisations working inside the settlements that are only semi-legal and if these state bodies are aware of the situation, this makes them indirectly complicit in what actually amounts to illegality.

Another measure linked to the Nomad Emergency Decree was the fingerprinting of children over fourteen years of age – something that also attracted the criticism of the Human Rights Commissioner. The justification offered for this action was that the authorities believed these children might be following 'Romani cultural patterns' and could already be involved in criminal activities. **Nicolae Gheorghe:** No, the finger-printing was a rather primitive technique to help establish their age as they had no documents. There was no assumption that they were criminals.

Elisabetta Vivaldi: Biometric tests were also made and people living in the camps were photographed. The same information could have been obtained more humanely by simply asking witnesses about the children's ages. People felt violated by such intrusive methods, which were not used on Italians – especially young people subjected to these checks.

This is something that may also create fear among Italians of Romani origin, because they do not want to be portrayed as nomads. If the authorities start trying to pin that label on them, then if an Italian Romani is involved in a crime, the media will say it was committed by an 'Italian nomad'. In that way, criminality will be associated with nomadism and Italian Romani will be associated with nomads. In a country where, constitutionally, everyone is equal and there are no ethnic minorities, that would be total nonsense.

The actions following the Nomad Emergency Decree may also make Italians of Romani origin feel afraid that they, too, might be portrayed as 'nomads' – even if they didn't live in camps. If the authorities were to start labelling them all in this way, then if an Italian Romani were involved in a crime, the media would say it was committed by an 'Italian nomad'. This would result in criminality being associated with nomadism and Italian Romani being identified 'as nomads' and therefore as offenders.

Official responses to Roma migration

Iulius Rostas: Let's now discuss how Roma migration is represented by the mainstream. In Italy, France and at one time also in the UK, the main reaction has been to present Roma migrants as criminals. Since this mainly concerned Romanian Roma, how did the Romanian government respond? Well, it not only adopted and confirmed all the media stereotypes but also specifically linked Roma migration to criminality. A 2009 Ministry of Foreign Affairs memorandum – and I can quote it if you want – gave clear instructions to various state authorities and embassies on how to react to Roma migration. Basically, they were told to blame the Roma and brand them as criminals, denying that the real problem is the state's failure to implement policies to integrate Roma. The government's aim is to Europeanise the Roma problem and thus hand over the national state's responsibility for its Roma citizens. This isn't just a matter of politicians talking – it's an official document.

But also relevant is what senior Romanian officials, such as the Minister of Foreign Affairs and the Prime Minister, said when they met their French counterparts to discuss migration. An important agenda item had been Roma, which had been inseparably linked to criminality. Yet at these meetings nobody raised questions of why Roma had migrated or what changes had occurred – not only in destination countries but also in their home countries. In 2003, Roma migration became a critical issue in France. Instead of trying to find out what was happening, the Romanian embassy in Paris reacted extremely defensively and simply offered apologies.

When a delegation of Roma activists led by Costel Bercus[12] went to investigate, they discovered that more than half the people at the location concerned weren't, in fact, Romanian Roma. The media had just assumed that, since they were Roma, they had all come from Romania.

Will Guy: When defending itself against criticism in 2010, the French government didn't just talk about criminality. In addition it offered a political explanation of Roma migration from Romania in terms of the socio-economic conditions of Roma. French officials accused the Romanian government of totally failing to make use of European funds to improve the living conditions of Roma in their home country. So if we accept that there's some truth in this, shouldn't the role of activists be to put pressure, if they can, on the Romanian government to make sure these funds are used? Because they *are* available! This is extremely important now, when all governments have to produce an integration plan or strategy for Roma by the end of this year. Therefore there is political pressure from the Commission as well.

---

[12] Of Romani CRISS at that time.

Remus Anghel: I'd expect that funding Roma would increase migration, because we know that people without resources don't migrate. In general it's people with more resources who move around. But the question is *what form* will migration take? What will be the opportunities and institutional support for migration in future?

Christian Petry: We also have to bear in mind cities on the receiving end of uncontrolled migration, like Mannheim in Germany. Officials are completely perplexed when Roma turn up without warning and camp under bridges with their families. Local people, too, are shocked to see children living in such hazardous conditions and demand action from their municipal authorities. In Mannheim migrants came from Bulgaria but attempts to use a non-Roma Bulgarian interpreter didn't establish effective communication with these people. So perhaps we need Roma activists to act as mediators and advise local authorities what to do. Such cities are completely helpless and they could easily turn away from a humanitarian approach to a strategy of expelling migrants immediately. These cities are asking for assistance from activists like you and this would be a truly European response to a very dangerous situation.

Roma activism and the issue of criminality

András Bíró: A crucial topic, which I think is fundamental for the Pakiv book, is that of criminality. Or rather it's the attitude of Roma activists in relation to the commonly repeated assertion of a close connection between Roma and criminality. My experience in Hungary is that Roma leaders shy away from this topic but Nicolae Gheorghe is an exception and in this he is quite atypical. Somehow not talking about it, or not taking a position, is seen as expressing a strange kind of solidarity.

In particular Roma activists have avoided the issue of trafficking. It was simply not discussed, and this was for ideological reasons. For example, the European Roma Rights Centre (ERRC) took a high-profile stance on the screening of passengers at Prague airport to prevent would-be Roma asylum seekers from leaving the country. The ERRC had insisted on their right to travel freely but steered clear of examining *gadje* allegations that trafficking was sometimes involved. **Iulius Rostas:** Roma activists need to work out a position on migration – in non-ideological terms. Also they need to discuss begging as well as other sensitive issues. Maybe then our views are more likely to be accepted by the authorities. **Christian Petry:** So will you give us a statement of your position? **Iulius Rostas:** Well, I think we need to say quite clearly: 'Migration, yes. Trafficking, no.' Roma activists must take a stand on this.

Nicolae Gheorghe: It is evident that a number of crimes are committed by people who are identified as being Roma. Although these cases are over-exaggerated, it is nonetheless a fact. However this leads to the deliberately misleading, constructed representation of Roma as criminals. While there is a grain of truth in this, it is minimal in relation to the level of fantasy involved. As for migration, a fragment of the Roma population is mobile and will continue to move around taking advantage of their freedom of movement, just as any other EU citizens as Roma are part and parcel of the societies in which live. This mobility can't be prevented but what happened in Italy, for example, was entirely different and an abuse of freedom of movement, which is an individual right but with conditions attached.

In Italy people are using the stereotype of Roma as beggars and criminals in order to make money. So when hundreds of people happen to arrive at the same point, the same bridge, with their families, without any food for them, are they just exercising their freedom of movement? No! These people are being trafficked. They are being exploited but are also complicit in that abuse, since their actions are intentional. What happened in Naples, where irresponsible parents deliberately placed their children in jeopardy is indefensible. I can't agree with such actions. Never!

Thousands of people were herded under the Ponticelli Bridge in Naples with the aim of drawing public attention to their misery and forcing the authorities to put them into traditional caravans (*roulottes*) and turning them into nomads. And people were actually paying to live there! Deliberately organising Roma to live under bridges or in derelict factory buildings without any amenities is not just a breach of urban legal regulations but amounts to criminal abuse.

In August 2007 there was a similar situation in Livorno when four children died. I can't simply categorise this as an act of racism perpetrated by others since their parents, who put them in such a dangerous situation, also bear responsibility for their deaths. It was this critical incident that led Romano Prodi, the Italian Prime Minister at that time, to declare: 'We have to tackle this issue of migration at European level.' However this was not intended in the same way as when the Romanian government had said: 'This is not our problem. This is a European problem.' Soon after, in December 2007, the issue was put on the agenda of the European Council and that started the process which led to the adoption of the framework strategy in 2011.

Migration as a political weapon

Nicolae Gheorghe: Some Roma leaders have suggested that activists should incite people to leave their home countries in order to use their migration as a political weapon on behalf of the Roma people. They say: 'This is our gun! This is how we can make people pay attention to us.' Among these are the Roma National Congress (RNC) and Rudko Kawczynski, one of the most prominent and charismatic Roma leaders. This isn't gossip but documented.

In 2010 there was a debate in the Romanian Parliamentary Commission on Human Rights, organised jointly by the European Roma Forum and the Commission's president – the Roma MP Nicolae Păun, head of the Roma Party. Both Rudko Kawczynski and Nicolae Păun declared that the situation of Roma in the EU was so disastrous that the only solution was to organise mass emigration to the United States and to ask for political asylum there. This radical idea was put forward by Roma politicians in a Romanian parliamentary briefing given in the presence of embassy representatives from Spain, the United States and others. It was *our* politicians saying this!

In 2003 we organised a demonstration near Bitola on the Macedonian-Greek border. We had eight hundred Roma camping at the border for three months from February 20 to May 18 with the aim of pressuring the EU to acknowledge the Roma issue at a time when Greece held the EU presidency. This was a huge responsibility for us and I still haven't fully recovered from it. We justified this planned strategy on the grounds that we had no way of forcing the issue onto the international agenda other than using migration. It was after this that Rudko Kawczynski and Nicolae Păun said: 'We'll send Roma to the United States to ask for political asylum.' But just a few days ago a Romanian senator from the ruling party declared: 'We'll send one million Roma to France, just to give them rights in France.' However similar statements had been made previously, as when the Romanian Roma king said in 1990: 'To compensate us for the Holocaust, we'll send one million Roma to Germany.' I think that the Germans took it seriously because in September 1992, the Repatriation Agreement was made.

Iulius Rostas: But these were hollow threats – a kind of Romani *butji* [Romani work] or *schmekeria* [trickery] – since these Roma leaders are generals without an army. I don't know if it's good or bad that they can't mobilise even 10,000 Romanian Roma to send them to Switzerland, Germany or wherever to apply pressure. But in any case they were just bluffing. Also these organisations were expressing an ideological position and are not really in touch with what's going on as regards migration. **Nicolae Gheorghe:** When Rudko Kawczynski spoke about the *Bleiberecht* [right to stay] in Germany and organised the demonstration of former-Yugoslav Roma – blocking the road between Germany and Switzerland – that wasn't ideology. It showed he was very much in touch. **Iulius Rostas:** At that time, yes. But they can't adapt to what's going on now.

Roma migration in comparative context

András Bíró: One question we should ask is why is it that some countries generate huge numbers of Roma migrants and while from other countries there are far fewer or even none – such as from Hungary?[13] I'm not offering an answer but perhaps our analysis should look at government attitudes. The mind-set of officials in Romania is horrible, really criminal, but in some other countries is quite different.

Iulius Rostas: There's a wide variety of Roma migration types, which makes it hard to generalise and also difficult for Roma organisations to respond to these developments. Many Roma left the Western Balkans as a result of the wars in the early 1990s, while many Roma fled Kosovo to escape Serbian revenge attacks following the 1999 NATO war. In the late 1990s, too, Czech Roma initially sought asylum in the UK and Canada but then travelled to western EU countries, and a little later Slovakian Roma headed for similar destinations. There was also Roma migration from Romania and Bulgaria during the 1990s and after but this gathered pace particularly after the 2007 EU enlargement.

There is a particular problem due to the high visibility of Roma migrants which often leads to mistaken understanding and false inferences, exaggerating the extent of Roma migration. Also perceptions of Roma criminality are also based on their visibility rather than on objective reality. A 1999 study by a French institute found that, contrary to media reports, Roma were not over-represented among total migrants from Romania at that time. Their 5 to 10 percent share in France corresponded to the estimated proportion they formed of the entire Romanian population.[14]

Remus Anghel: There are many types of Roma migration and often multiple motives underlying these journeys but one of the most important of these is economic reasons. This motive also drove non-Roma migration from CEE countries to prosperous, older Member States of Western Europe in search of work. For example, there is currently

---

[13] In fact some Hungarian Roma sought asylum in Canada in 1997 and again in 2010-2011.

[14] Even more extreme pictures were presented by UK tabloid headlines. In 1997 the *Daily Mail* portrayed the arrival of Czech Roma as 'the Dover deluge' and reported 'pleas for action as port is flooded by gipsy asylum seekers', while the Express reported that the 'gypsy scam grows' as 'thousands on the way seeking benefits cash'. The Express followed this up in 2004, shortly before EU enlargement, by confidently predicting that '1.6 million gypsies [are] ready to flood in[to]' the UK from CEE countries, ignoring a 2002 survey by the consultants PricewaterhouseCoopers. This had found that six million [ethnic] Poles wanted 'to live and work in another European country' and indeed it was Polish migrant workers who came to Britain in their thousands and not Roma.

temporary labour migration from southern Transylvania to Germany for agricultural work within the framework of a Romanian-German agreement. Eastern European migrant workers are generally preferred for such schemes because they only remain in Germany for limited periods of three or four months before returning home. Also a Spanish agreement on labour migration is being implemented.

But the equivalent system for Italy is ridiculous for several reasons. It is not regulated, the legal framework is inadequate and in any case the planned numbers are insufficient to meet Italy's economic requirements. Another problem with Italy is the lack of management of migration in comparison with some other countries. Almost the entire burden is borne by Italian local authorities but they are not provided with any financial support. To the contrary, in Spain there is a better management of migration at the local level. There have been very interesting policy-making initiatives both by local authorities and by migrant organisations in Madrid and Barcelona, for instance. Consequently I would hardly recommend Italy to Roma as the best destination at the present time.

Nicolae Gheorghe: A particular problem, already referred to, is that of stateless Roma from former Yugoslavia who are now living as refugees in Western European countries, for example Bosnian Roma in Italy and Serbian and Montenegrin Roma in Germany The most critical case is that of Roma who fled from Kosovo. My feeling is that ultimately the right place for refugees from Kosovo is in Kosovo and those from Bosnia in Bosnia – but a democratic Bosnia that is part of the EU. But I think these people are going to be kept in cold storage for another twenty years, under temporary humanitarian protection, until we have a clearer idea of future prospects.

In the meantime collective status for Roma refugees in Western Europe is not possible. I hope EU states won't agree to this since it would set a dangerous precedent. There are Roma activists who have the courage to say: 'Kosovan Roma, go home. That's your country. Fight for your homeland.'

Željko Jovanović: But it doesn't depend only on them. You have to tell the Kosovo government to give them back their property first and then they'll go back.

Nicolae Gheorghe: Of course. But I went to the European Roma Forum with the message: 'You have to take a decision.' That forum was created to make a stand on controversial issues, to express clear-cut views. But what responsible politicians wanted to hear from accountable Roma politicians was how the burden of managing this issue of refugees from the Balkans could be shared between them. **Željko Jovanović:** But that's not possible because, as Iulius Rostas said, these are generals without an army. We need to build an army first, then worry about generals. **Nicolae Gheorghe:** In ancient Rome, there were soldiers who later became generals. We are the soldiers who will become generals but we definitely need to recruit other soldiers.

Assisting beneficial Roma migration

Remus Anghel: Looking at the positive aspects of migration, my suggestion for Roma activists is to try and get people to enrol in the temporary labour schemes I already spoke about in those European countries that have them. When we talk about migrants, we need to talk about motivation and guaranteed earnings will offer them sufficient motivation. If Roma go to Germany, where the system is regulated, there will be fewer problems – for example, if they bring a car back with them, their ownership will be properly documented. But in Italy things are far more chaotic, which is one reason why the camps are expanding. Roma could also investigate other European destinations. However Europe is experiencing a crisis at present and the Italian economy is not expected to expand much in the coming years. And there is now 20 percent unemployment in Spain, where Eastern European migrants were mainly men working in the construction industry. So it's high time to stay at home as insecurity has increased. Nevertheless trying to convince people to move into legally regulated schemes wherever possible would be a very sensible strategy.

As for Roma women, one opportunity for them is employment as care-workers in Italian, German or Spanish households but the intimacy involved in such work can cause difficulties. There was a very interesting film made in Italy, featuring a Roma woman who initially dressed in traditional clothes but then was persuaded by some Italians to adapt to the Italian way of life. When she started dressing like an Italian or a Romanian, she found work. This is a very sensitive issue, since it is very much bound up with identity.

Longer-term migration generally leads to underdevelopment and dependency in regions of origin, whereas temporary migration can produce greater effects in terms of providing people with new role models. If somebody works for a time in Germany, then returns home and invests their earnings in their family's education, this is a fundamental shift. People learn from what they see around them. But if you go to Italy and live in the camps, you will acquire different attitudes than if you had gone to Germany and had been treated decently by your employer – incidentally, a far more likely occurrence than in Romania. Then you might say: 'OK. Life can be better.' Such experience can really transform people's motivation.

There are other possibilities too. Roma living in Romania and elsewhere need better advice if they are considering migration. Would-be migrants often rely on information which is false and travel to the West but find nothing there for them. What they were told was all lies. Therefore future migrants should be given accurate information and provided with viable avenues of migration. In this way they could be motivated to avoid living in marginal conditions but instead to adopt a strategy of returning home from time to time and using their savings to invest in education to improve their chances of social mobility.

Iulius Rostas: We don't have a clear view from Roma activists from Romania and Bulgaria as to whether migration is good or bad. I visited several communities in Romania, including Orbic in Buhuși, and the remittances sent back by Roma migrants made a real impact on those communities. After only a few years, they were quite unrecognisable. No government policy has had such an impact on any Roma community I visited. So, migration brings about social change for the better within Roma communities.

The status of Roma in Europe: alternative conceptions

Nicolae Gheorghe: All activists want more attention paid to Roma issues but there are very different visions of the desired status of Roma that might result from increased attention and resulting policy decisions. Migration is the best-articulated area in which we have clear statements of such alternative and conflicting agendas put forward by leaders and organisations

Nadir Redzepi: Four resolutions were agreed by the first World Romani Congress (WRC) in 1971. The last was that Roma should stop moving around, should settle in houses, should send their children to school and should have proper jobs. This fourth decision has never been promoted by Roma NGOs. Roma migration is not a new issue and most officials consider this a security threat – on political and economic grounds – but Roma activists lack an adequate strategy and arguments to change their minds. We have frequently tried to convince donors that Roma activists should be supported in projects to prevent migration and especially to counter manipulation by Roma leaders who support organised migration.

Nicolae Gheorghe: But it's not just that we lack a strategy. There's a trend among some Roma leaders who believe that promoting migration is the solution. They say: 'We have to be Europeans. We must have a European passport. We are European citizens, which means that we can travel whenever we wish, wherever we wish and in whatever manner we wish.' And that's dangerous. I can understand those who see this as a security threat, because we use this as a security threat.

Nadir Redzepi: It is entirely natural for people to seek new opportunities and a better life. This cannot be prevented but we could set up projects, programmes and activities to convince people to stay where they are. However this isn't happening. Although we have a range of different programmes on education, human rights, women's rights and other areas, in the last ten to fifteen years there have never been programmes targeted at migration. Now the main priority for Roma activists should be to aim at preventing migration and to convince not just donors but also state authorities to work together on this.

Nicolae Gheorghe: I've already mentioned that some Roma activists have adopted a contrary, pro-migration position. They argue that since Roma are spread throughout Europe in a diaspora, this should be acknowledged by the EU by granting them legally binding recognition as a stateless people without citizenship of any nation states. Furthermore they maintain that this status should be supported by the Charter of Roma Rights already adopted by the European Roma Forum.[15] If adopted, a possible consequence might be a *Flüchtlingenquote* [refugee quota], as for Jews.

In contrast the Roma leader, Romani Rose, takes a diametrically opposed position, arguing that in Germany Roma are long-established German *Bürger* [citizens]. Consequently he and his supporters didn't welcome the arrival in Germany of tens of thousands of Romanian Roma in the early 1990s but took the view that they should remain in their homeland where conditions needed to be improved. However the controversy between the Central Council of German Sinti and Roma and the Sinti and Roma in Hamburg, that is to say between Romani Rose and Rudko Kawczynski, was politically productive in the sense that it generated debate about these opposed agendas among Roma in Germany and beyond.

The International Roma Union (IRU) offers yet another alternative. As Nadir Redzepi said, the first WRC focused on the sedentary Roma population of CEE countries and the Soviet Union, emphasising their citizenship and need for better integration. This was because Roma delegates from these regions were in the majority at congresses. Much later – during the EU enlargement process when many states saw the entry of CEE applicants with large Roma populations as a threat – the fifth WRC adopted a policy of stabilising Roma within the EU. So partly for pragmatic reasons, but also in order to differentiate itself from the RNC, the 2000 Prague WRC voted for Roma to remain where they were already living and for their conditions to be improved. In return it hoped that the Roma would be recognised as a non-territorial nation and would be granted representation within the EU as a distinct people. This vision was set forth in a manifesto.[16]

Salomeea Romanescu: I disagree with these scenarios since we're now living in a European Union, where the trend is to integrate all states and construct a federation. Do you think that each federal state in the US or Canada would tackle Roma integra-

---

[15] This is toned-down version of the Charter that Rudko Kawczynski had presented in 1994 in Seville.

[16] IRU (2001) *Declaration of a Roma Nation*, 1 January <http://www.hartford-hwp.com/archives/60/132.html>

tion separately? A European federation will be the model for the future and I'm very optimistic about this prospect. **Nicolae Gheorghe:** But the scenario based on nation states is still valid. They still exist – unlike this federation.

> EU expansion to include Central and Eastern Europe was seen as a win-win scenario, based on the neoliberalist ideological credo that markets worked perfectly and had the potential to enrich everyone, especially the poor and marginalised like many Romani people. Nothing could be further from the truth. This presumption prevented governments fulfilling their essential role of regulating economic growth and preserving social protection. However governments can and have intervened to mitigate market failure and ensure social justice for the most vulnerable, as in Sweden.
>
> *Salomeea Romanescu*

Salomeea Romanescu: Well, maybe you don't have all the information. I spoke with the EU Budget Commissioner at a conference and also with Leonard Urban, the current Romanian Minister for European Affairs, who confirmed that the trend is towards more Europe – more EU intervention in national policies. This will enable the transfer of resources from richer to poorer countries to allow the problem of unemployment – a great threat to internal security – to be solved. If states fail to carry out specified policies they will be penalised and structural funds will be withheld. This is the context in which to think about the European Roma minority. But in any case they are not really a minority but citizens of Europe. We have to make this qualitative shift in our thinking. As a human being I would not be happy about working and studying in Europe without taking my family with me and, as European citizens, Roma should be free to migrate with their families.

Political construction of the Roma people

Nicolae Gheorghe: I just want to remind you that, when Nadir Redzepi introduced himself, he said: 'I'm still speaking about the Roma nation.' That's something he took from the first WRC in 1971. Among Roma activists, we speak about the Roma nation in cultural terms – not as a nation state with territory – but we are not only a collection of individual citizens. If we integrate in Europe, we should integrate as a political people. But this people has to be politically constructed – by us – and this is what we're not doing. Activists talk about 10, 15 or 25 million Roma as though they're a faceless, demographic mass but with no attempt at political construction on our part. It's *our* responsibility to undertake this task; it's not the job of the EU although we might take advantage of EU resources in the process. This is what we have to do to achieve collective integration of Roma in Europe – not only collective travelling.

So one message for our Pakiv book is: How are activists constructing our people politically, from the grassroots level – the neighbourhoods, villages, etc. – all the way up to a Roma people at European level? Carlo Maria Martini, Altiero Spinelli and the founding fathers of the EU spoke about a Europe of peoples, not a Europe of nation states. The dream is still there but it will be achieved in a hundred years, not a hundred days. So I suggest that the book should state explicitly that Roma activists are not solely working on issues like poverty, exclusion and cases of discrimination before the courts. Our job as the political and intellectual elite is to construct our people politically and to have a vision of that goal. This is something we are simply not doing.

WHAT NOW?
TAKING THE PROJECT FURTHER

András Bíró: In this final session I would like to start by reminding you of the original aims of the project. We started with three core texts to be followed by a conference – all of which was to be included in a published book in the hope that it would be translated into several national languages. The original plan has been modified by the idea that the content – a collection of ideas and debates about Roma issues – will serve as an intellectual and emotional challenge to a wider range of activists in order to strengthen the Roma movement. This was seen as an essential development at a time when a new generation of actors could emerge to increase the movement's impact. I very much agree with this shift in orientation and objectives. However if the book is to be published in the name of the Pakiv Fund, as planned, it will be necessary to think about the public being addressed and adapt the language, bearing in mind the target audience.

Christian Petry: From the start we had a dream that this would be the beginning of a discussion within the Roma movement itself. Therefore all involved should do what they can to turn the published ideas into activities within the Roma movement. Of course, not all of the material is capable of being digested by everybody. So, in addition to the book version, the content will need to be edited and re-expressed more concisely in a variety of ways – as pamphlets and as a manifesto to highlight the most pressing issues so that NGOs can grasp them.

Nicolae Gheorghe: Romani CRISS has already translated my text into Romanian and they would like to translate the other two core texts into Romanian.

András Bíró: I am not happy that a manifesto should be among the first outcomes. It would be preferable to first hold a series of meetings in different CEE countries to debate the issues in the book in a broader way than has been done up till now. This would involve not just the three texts but also the debate and critiques – the whole collective product. This would demonstrate whether the process was working and if the message was reaching the required levels to produce the desired level of discourse. This would all need organising, an administrator and funding support.

Jennifer Tanaka: I still think that from all the texts and discussion, there should be prioritising of issues and a brief statement of the main points on migration, citizenship and other topics. The assumptions underlying the situation as presented in the book should be made explicit – for example, to justify why citizenship is seen as an important way forward. It would not be feasible to hand out a text of 120 pages or more to all the activists and NGO people who were busy working and hadn't the time to come to the conference. What we need is something shorter and in simpler language, where issues have been prioritised and assumptions made clear.

Will Guy: Željko Jovanović and I thought that a range of versions should be produced for different purposes, while retaining the intention that the main text should be circulated for discussion leading to the publication of a book. **András Bíró:** Various methods of dissemination could be used including print and the internet but should include a book. As a result a younger generation of Roma intellectuals could make a totally different contribution than the reactions we have already received.

Nadir Redzepi: This direction for developing the project is mistaken since a variety of outputs would continue to give to policy makers, donors and also activists the impression of inconsistency. Instead, the project should shift in the direction of filling gaps in existing Roma demands.

Željko Jovanović: Well, it depends on the direction but I don't think this book should formulate demands. Rather it should give us food for thought about demands, since we didn't do our homework on introducing democracy and legitimacy into our options. I think this book might help all of us who are putting into practice different approaches to Roma issues on a daily basis. The outcome might be an ideology, or a set of ideologies, to inspire managers when defining project proposals, donors when defining criteria, politicians when interfacing with the mainstream and media practitioners when reporting on the Roma. The outcome should be a collection of twenty years of experience and ideas, formulated in such a way as to provide a challenging ideology and a set of visions for the future.

The significance of this book is not in its publication. Its main significance lies in whether it becomes a topic of coffee-break discussions between Roma working daily in

NGO offices and Roma speaking with grass-roots communities. Only then could the book become significant. One target group might be intellectuals and academics, who would read the book. But it is necessary to ensure that the book will be translated into everyday language, so that Roma and non-Roma could develop an alternative ideology. **András Bíró:** An approach, not an ideology. **Željko Jovanović:** I prefer to speak of an ideology rather than approach since we are trying to define very abstract political theory about the Roma issue. Ideology, with its positive sides and its negative sides is something we lack every day. It doesn't have to be a dogma but we need something to challenge.

Iulius Rostas: I don't have such high expectations of the book as Željko Jovanović seems to have. I remember when Andrzej Mirga and Nicolae Gheorghe published their seminal article in 1997 which inspired me to develop a discourse on civil issues. So my hope is that this book will inspire others in a similar way to develop a more coherent and articulated discourse on various issues. But the book isn't something for the entire Roma population simply because the majority of Roma don't read books.

András Bíró: And what about the younger people who have completed their university education?

> Ever since 1989 reports, research and studies have presented Roma as victims – a population in need of assistance – and this is a characteristic of the development industry. Although not admitted openly, an agenda is created with the aim of attracting funding, and therefore there is significant concern to create and maintain a positive image of the organisations and institutions which promote the agenda. Consequently the resulting activity is report-driven, focused on inventing procedures and generating appropriate data. Both NGOs and state agencies are more concerned with producing polished results and creating an image of reliable partners for donors and EU institutions rather than investing in social partnerships with the intended beneficiaries.
>
> *Florin Nasture*

Željko Jovanović: If Roma activists don't read books, it's not because they're illiterate. It's because they don't have the time. One activist told me: 'It's as if we were trapped in a cage. First of all you see what donors want. Then you write a project. Then you do the organisation. Then you report back. Then you do the research. Then you hold a conference. Then you do the lobbying. And then you start the process all over again. It's like a factory production line.' There's no innovative thinking and people are discouraged from talking about Roma issues since they feel this would only be repeating the same old ideas.

Martin Kovats: During the last two days, or in the book, do you feel that there were any new ideas? **Željko Jovanović:** For me, there are a lot of ideas that we will definitely promote. One idea is to continue the intellectual talking-shop. Another is that we start thinking about doing more on migration along the lines that we discussed. So for me, it was excellent.

Christian Petry: Is there anything we haven't discussed that anybody thinks we should have discussed? **Željko Jovanović:** We didn't really discuss how Roma issues could be understood in economic terms or the impact of countries' changing economic situations. Debates included consideration of perceptions and concepts but very little attention was paid to numbers. **Livia Plaks:** Also we neglected the role of the EU, and how it could be more influential. **Ioana Vrabiescu:** I'd like more meetings like this one. **Iulius Rostas:** We should concentrate more on the effects of new funding on Roma. **Jennifer Tanaka:** We don't think about civil society in its broader sense. Instead we just talk about NGOs and projects.

Fifteen years ago, when income generation and economic development were the main focus of Pakiv, I really believed that we could make a difference through small-scale investment (whether by grants or loans). I think their importance has not diminished, as we see that EU-funded labour activation programmes have not made a significant difference. At the end of 2010 the Polgar Foundation was reporting its initial success with Grameen-type micro-credit loans, funded by EC Pilot Programme. Yet, they also stated that self-employment is not the preference of the participants, who would rather have a steady job. But perhaps this is all we can do, given that larger scale investments are more about the political economy?

Therefore can we launch grassroots organising among Roma (and non-Roma) without also creating or making linkages to the question of jobs and income? We have to start with the status quo but what can really be offered? This was really not talked about much in any of the papers, though is actually what the vast majority of local Roma, local constituencies – the target of social inclusion policies – will tell us they want.

Jennifer Tanaka

 Nadir Redzepi: We haven't really talked about the Romani movement.
 Gergő Pulay: When we debated gender issues, we could have extended this discussion to include other categories, such as disabled people, which also intersect with the so-called broad Roma category. It might be useful to compare Roma to other minori-

ties, such as the Hungarians and the Turks, but also to indigenous movements elsewhere, because we can learn a lot from them.

Will Guy: I would add EU funding but also we didn't really have much on bad behaviour. Jennifer Tanaka mentioned usury, for example.

Christian Petry: Another neglected subject was good practice – concrete cases involving cities, mayors and Roma communities – where things have worked well. These golden nuggets were mentioned in conversation but not in formal sessions. Roma activists and the Roma communities could be convinced by examples where good strategies have been successful.

Nicolae Gheorghe: Yesterday it was said that new ideas for projects and action were needed. So I'd like to put forward a project proposal where we try to make use of the ideas in the texts. It's not yet good practice, because it's not yet a project, but I'd like to be able to say that these ideas we have formulated are not left floating in the air. **Christian Petry:** I think specific proposals are wonderful to have but in the end, it comes back to having a clear structure for the book. We want concrete outcomes from what has been discussed. **András Bíró:** And then we can go further.

VALUES, LEADERSHIP, POWER

ŽELJKO JOVANOVIĆ

> When a people are mired in oppression, they realise
> deliverance only when they have accumulated the
> power to enforce change.
>
> *Dr Martin Luther King*[1]

These thoughts are a reflection upon the writings of András Bíró, Nicolae Gheorghe and Martin Kovacs. But they are also a response to views expressed during the two days of debate among participants at the workshop.

The authors who initiated the interactive creation of this book have put forward insightful and challenging views. Like András Bíró, in his preface to the edited account of the workshop discussions, I do not see the purpose of this book as producing a straightforward 'answer' to the multiple and complex problems confronting Roma. Instead the authors intended to open up a further debate or series of debates as a way of clarifying what might be the most productive strategies for Roma and those concerned with issues surrounding them. I hope that this book will stimulate critical reflection and, following this, encourage incisive action.

I do not see my role as speaking for everyone or arguing with the views of the three authors. Instead, in my paper below, I humbly offer my own vision of steps along the way forward. My reflection is based on the belief that at the root of the Roma question lies the issue of power. Integration, as a permanently changing process, has to be continuously negotiated and the terms of these negotiations are determined by those who hold power. This book, I believe, presents an analytical perspective on these negotiations but also offers potent ideas to be used in them.

We, the Roma, are a people *mired in oppression*. We comprise Europe's largest ethnic minority; our population in Europe today is variously estimated at between 10 and 12 million people. The oppression we suffer registers as the most critical of democratic deficits both within and beyond the European Union. The twentieth was the century of pogroms and genocide. The twenty-first has begun as the century of discrimination and segregation. Our people have endured too much.

Despite this legacy of oppression, there are encouraging signs that we are on the way to *accumulating power*. How far have we come? At this moment the brutal truth is

---

[1] NY Times (1967) 'Martin Luther King defines Black Power.' *The New York Times Magazine*, 11 June, 26-27.

that, while a degree of institutional participation has been granted to us, we have no political power to *enforce change*. In terms of political, economic and social development we are not yet, in any sense, masters of our own destinies. Our elites, in their struggle for status, are controlled by far greater powers. Our communities, immersed in a daily struggle for survival, have been defined as target groups of beneficiaries and not recognised as a political constituency of rights-bearing citizens. The change we need has been halted, having reached an uneasy accommodation between our community, our top-down appointed elite and our democratically elected governments. As a consequence of this *status quo*, top-down governmental policies on Roma remain ineffective – they do not reach down to community level; they only justify the existence of those on top. So, let there be no illusion, there is still a long road ahead of us. But we can and must walk ahead, because our hunger for change remains stronger than the oppression confronting us. Where are we going? We have to accumulate political and civic power proportionate to our numbers. Only then, will governments listen our demands, and only then can we *realise deliverance*.

The participation we have achieved

This is not to diminish our achievements in terms of institutional participation over the last ten years. The rhetoric, if not the substance of Roma participation has become a mantra for all national and international, governmental and intergovernmental institutions in a way that was formerly inconceivable. Central to the vision and organising principles of the Decade of Roma Inclusion 2005-2015 is a commitment to Roma participation.[2] It is frankly acknowledged in the Decade vision statement that 'Roma participation will make or break the Decade'. This would seem to suggest that the principle of Roma participation has finally been embraced but, as ever, there remains a gap between rhetoric and substance. The political challenge is to move beyond simply paying lip service to the notion of Roma participation.

Years of empowerment and capacity building have produced a tiny stratum of our elites capable of institutional participation. One consequence of progress in this area is that some of the brightest and best of our civil activists have become civil servants. At national level, former Roma activists have been appointed to serve in governmental offices. At local level, Roma participate as municipal Roma coordinators, Roma health mediators, and Roma teaching assistants. Roma activists moved from the streets into offices and from mobilisation to administration. The struggle for change

---

[2] For more on the Decade of Roma Inclusion 2005-2015, see: <http://www.romadecade.org/ about#[1]>

became more removed from our communities and more immersed in bureaucracy, where 'the problems of ordinary people [...], become a distant echo rather then palpable reality, abstractions to be managed rather than battles to be fought' (Barack Obama, 2004).[3]

The modest concessions in terms of institutional participation have created a distinct niche role for former Roma activists, and an almost uniform type of apparatchik, recognisable across Central and South-eastern Europe. We might call this type the *Roma-in-charge*: a person of Roma ethnic origin, nominated by government, accorded an advisory role, but denied any decision-making powers. Co-opted, and possessed of a sense of purpose, the *Roma-in-charge* enters a higher comfort zone in terms of income, status and recognition – a comfort zone at some remove from the quality of life of the average Roma citizen.

Such comfort functions as a sophisticated tool of financial and political control. Both the *Roma-in-charge* and our civic organisations have been controlled by financial dependency – either by personal remuneration for the *Roma-in-charge* or access to governmental or EU funds for many of our organisations. As governments increasingly use European funds to outsource a range of service provision to NGOs, many organisations – with the best will in the world – have unthinkingly mutated from independent civil society watchdogs to utterly dependent clients. As a consequence, governments have muted our critical voice.

In terms of political control, the *Roma-in-charge* finds himself in the worst of all positions – seen to be powerful but actually powerless. Usually a high-profile appointment with a lot of attendant media publicity heralding a 'new departure', or signalling 'real political will' on the government's behalf, the *Roma-in-charge* is burdened from the outset by the weight of great expectations and the depth of power constraints. The heads of the Roma National Strategy Secretariat in Serbia, the National Agency for Roma in Romania, or the Office of the Plenipotentiary for Roma Communities in Slovakia – all *Roma-in-charge* at central government level – have possessed no power: no power to decide over paving roads or piping water into a Roma *mahala* (quarter). If appointed at local level, as were the Roma municipal coordinators in Serbia, *Roma-in-charge* have had no power over bussing our children to school from a remote *mahala*; nor have the Roma teaching assistants had the power to desegregate a school. Institutional participation has empowered institutions for window-dressing rather than our people for influencing governmental policies.

---

[3] Obama, B. (2006) *The Audacity of Hope: Thoughts on Reclaiming the American Dream*, New York: Crown/Three Rivers Press.

Institutional participation is our achievement but at this point it is inevitably controlled by higher powers. However, we have no choice other than to keep walking ahead. Therefore, we must see the institutional participation of our subordinated elite as only a stage along our way. Political power derived from a mobilised constituency is the next step from here.

The power we need

To make it clear and properly understood, the power we need is to enable us to assume responsibility for our own future. Those in authority have allowed us to participate but real power will never be given to us. Using every available democratic means we must take it ourselves. Voting is only one of those means and in my view the most critical in the today's context.

In today's democracies the vote of every individual citizen – literate or illiterate, rich or poor, Roma or *gadje*[4] – carries equal weight. We are many, and however poor, illiterate, or oppressed we may be, we can wield power proportionate to our numbers. Our social and political circumstances today are incomparably better than those of African-Americans in slavery or black South Africans under Apartheid. Yet, it is clear today that we do not exercise voting power corresponding to our numbers. A widespread myth exists that the Roma vote cannot be effective, that it is a vote to be bought and sold due to high rates of illiteracy. This is a fallacy. Nelson Mandela in his autobiography, *Long Walk to Freedom*, famously refuted this argument in terms that still resonate today:

> A man stands up to contest a seat in a particular area; he draws up a manifesto, and he says, 'These are the ideas for which I stand'; in a rural area he says, 'I am against stock limitation'; then, listening to the policy of this person, you decide whether this man will advance your interest [...] and on this basis you vote for a candidate. It has nothing to do with education [...] a man looks at a man who will be able to best present his point of view and votes for him.[5]

However, illiterate people are easier to manipulate; it is easier to manipulate the powerless than the powerful. Majority parties have recognised the equality in weight of votes before elections, but not the equality in rights after them. They only stop by our communities, buy our votes cheaply, and never return again before next elections.

---

[4] Non-Roma.
[5] Mandela, N. (1994) *Long Walk to Freedom*, London: Little Brown & Co., 228.

Roma leaders, campaigning for majority parties or their own, have mostly followed the same practice. Roma voters are not blind to this. In Romania, a country with constant Roma representation in the national parliament since 2000, 59 percent of Roma expressed the view that their MPs were completely ineffective in addressing their problems.[6] In Serbia, only one in a hundred Roma trusts Roma political parties and only five in a hundred trust Roma NGOs.[7] In 2007 two candidates of Roma parties were elected as Members of Parliament. This was a unique case in the history of Roma in Serbia where about 35,000 people, mostly Roma, voted for these successful candidates. Eight months later they lost their seats in early elections and vanished from the parliamentary life of Serbia. Afterwards a grassroots leader made a sharp comment about loyalty to one of the former MPs:

> We, the Roma, didn't vote for you a second time. We're not stupid not to know that on your own you couldn't do much for us during only eight months in parliament. But you behaved just like the *gadje*. You came to speak to us only before elections but you never came back after you were elected. All we needed was for you to stay in touch with us and listen to what we had to say.

We need to nurture a new generation of leaders, committed to empowering others; leaders, whose ethnic origin will not be considered as an exclusive entitlement to support from our communities, but instead as a moral imperative to serve for the betterment of others who face injustice. The words of Martin Luther King are worth recalling:

> And so we shall have to do more then register and vote; we shall have to create leaders who embody virtues we can respect, who have moral and ethnical principles we can applaud with an enthusiasm that enables us to rally support for them based on confidence and trust.[8]

To meet the challenges and uncertainties that lie ahead this next generation will need resolute determination to exercise leadership of a political community while drawing on the collective power of our citizenship-given rights. We need leaders who before elections can organise and mobilise citizens to turn out and vote; and after elections to

[6] NDI (2009) *Assessment of Barriers to Roma Political Participation in Romania*, Washington D.C: National Democratic Institute <http://www.ndi.org/files/Assessment%20Report%20Final%20(complete).pdf>

[7] Milivojević, Z. (2008) *The Decade and Position of Roma in Serbia*, Belgrade: Roma Centre for Democracy <http://www.romadecade.org/files/ftp/The%20Decade%20and%20Position%20of%20Roma%20in%20Serbia%20-%20Final%20(2).pdf>

[8] King, M. L. Jr (1968) *Where Do We Go from Here: Chaos or Community?* Boston: Beacon Press.

hold those elected to account and challenge them when promises are not kept. We need leaders who can get people to participate as often as possible and to protest as often as necessary; leaders who can make our vote matter on each and every day between elections.

We need to continue to support and expand the politically active elite that will emerge as a result of the affirmative actions and educational scholarships which were institutional responses to the perceived disadvantages of our community. We have no other option than to overcome intergenerational discrimination and offer these young Roma the chance to acquire skills to carry out policy and political work. They need know-how and opportunities to become politically engaged and fully express their commitment towards their communities. Together with the grassroots this new generation of leaders should act to take advantage of the space afforded by democracy to empower others in Roma communities to participate as citizens by exercising their rights and demanding equality for all.

This is no easy task. The coming of democracy did not bring deliverance but rather disenchantment and a loss of trust. Our exclusion worsened; our sense of security was threatened as never before by violence from state and non-state actors alike. The experience of police harassment, brutality, and ethnic profiling has meant that law enforcement authorities have yet to win the trust of Roma communities in Italy, Slovakia and elsewhere in Europe. It remains absurd that because of the colour of our skin, so many of us have experienced brutality by the police so frequently. We do not trust parliament – the institution at the heart of a country's democratic life. 76% of Roma from Romania say the Romanian National Parliament is not effective. Only 10% of Roma in Serbia place their trust in parliament, while around 30% declare that they have no trust at all. Democracies, old or new, east or west, have yet to deliver us from oppression and have yet to earn our trust.

Despite all of this, we must not lose hope or abandon our conviction that things will improve in future. We are no longer at the start of our journey. Increased participation at various levels of state institutions demonstrates our real progress and represents a significant step forward. No one should disparage this and we should be proud of what has been achieved to date with an eye to what can be achieved from now on. To be cynical about how far we have come is to negate the efforts of all who justly struggle for increased and meaningful involvement. If we dismiss participation as unnecessary, we will blind ourselves to the possibilities about how best to participate. However, the institutionalised role of the *Roma-in-charge* is just not enough. To move from this ineffectual, top-down 'participation' driven by tokenism, we need bottom-up organising, driven by values. And when it comes to values, the words from the inaugural speech of one former community organiser, Barack Obama, are inspirational:

Our challenges may be new. The instruments with which we meet them may be new. But those values upon which our success depends – hard work and honesty, courage and fair play, tolerance and curiosity, loyalty and patriotism – these things are old. These things are true.[9]

---

[9] Obama, B. (2009) 'Inaugural speech', *New York Times*, 20 January <http://www.nytimes.com/2009/01/20/us/politics/20text-obama.html?pagewanted=all>

THE PAKIV EUROPEAN ROMA FUND is a charitable foundation governed by German law. It was created in 2002 with private funding from people linked to four organisations: the Romani CRISS (Bucharest), the Freudenberg Foundation (Weinheim), the Autonómia Foundation (Budapest) and the Roma-Lom Foundation (Lom, Bulgaria).

The first major project of the Pakiv European Roma Fund was the trainee programme, Training, Mentoring and Community Development – Facilitation for Building Capacities amongst Roma, which ran from 2001 to 2003 funded mainly by the World Bank. Former trainees have set up a European alumni organization, the Pakiv European Network, and in addition established local and regional Pakiv organisations in various countries.

All organisations bearing the Pakiv or related names have launched practical projects to promote the social, educational, economic and political inclusion of Roma in their national, regional and local societies, and also fostered mutual feedback amongst them. As the basis for their active involvement, they all share the idea expressed by the word *'pakiv'*, which comes from Romanes meaning *trust, honour, credibility, wisdom and balanced conduct, belief,* and more. The intention is to develop an ethical mindset, a culturally-rooted civil code for their own engagement with civil society and a vision for the participation and integration of varied Roma groups in their local societies that is derived from the cultural tradition of the these specific Roma individuals, extended families or groupings. The Pakiv European Roma Fund sees its core remit primarily as self-examination of its members' and trainees' existing practices and efforts to promote Roma inclusion in Europe. Accordingly it formed a Reflection Group, which has published this book and hopes to shape the discussion process it has triggered.

At present the Pakiv European Roma Fund is attempting to encourage the growth of a Europe-wide 'Pakiv family', that can bring together the varied practices (at local, national and European levels) of those individuals, groups of activists and associations who wish to foster an embryonic vision of Roma-related policies and politics, organisational languages (including Romanes) and conceptual approaches. The eventual goal is the emergence of 'ideologies' of Roma community development, involving communication, mobilisation and Roma self-organisation.

The Chairpersons of the Board of Trustees are currently Christian Petry (Executive Director) and Nicolae Gheorghe, who also chairs the Reflection Group, as well as András Bíró. Other board members include Emil Metodiev and Iulia Dimitrita as representatives and promoters of the Pakiv European Network.

Contact: PAKIV EUROPEAN ROMA FUND
C/O STIFTUNGS- UND FÖRDERGEMEINSCHAFT MODELLPROJEKTE GMBH
Babostr. 3
D-69469 Weinheim
T. +49 (0) 6201 2 559 661 • F. +49 (0) 6201 18 29 60 • pakiveuropeanfund@sfgm.de
Pakiv European Network: http://pakivnet.org/